CENTERING

CENTERING

A
GUIDE
TO
INNER
GROWTH

Sanders G. Laurie & Melvin J. Tucker

Destiny Books
Rochester, Vermont

Destiny Books
One Park Street
Rochester, Vermont 05767
www.gotoit.com

First quality paperback edition: October 1983

Second edition: 1993

Library of Congress Cataloging-in-Publication Data
Laurie, Sanders G.
     Centering : a guide to inner growth / by Sanders G. Laurie
and Melvin J. Tucker. —2nd ed.
        p.   cm
     Includes index.
     ISBN 0-89281-420-9
     1. Success. 2. Meditation. 3. Centering (Psychology). 4. Medita-
tion—Therapeutic use. 5. Psychic ability—Problems, exercises, etc.
6. Success—Psychological aspects. I. Tucker, Melvin J. II. Title.
   BJ1611.2.L423 1993
   131—dc20   92-44726
                                             CIP

Text design by Charlotte Tyler

Printed and bound in the United States

10 9 8 7 6 5 4

Destiny Books is a division of Inner Traditions International

Distributed to the book trade in Canada by Publishers Group West (PGW), Toronto, Ontario

Distributed to the book trade in the United Kingdom by Deep Books, London

Distributed to the book trade in Australia by Millenuim Books, Newtown, N.S.W

Distributed to the book trade in New Zealand by Tandem Press, Auckland

Distributed to the book trade in South Africa by Alternative Books, Randburg

Contents

⋅◆⋅

Preface

Meditation?

In the 1970s it was a dubious practice. The general public suspected its far Eastern background and the hippies and cultists who proclaimed its benefits. At best, the public considered it an aberration of psychic practitioners; at worst, the devil's way of luring honest individuals into loss of faith and grievous sin.

But a few upstanding members of society were intrigued by its reputed benefits and found psychics who could teach them how to meditate. When these brave novices began to experience improvements in their lives, they spread the word that meditation was the answer to modern problems.

The new believers' success with healing themselves and others began to attract attention, and they buttressed their claims with books on faith healing by noted psychics like Catherine Marshall, Agnes Sanford, Olga Worrall, and Ruth Montgomery. To quash the concept that practice might be anti-Christian, meditators cited the written works of Father Francis McNutt.

Several medical doctors added a stamp of legitimacy to meditation and its by-product, healing, in lectures and publications. Dr. Henry K. Puharich's professional papers and books for the general public told about his research into faith healers and healing. Dr. C. Norman Shealy's book described a new treatment for patients with severe back problems; in it, the nationally famous surgeon explained that he had cut back on spinal operations and was teaching his patients how to meditate the pain away. Along with Dr. Terry Friedman, Dr. Shealy further promoted a combining of meditation with medication by founding the Holistic Health Association.

At the same time, other medical doctors tested the self-healing powers of various adepts. Dr. Elmer Green and his associates at the Menninger Foundation in Topeka, Kansas, ran experiments on the Dutch yogi Jack Schwarz, and the Indian Swami Rama, while Dr. Wilbur Franklin at Kent State University worked with the American yoga master Komar.

Prominent universities also contributed to the public's understanding of the healing process. Harvard University's Dr. Herbert Benson published *The Relaxation Response* in 1976. Notable educators who conducted laboratory experiments that proved the existence of healing energy included Dr. Thelma Moss of UCLA, Professor Douglas Dean of the Newark College of Engineering, and Dr. Shafica Karagulla of McGill University in Montreal, Canada.

Two additional books by practitioners, one by Dr. Lawrence LeShan and the second by Dr. O. Carl Simonton, outlined ways of healing cancer. And Dr. Simonton went beyond teaching local patients when he provided instructional tapes to help people around the world cure themselves of the dread disease.

Other life-threatening illnesses have similarly yielded to the combination of meditation and medication, and AIDS will soon respond to the powerful combination.

That it has not done so already is due mainly to "conceived opinion." The belief that individuals who acquire AIDS are only "getting what they deserve" for "sexual misconduct" is entrenched in public consciousness. So far, AIDS sufferers have been unable to combat this widespread idea. But knowing the reason for failing to cure oneself is half the cure. The other half is finding the right way to reprogram an AIDS-afflicted body back to health. At the moment, the cure may seem impossible. So did the four-minute mile, until one athlete broke the time barrier. Once a single person heals himself or herself through meditation and medication, others will be able to turn their immune deficiencies into sufficiencies.

The success people have had with healing themselves of cancer and other terrible diseases has borne fruit. Self-healing, and the meditations that promote it, have proved their worth. Meditation has entered the mainstream of modern belief, and those who are unaware of its techniques are out of step with progress. Moreover, our lack of knowledge prohibits us from using it to lead healthier and more secure lives.

Centering has been designed to acquaint you with the basics of meditation. It is comprehensive in scope, able to take you from where you are at present to the point where you can handle your world with ease. It is a do-it-yourself project. Unlike some meditation programs, there will be no one ripping apart the fabric of your personality to shame you in public. Any dissatisfaction with your condition will be private and personal, and you can retain your secrets while you improve your personality. You will also proceed at your own pace, as slowly or as quickly as you like. You set your own timetable.

Little will be required of you. All you need is a few minutes a day, a determination to better your life, and the persistence to overcome obstacles so you can become a whole person. When you reach this goal, you may discover that material desires no longer occupy your thoughts, for attunement with the universe is bringing whatever you need.

The effect of meditation, the becoming whole—otherwise described as psychic integration, psychosynthesis, or a holistic state—can be difficult to attain. Many of us resist change or lack the determination to succeed. Not everyone who begins a program of this nature will complete the process of individuation (becoming whole) immediately. Some people stop meditating, thereby cheating themselves of a greater good. Yet those with the greatest problems will succeed. When a need is so compelling as to make one say, "Anything is better than to continue to live like this," success is assured. Individuals who fervently desire change will persevere with their meditations and overcome every obstacle.

Those of us with lesser needs are tempted to improve a little and rest, or settle for less at some point along the way to individuation. The psychic stage of development, at which one becomes able to use telepathy or another of the psychic arts, is a trap that ensnares many. But prior to discussing these arts, let us examine the steps of our self-study program.

We begin with a questionnaire that will reveal our present approach to the world.

Next, we will learn the basics of meditation.

In exploring the basics, we will discuss common attitudes or habits that are detrimental to our welfare, and the constructive patterns that lead to holism.

Subsequent chapters will help us deal with meditation techniques and various ways of improving our attitudes. The chapter on healing will start with procedures for assisting others and conclude with self-healing exercises for diseases like cancer and AIDS.

As we become accustomed to meditation, we may find ourselves developing talents that seem new but are not—we have had them all along without knowing it. An exploration of psychic abilities will help us understand why they occur and how they help us reach the goal of our study—wholeness.

Since wholeness is a twenty-four-hour-a-day affair, we shall discuss dreams and their importance to our psychic and spiritual growth.

We shall conclude with a questionnaire that will assess our progress. All of this will be achieved through meditation.

Essentially, *meditation* means stilling our minds so we can find within ourselves the solutions to problems, answers to questions, and alternatives to circumstances that confront us. The rewards of meditation are many. The practice reduces stress. It leads to an expansion of awareness, easy learning, a general heightening of our present talents, and a first-hand knowledge of what is known as PSI or ESP.

The acronym ESP stands for extrasensory perception, and PSI, a coined word, is its synonym. Don Fabun, publications director of Kaiser Aluminum, said in his *Dimensions of Change* that PSI is actually a process or force within that connects us to exterior energies and thereby to a higher power. He added:

> There seems to be something going on inside us that we do not understand. Some sort of cosmic transcendental forces flow through us, as if we were a telephone line. Call these forces God, or ESP, or PSI—the labels do not matter. But we do not make use of these forces, although every preceding culture of which we know has done so. We shiver, lonely in the cold wind of a technological culture, standing on the runway with a dollar in our hand, while all the time the warmth is within mind's reach. But may the mind not be a way to breach the wall? Think what delights may be on the other side! Come along?

What we now call PSI or ESP has been around for untold generations, so we are only pasting labels on what has been built into the human psyche. On our progress to the higher power, or what Fabun terms the "warmth within mind's reach," we may encounter one of the ESP abilities, which include mental telepathy, clairaudience, clairsentience, clairvoyance, and psychokinesis.

Mental telepathy refers to knowledge of circumstances or events that happen at the same time as we "receive" the information. It can be a sort of wireless telephoning in which you and a friend deposit messages in each other's minds. Edgar Mitchell conducted telepathy experiments while he was on the moon, sending back his thoughts to a receiver on earth. Perhaps you, too, have experienced mental telepathy without recognizing it for what it is. Maybe you have known something before a friend or close relative has said it aloud. Or maybe you've thought of someone and he or she has mailed you a letter at that time or telephoned you soon afterward. Mental telepathy happens too often to be coincidence, and once you recognize it when it happens, you will be able to use it to your advantage.

Clairaudience, clairsentience, and the more frequently occurring clairvoyance refer, respectively, to hearing, feeling, and seeing what has happened in the past or will happen in the future, at your present location or at a distance. Such experiences give you knowledge of remote or otherwise unknown events.

Retrocognition means looking into the past, while precognition refers to prophesying (foretelling the future). At first you may find it difficult to identify whether an event belongs to the past, present, or future, and to feel comfortable in an apparently timeless dimension. But persevere and you will be able to pinpoint the time frames.

Psychokinesis is the ability of the mind to influence objects: to make them move of their own volition, or regulate the throw of the dice or turn of the cards.

Any of these phenomena, which can occur as you move toward individuation, will be proof of your progress, a proof you may need at certain points in your development. But they should not be sought for themselves. You will cheat yourself if you settle for being a psychic, medium, mental telepathist, or mental magician with the powers of a Uri Geller, the Israeli who bends strong and rigid metals by mental force. Though these stages may appear glamorous, you will gain far more by using these mysterious PSI powers to perfect your personal life.

PSI talents, though seemingly rare and unusual, are in no way supernatural. The laws of the universe are established, unchanging, immutable. If they appear to be broken, it is because universal laws extend beyond the bounds of what we term reality. Our previous inability to use mental telepathy or the other phenomena is due to our not having achieved the mandatory mental control.

Levitation, for instance, does not break any universal law. Saints and certain mediums such as Daniel Dunglas Home (1833–1886) have been known to levitate. Home was described by several responsible spectators as having floated out of a second-story window and back into another window of the same building. St. Bernard, St. Dominic, St. Teresa of Avila, and others were observed to rise from the ground without physical aid. Levitation also occurs in poltergeist manifestations. If certain individuals can produce the effect, then it must lie within the province of universal law and require only a correct frame of mind and attendant body circumstances to trigger it. Thus, when we try to focus our minds on the unconscious processes that trigger the so-called supernatural experiences, we may learn to control them consciously and so discover that all is, in fact, super-mental. Centered individuals are those who have attained this level of control and understand that the achievement is not an end in itself but a guidepost to far greater benefits.

But ESP isn't confined to the odd and unusual. It has numerous practical purposes. It can make it easier for you to master new materials, to discipline your mind so you can learn without effort and easily remember what you've learned. Meditation and its results will fill you with joy as you educate yourself, whether in a classroom or through a program of self-study. All the same, education is only a part of life, and the kind most valued is of the psychic and spiritual nature. To attain it, we must be able to control ourselves fully.

The next requirement is a commitment to having a better life as well as a more successful career. We must recognize ourselves as important people who have specific missions in life. Our individual missions demand that we make the most of our talent and possibilities. We speed the process by knowing what we are and how we react, and by learning how to control our body, mind, and spirit. Meditation thus becomes an exciting journey, on which we discover not only the techniques of exploring the inner self but also the way to tune into what some psychologists believe is a universal fund of information that is called the collective unconscious.

The universal or collective unconscious lies beyond the personal unconscious. Only by conquering the personal unconscious can we expand our mental processes and thus begin to use more than 10 percent of our brains identified as our normal usage by the American psychologist William James.

Our means of expansion is to attain an altered state of consciousness.

Each of us should be able to find a method suited to our personalities and needs, for the human potential movement has gathered such momentum that newspapers and magazines abound with articles about methods or techniques for getting "one's head together."

Some of these methods are centuries old and have been merely adapted to Western use. Yoga is one that has been translated more or less intact and has become so popular that several TV channels broadcast yoga exercise programs. Many viewers achieve wholeness through yoga, but others require a method more geared to hectic schedules and fast-paced living.

In the 1970s and early 1980s transcendental meditation (TM) and Silva Mind Control taught meditation techniques to thousands of American seekers. Students were wildly enthusiastic about their offerings, and the programs became famous enough to rate mention in *Time* and *Newsweek*. But TM destroyed its credibility when it promised to teach everyone to levitate. Serious meditators resented the discipline's being used for a parlor game, and TM failed to fulfill the promise. Silva Mind Control, on the other hand, has remained a viable method of learning meditational skills.

Courses in meditation do not come cheap. They can run into hundreds of dollars, placing even the best of bargains beyond the reach of many earnest seekers. Nonetheless, many people believe that they get only what they pay for and that whatever costs the most is best.

Transactional analysis (TA), primal therapy, and Gestalt therapy have long been alternative methods of integrating the personality. Others, such as psychosynthesis, Arica, and Rolfing are less popular than they were, though still effective. Each serves its purpose, for those who are so oriented. Biofeedback, which monitors body reactions and thus assists people in learning how to control the physical self, has retained its great appeal—perhaps because it requires machinery and thereby attracts the scientifically minded.

On the whole, however, most individuals have lost interest in spending thousands of dollars and years of their lives in searching for themselves. Even people who learn the basics of meditation in organized courses must go it on their own sooner or later. The search for self is an individual effort, and any consciousness-raising technique that does not equip a student to be his own guru is a waste of time and money.

Yet each of us must make a start somewhere, and some prefer to work with a group. Fortunately, there are hundreds of psychics across the nation who are willing to teach meditation for reasonable fees. A course or two taken from a proper leader—that is, one who does not attempt to perpetuate his or her hold on students—is an excellent way to start. But remember that when those classes are over, you must proceed on your own.

Or you can start from scratch with the private course that we call *Centering: A Guide to Inner Growth.*

We repeat: it is received opinion in our society that you get what you pay for. This does not hold true for consciousness-raising. What you gain from meditation depends on what you put into it in terms of effort and persistence rather than dollars. The most expensive study will not benefit you in the slightest if you don't follow directions. Do not be deluded, then, by the modest cost of the *Centering* technique. It is a proven one. Thousands upon thousands of students—TM, Silva Mind Control, and yoga graduates among them—have learned the *Centering* method and benefited immeasurably from it. Many have written to report on their experiences. A few even credit *Centering* with saving their sanity or preventing them from committing suicide. But the majority tell how meditation enabled them to cure their diseases (especially cancer) or—when they learned meditation techniques too late in an illness to cure themselves of the disease—to control their pain and so ease the quality of their remaining days. The successes of cancer survivors could pave the way for a breakthrough by those with AIDS.

Besides its effectiveness, the *Centering* technique is safe. You need not fear that you will go astray or attract harmful "entities" to yourself. The horror stories seen on TV or in the movies about people with obsessions or demonic possessions are mostly fiction. The few people who could be called "obsessed" or "possessed" usually became so by trying to use psychic abilities for the wrong purpose. You cannot and will not make that mistake if you follow the steps outlined in *Centering.*

Because each of us is at a different level of understanding, or operates best from a different perspective, you will be offered several meditative techniques. Experiment with each, and select what is best suited to your temperament and current needs. But be flexible, for as you advance you will require different meditation exercises.

You are now ready to consider the course itself. If you use it for self-study, instead of working on it with a group, you can proceed at your own pace. Any questions that arise can be answered by your subconscious or by reading positive works on the subject. At the start, you may wish to discuss some of your experiences with friends who are also reading *Centering* or otherwise privately working on themselves. But this should be done only at the beginning. Once you are into the work, it's best to keep your experiences to yourself and rely on your subconscious for whatever help is indicated.

The advantages of self-study are numerous. In concentrating on your interior self, you will not be distracted by others. Many of the most famous mystics and psychics of the ages were self-taught. Among the Christians are St. Francis, the author of one of the prayers we will use; St. John of the Cross and St. Teresa of Avila, both of whom wrote instructions that can be found in translation by E. Allison Peers (*Dark Night of the Soul* by St. John of the Cross and *Interior Castle* by St. Teresa of Avila); Meister Eckhart; and Therese Neumann. Noted Indian mystics include Lahiri Mahasaya, Ananda Moyi Ma, and Giri Bala. In all cases—whether Christian or Oriental—it is difficult to determine how much of their knowledge was self taught and how much was inherited from their respective religions. Nevertheless, their inheritances had to be meager, since only the aforementioned and a few hundred more spiritual individuals were able to "break through" and claim the immortal gifts. Perhaps more would have done so had religions and governments been more tolerant of those who tried to heighten their spirituality on their own—especially during the 16th and 17th centuries in Europe, when authorities put hundreds of thousands of people to death for practicing "witchcraft."

Time has changed the picture. On the American continent, at least, the private search for transcendence is no longer considered outlandish or eccentric. Human beings are free to look for their greater good on their own, and what has been accomplished by a few who have achieved transcendent experiences can be repeated. The ability to break the bonds of what we consider reality is not confined to a chosen few. Each and every one of us has that ability. We need only reach out for it, work to make ourselves worthy of reaching a higher consciousness, and persevere until we have achieved it.

The methods we will use are as positive and successful as those taught by Alcoholics Anonymous. In fact, members of AA who have already learned to discipline themselves would find the *Centering* techniques a perfect followup to AA procedures as well as a safe and speedy way to improve their lives.

This is not to say that everyone who begins the work will become whole and thereby truly centered. We all have the ability, but some of us do not feel the need for what we call holism or individuation. Still, there is nothing wrong with improving a little, and we each must decide for ourselves. Those who are interested in meditation but not are yet committed to change might well read the following chapters as one would an interesting story. Perhaps later they will return and begin work on the course.

Those among us who sincerely want to benefit from integrating ourselves will do well to read a chapter at a time and put the suggestions into practice before continuing to the next assignment.

With these thoughts in mind, let us begin to be more than we ever dreamed we were capable of being.

(Margaret) Sanders G. Laurie

1

Brain Waves and Meditation

Meditation, which can be loosely described as a solitary exercise in which one focuses the attention within oneself, is by no means a modern discovery. It has been practiced for centuries, and in the Western tradition it probably began with the Egyptians, who used it for religious purposes from about 4000 B.C.E. to the fall of their civilization. The ancient Hebrews were certainly meditators, and the earliest mention of the practice in the Old Testament concerned Isaac, who "went out to meditate in the field at eventide" as he waited for his betrothed, Rebekah, to arrive at his kingdom (Gen. 24:63). Later in history, Joshua instructed his people: "This book of the law shall not depart out of thy mouth; but thou shalt meditate therein day and night, that thou mayest observe to do according to all that is written therein: for then thou shalt make thy way prosperous, and then thou shalt have good success" (Josh. 1:8). The Psalms contain several references to meditation, particularly Psalm 119, which stresses the importance of meditating, "in thy precepts" (Ps. 119:15, 23, 48, 78, 148).

The early Christians used meditation frequently, and at the start of the Christian movement it must have been used by all, for Jesus advises: "Settle it therefore in your hearts, not to meditate before what ye shall answer" (Luke 21:14), and Paul charged Timothy to "meditate upon these things; give thyself wholly to them; that thy profiting may appear to all" (1 Tim. 4:15). Later the practice became the province of those in the religious orders, among them the Spanish St. Teresa of Avila, whose *Interior Castle* treatise describes the stages one passes through on the way to God as he or she continues to meditate. This 1577 testimony was continued in spirit by the humble Brother Lawrence, who became a Carmelite In Paris in 1666 and whose letters indicate he carried meditation into his every waking moment.

Yet meditation was not confined to the clergy. Countless lay people used it and praised its benefits because they found that it worked.

1

Of course, no one knew exactly how it worked, and its advocates—like St. Teresa and Brother Lawrence—were able to instruct others only according to their individual experiences. Now, however, we are beginning to see why and under what circumstances altered states of consciousness like meditation can occur and to accept them as natural functionings of the mind.

Alpha Rhythms

Dr. Hans Berger, a German psychiatrist, ran some experiments in the 1920s in which he connected patients to an electroence-phalograph. He found that his patients' brains emitted vibrations that differed in frequency and nature, but fearing the ridicule of his medical peers, he withheld his data. When he finally published the results in 1929, the world learned that the brain emitted oscillations that ranged between eight and thirteen cycles per second. Berger called them alpha rhythms. As W. Grey Walter explained in "The Electrical Activity of the Brain," alpha rhythms "can be identified by the part of the brain they come from; they are nearly always largest at the back of the head, where the nerve signals from the eyes reach the brain. They are usually larger and more regular when a person has his eyes shut and is not thinking." The pattern that identified when human beings used all five senses and produced thirteen to eighteen vibrations per second became known as beta rhythms. A slower frequency of five to eight oscillations was named theta, and below five, delta rhythms.

What this means to us is that whenever we are involved with the five senses, we produce thirteen or more brain vibrations per second, a very rapid set. When we close our eyes or relax, we can reduce the vibrations to between eight and thirteen. That is, we exclude the sensory stimuli and arrive at a stage where the mind is capable of extrasensory perception. If we go further, into the theta or delta levels, we descend into sleep, as modern dream researchers have discovered.

Berger's scientific successors studied the brainprints of babies in their search for clues to the riddle of changing brain patterns and found that newborns produce delta rhythms during sleep; year-old infants emit theta waves of five or six oscillations; two- and three-year-old children begin to develop alpha rhythms and continue until they are seven or eight years old, when beta waves become dominant. W. Grey Walter confirmed these results in his own scientific investigations.

The effects can be observed by anyone who studies a child between the ages of two and seven, when he is operating primarily on the alpha level. During this span, children are veritable sponges for absorbing information. They can hear a television commercial only once and recite it verbatim. Their insatiable curiosity frequently erupts in a spate of questions that try the patience of adults. Their insights are often remarkable, and their observations startling to more jaded senses. One four-year-old, for instance, had a hole in his sock, and when asked where the material that had covered his heel had gone, responded lightning-quick, "down the drain." Any child over seven might have difficulty with the question—as would an adult—for after seven the ease and facility of perception that are characteristic of the alpha level are lost. School and its regimentation have borne the blame for the loss. Now it appears that beta rhythms are the culprits, and those who operate on the beta level are sense-reacting to the world rather than thinking about it, solving its problems, or creating new worlds, as one may do in the alpha state.

Alpha, therefore, has great implications for learning, particularly in an industrialized nation such as ours. We have become a truly "tuned-in, turned-on" society, having so immersed ourselves in sensory stimuli that we have forgotten how to employ our mental abilities to full capacity. Young people in particular can be seen on the streets or the beaches with earplugs in place and transistors set at full volume. Adults are often no better, for after a day of reacting to sensory stimuli—conversation, the shrill of phones, or the hubbub of traffic—they plunk themselves down before their television sets for an evening of sensory barrage. Small wonder, then, that so many individuals in industrialized societies suffer from stress-related ills. A natural functioning of the brain is being denied. The body suffers from the loss, but so does the mind, for it is prevented from problem-solving.

Meditation has never been more needed than it is at present, for in meditation one is required to abandon the five senses and move down into the "underworld" of the inner self. In so doing, the body relaxes and the brain slows down to the alpha level. After a suitable rest, the brain can resume its normal beta activity with renewed vigor, for the body and spirit have—temporarily at least—been brought into alignment with the mind.

Attaining the Alpha State Spontaneously

This process can and often does occur spontaneously—for instance, in those moments when one is so absorbed in a book, one's thoughts, or an outside activity that it requires a jolt to bring one back to "reality." This absorption is uncontrolled alpha, and while it lasts one learns rapidly and can apply one's knowledge to solving old problems or rearranging previous concepts to generate new ideas. In short, it is at the alpha level that we do our real thinking. At the beta level we operate on our five senses to cope with the environment, but in alpha we tune out extraneous stimuli and focus our attention on the thought or object at hand. Furthermore, once the senses are ignored, physiological changes take place in the body. Respiration and heartbeats slow, and we become more relaxed.

Methods of attaining the alpha state are varied. The Eastern religions have centuries-old methods, which require years of practice before one can become proficient in their use. Yoga is but one example. Modern means for Western man include biofeedback: training the body to respond to signals from machines. Both are salutary, although the Eastern method is too time-consuming for a technologically oriented culture, and biofeedback requires costly equipment not readily available to everyone. Fortunately, we have a natural alternative, one requiring a minimum of time and effort: meditation.

What we will outline is not hypnotism, however. That is an altered state of consciousness that should be avoided. During hypnotism the subject grants control of consciousness to an outsider and *may* leave the self open to suggestions that could contravene the normal. There is no necessity for surrendering self-control. In fact, there is every reason to retain it, for the meditation techniques require a subject to be fully aware of what is happening and always conscious of the results while working on the subconscious to achieve his or her goals.

We shall describe the process first and, at the end of the chapter, list the steps to be taken in their proper order.

Pharaoh's Position

Begin by seating yourself in the position used by the pharaohs of ancient Egypt. The oriental postures of squatting on the calves of the legs or crossing the legs in the lotus position may be used, if comfortable, but the seated position is recommended, since it can be practiced without attracting undue attention in public—and in the future you may wish to meditate in those spare moments when you wait for a meeting to begin or for a plane or train to whisk you to another location.

The pharaoh's position is simple. Seat yourself in a comfortable, straight-backed chair so that your spine is straight from hips to head. (Lying prone also allows one to hold the spine straight, but it is not advised, since it is conducive to sleep and does not lend itself to meditating in public.) Place your feet firmly on the floor, side by side, with one hand palm down on a thigh and the other hand resting palm up on the other thigh.

So much for the posture. Now pay attention to your body. To achieve the desired state of relaxed awareness needed for a good meditation, it is best to loosen any tight clothing and, if possible, to slip off your shoes. You may also wish to dim the lights of the room, leaving a soft reading light until you have mastered the instructions.

Plan to meditate each day at the same approximate hour and in the same location. Should this prove impossible, do not give up. Brief attempts and at random times and places are better than none at all.

Now close your eyes and become aware of your body. Note your tensions. Then, relaxing the rest of the body as much as possible, tighten the toes of both feet. Strive to tighten just the toes and no other part of you. Where you place your attention, you can place the tension, so bring all your senses to bear on your toes and feel the tension in them. Hold it for a few seconds, then relax your feet. Notice the difference between the tension and the relaxation.

Repeat the process with the calves of your legs: tighten, observe; relax, observe.

Repeat for the thighs, then work your way up your body, tightening, observing; relaxing, observing, as you focus on your abdomen, chest, hands, arms, entire head. Conclude by tightening and relaxing the entire body at once.

Now permit your body to become as limp as a rag doll's. Breathe easily. Do not force the breath, but let it come and go at will while you direct your attention to it. If you become excited and start to breathe heavily or fast, relax a moment, think of something pleasant, and then resume the breathing exercise.

Breathing

Breath is the key to any altered state of awareness. It is your means of exchange with the world about you. You breathe the world in, you breathe it out. The process is natural. You do not have to think about breathing, for it is an involuntary action. Now, however, you are going to use your breath to screen out portions of your world. As you exhale, you will allow yourself to sink down into your mind. To assist in the descent, imagine you are on a private elevator. If you suffer from claustrophobia, use a down escalator or take the stairs. Later you will be able to cure yourself of this fear through reprogramming, but for the present make the best of it. When the doors of your elevator close, begin your countdown, descending as you exhale and pausing at each floor as you inhale. You will ascend in reverse: rising on the inhale and pausing at the exhale. As a further aid, see the number of the floor to which you are descending. Let it flash before your eyes three times, and say it three times.

As you relax to begin your elevator ride, remember that you are not doing anything that could be considered weird or unusual. You are merely using an idea that intelligent people from thousands of years ago up to the present have used to improve their lives. Only the mechanics of the technique have been updated, and these are temporary. Soon you will be able to dispense with your private elevator and sink naturally into the meditative stage. But for the present, use the summarized instructions at the end of the chapter.

Giving Yourself Instructions

Once you familiarize yourself with the basic procedure and can move into and out of the alpha stage without checking directions, you are ready for your first experience. If you have access to recording equipment, tape your instructions. Be sure to relax your throat before starting to tape, then speak slowly. Your voice should become deeper, softer, and more relaxed than usual, and you should remain silent for long periods of time. If you do not have access to tape-recording equipment, give yourself instructions in the same manner, remembering to stay relaxed and to pause frequently. Memorize the general order of the steps, but don't worry about using the precise words, except for 2a and 2b below. Instead, focus on your personal experience. Above all, relax, knowing that in a few sessions the procedure will become automatic and you will remember without strain.

When you are ready for your initial descent, dim the lights of the room, loosen any tight clothing, and seat yourself in a chair, spine straight from your hips to the top of your head, and hands resting on your thighs. Do not cross your legs at the knees or the ankles, or clasp your hands.

Begin the tensing, observing, relaxing, observing exercises, starting at your toes and proceeding up to your head. Conclude by tensing the entire body at once, noticing the tension and the subsequent relaxation. If any part of you begins to feel tense or uncomfortable during the meditation, tell it to relax by saying, "Relax, shoulders," or "Relax, leg."

Let us begin. Close your eyes. Close your mouth, also, and breathe only through your nose.

1. Step onto your private elevator, face the doors, and watch them shut. Inhale. Exhale and drift down to 5, 5, 5. (Visualize and repeat the numbers.)

   Inhale. Exhale and descend gently to 4, 4, 4.

   Inhale. Exhale and float down to 3, 3, 3.

   Inhale. Exhale and drift softly to 2, 2, 2.

   Inhale. Exhale and descend to 1, 1, 1.

   Inhale. Exhale and float gently to B, B, B.

2. Your elevator doors open and you step out into a shaft of light that shines down on you from above.

   a. Say, "I am now in the healthiest possible state of being."

   b. Say, "In this state, I and I alone will control my mind. No one or nothing else can or will ever control my mind."

   c. With your eyes still closed, imagine before you a mental movie screen. Its surface may be white or dark, but picture it in your mind's eye. Then allow whatever images that come to flash across the screen. These will be your thoughts, which normally surface as images.

   d. After a few minutes, erase your screen and focus on the blankness. If a thought picture attempts to cross your mental screen, do not fight it, do not resist it, but let it pass. Firmly but gently bring the screen back to blankness.

   e. Keep your screen blank as long as possible, then say, "I am now in the healthiest possible state of being." (Pause.) "In this state I am completely relaxed." (Pause.) "Every part of my body is now relaxed."

   f. Say, "In this healthiest possible state of being, I am absorbing energy from the atmosphere." (Long Pause—to be identified hereafter as L.P.) "When I bring myself out of this state, I will be completely refreshed—as refreshed as though I'd just wakened from a night of deep and restful sleep after a month at my favorite vacation spot." (L.P.)

g. Say, "My body will feel as though it were new-made, with every part in perfect working order." (L.P.)

h. Say, "My mind will be open to learning, and whatever I see, whatever I hear, whatever I read, I will understand and utilize." (L.P.)

i. Say, "I will be bursting with energy." (L.P.)

j. Say, "I will be filled with joy—a joy that will last for days." (L.P.)

Say a prayer of thanks for these blessings, and step into the private elevator, which will bring you up to waking level.

1. Your elevator doors close, and you inhale and rise slowly to 1, 1, 1. Exhale. Inhale and drift up to 2, 2, 2.
   Exhale. Inhale and float softly up to 3, 3, 3.
   Exhale. Inhale and drift up to 4, 4, 4.

2. Your elevator doors open and you step out, snap your fingers, and come wide awake and feeling great.

You may have noticed that you descended six floors but ascend only to the fourth floor. This has been deliberate, since most of us operate at a high beta level (i.e., with brain oscillations well above the thirteen per second of the lower end of the beta scale). You will want to be at low beta level when you emerge from meditation. The fourth floor is a reminder.

This is your basic framework for meditation. Various exercises will be added to these basics as the course progresses, but the instructions will not be repeated for a couple of chapters. Then we shall revise and streamline the procedure. Thus it would be best to mark this page so you can find it readily. Also, familiarize yourself with the steps, though you need not worry about reciting them verbatim. While it is advisable to follow the order of the instructions at first, the precise terminology isn't necessary. There's nothing magical or sacred about the wording. It will do nothing for you except act as a guide. The steps, however, should be followed closely for a time, since they have been carefully designed to provide the quickest route to mastering the technique. If you forget a step, nevertheless, you do not need to panic. You can remember it during your next meditation. What is important is that you relax as fully as possible during the initial sessions. Worrying about words or the order of the steps is inimical to such relaxation.

Furthermore, you should drawl out the instructions and leave long pauses between them. Ease of delivery is particularly important for success. In an altered state of consciousness, you should not be rushed. Your mind must have time to hear, accept, and pass the ideas on to the subconscious. Just as you sink into meditation, so the instructions must sink into your subconscious mind.

During this first attempt you may have felt a bit self-conscious—even silly, perhaps. Do not let this disturb you. Uneasiness of all sorts will fade as you persist. So will any unusual bodily reactions you may experience. Light-headedness is a good example. Some people become so anxious during their first meditations that their bodies are affected, or they are so fearful of losing control that they can't get "down to B." Such unwanted sensations will cease when they learn to relax and breathe easily. Rushing down into or hurrying out of alpha or breathing at the wrong rate might also result in some slight dizziness or other discomfort. Learn to pace your breathing so it doesn't place any strain on your body.

In other ways your body may resist your alpha trials at the start. For instance, if you have been troubled with persistent neck pain, you could become acutely aware of it during meditation; in fact, your neck may resist every attempt to relax it. Accept this, knowing that in a few sessions, your neck discomfort and any other aches or pains you have been suffering will disappear.

Screening Out the Senses

We have described the alpha state or the meditative experience as a means of screening out the five senses. Your bodily reactions during the first trials may indicate otherwise. Your sense of hearing could become so acute you will be able to hear dogs barking at the other end of the town. Your sense of smell or sense of taste may similarly become keener rather than dulled. Surprisingly, this is normal. It happens because your body has convinced you (or you have convinced yourself) that it is in control. It will not yield until you have learned to tame it—as you shall in succeeding lessons.

Following early attempts, some meditators have described a sea of faces flashing before their closed eyes. Some report drifting, whirling, or exploding colors.

None of these sensations is to be expected. We should not anticipate specific phenomena during meditation simply because another and different human being has experienced them. We are each individuals and will react in our own way. To expect is to limit oneself. But if images such as faces do occur, be assured they are nothing unusual or alarming. Furthermore, they are unimportant. Ignore them. Let them pass as easily as they come, for the true visualizations of your alpha work lie beyond.

Sharing Your Experience

If any of your friends are studying along these lines, you may wish to discuss your first journey in order to share your experiences. This is understandable and could be of mutual benefit. But after the novelty has worn off and you are comfortable with the process—as you should be after a couple of weeks of daily meditation—it is best to keep your experiences to yourself so that you do not weaken them. The paths to perception are solitary. Keep the details of your trip to yourself if you wish to advance. This rule will become increasingly important as you progress. However, if you encounter any initial stumbling blocks, you may find it helpful to discuss them with others.

You have now taken the first step toward becoming holistic, which means arriving at a point where your body, mind, and spirit will function in perfect harmony. Everything you encounter in your meditation work will be for your benefit. You will be rewarded with a belief in a higher power if you have none at present, firmer religious convictions if you possess a faith, and the joy of living in a world where you love yourself and others.

To assist yourself in achieving these goals, review this chapter carefully. Do not rush on to the next chapter until you have put the foregoing ones into effect. Then, before you resume your study or reading, compile a list of all those things, circumstances, experiences, or human characteristics of yourself or others that cause you to be unhappy. When you complete your "negative" list, jot down everything that makes you joyous. Put the lists in a safe place so you can refer to them later. You will need them for the third chapter and also for checking your progress after you have completed the study of meditation.

Begin your lists now. Also begin to meditate at least once a day for as long a period as seems comfortable to you. Do not fret about the length of your meditations, for they will grow longer as you become more adept.

Above all, relax. You are in good hands—those of the highest power of the universe, which has brought you to this moment where you can begin to grow.

2

Attitudinal Profile 1

At the beginning of any new venture, it is best to take stock of ourselves so that later we can assess our progress. In this study, we should become aware of how we perceive the world.

The famous Swiss psychiatrist Carl Jung believed that everyone adopts a dominant orientation to experience—that is, each of us perceives the world in a particular fashion. He identified four ways in which our consciousness responds to the environment: thinking, intuition, feeling, and sensation, and he illustrated these functions, as he called them, in the following manner:

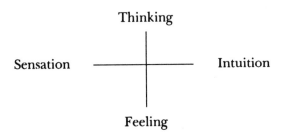

Although thinking is at the top of the diagram, it is no better than any of the other functions but is just one of four equally valid psychological adaptations. Of course, everyone uses all these functions at one time or another, and it is frequently difficult to determine which one is controlling our reactions to a stimulus. Nevertheless, one particular type exerts the most control and is assisted by a secondary or auxiliary function, which is adjacent to it on the diagram.

The attitudinal profile that follows has been designed to help you identify your dominant type. The situations described have been made as general as possible so they can apply to people of diverse tastes and backgrounds throughout the world. Further, they are basically simple, and we ask that you do not add any complicating factors that might influence your responses. Naturally you can think of more plausible circumstances or better solutions, but they might not indicate how you are oriented at this particular moment.

No answer is either right or wrong. There are no absolutes here and one response is as valid as another. Your answers will not reflect your morals, the way you feel about other people, or faulty or praiseworthy personality traits. Each will simply isolate the specific way you look at and react to the world about us.

In many cases there are no *clear-cut* differences between the choices, though the differences do exist, and we ask that you select the response that would be *most* appropriate for you in the given situation. Try to avoid any extraneous considerations, such as whether the individual involved can help or harm your career, how important he or she *really* is to your present or future, or how your relationship to the person would affect your decision. In short, be as objective as possible.

When you have selected an answer, write the identifying letter in the blank provided at the end of the profile or on another sheet of paper you can retain as a check against the retest at the conclusion of this course of study. Please answer *all* the questions. If in any of the questions there is no answer that fits your ideas exactly, then pick the one you think is closest.

Attitudinal Profile

1. At dinner the person you love is disappointed in his or her choice and wishes to have ordered your dish. You have an ample portion which you share because
   a. You recall a time when you made a similar mistake ordering.
   b. Food is evidently more important to the other than it is to you.
   c. The other's enjoyment of the moment is more important to you than the food.
   d. He or she doesn't want the food as much as the reassurance that you care.

2. You have invited a social acquaintance to have a cup of coffee with you and he or she refuses, pleading a previous engagement. You know this is not true and you
   a. Analyze the situation in order to understand the reason for the refusal.

    b. Are hurt because you feel that your acquaintance doesn't like you.

    c. Are not disturbed, since this is the other's problem, not yours.

    d. Pursue the subject in an attempt to discover the real reason for the refusal.

3. Some social acquaintances you met during a holiday have invited you to their home for dinner. You suspect it is a special occasion, such as a birthday celebration. You

    a. Take a gift. If it is not a birthday, you can pass it off as a thank-you for the hospitality.

    b. Play it by ear, taking a gift if it feels right to do so and nothing if it doesn't.

    c. Contact your host and ask if it is a special occasion, and act accordingly.

    d. Accept the invitation, knowing that you will do the correct thing when the moment arrives.

4. A film you are watching is very sad. You

    a. Enjoy seeing a film that everyone is talking about.

    b. Don't feel particularly upset, since it is only a film.

    c. Try to understand the problems that motivated the writer to develop such a situation.

    d. Cry, or feel like crying.

5. A social friend wants your approval of some work he or she has just completed. You think it is incredibly sloppy but you

    a. Ask yourself what you're supposed to learn from the situation, and act accordingly.

    b. Ask the friend what he or she plans to do with it.

    c. Spend considerable time discussing the work.

    d. Point out the areas where the work could be improved.

6. You are obligated to attend a lecture that your business is promoting in your area. None is more important to your work than another, but you have the following choices:

    a. A discussion of a recreational area plan for two years ahead.

    b. A debate on why the attitudes of young people have changed.

    c. A talk on the historical significance of your area.

    d. A panel discussion about the present crime rate in your region.

7. A fellow employee becomes ill and asks you to do part of his or

her work as well as your own. You do your best to cover both assignments because it is a rush job and
   a. The work has to be done.
   b. It is best for all concerned that you do the work.
   c. You are capable of handling emergencies.
   d. He or she would make mistakes that would take you more time to correct.

8. You receive a little less change than you believe you should. You
   a. Joke about the rising cost of living with the sales clerk but make no mention of the possible error.
   b. Call the sales clerk's attention to it, so he or she won't be careless in the future.
   c. Ignore the error, since you have made mistakes in the past and suspect you might have miscalculated the amount.
   d. Ignore the possible error, since it isn't truly important.

9. Your lost pet is returned to you, but the finder refuses your offer of a reward. You
   a. Are deeply moved by the refusal, though you would have done the same in that position.
   b. Inquire about the expense incurred in returning the pet and insist that the other accept that amount with your thanks.
   c. Express your gratitude for having met such a fine person as the finder.
   d. Know the finder doesn't need the money or he or she wouldn't have refused it, so you extend thanks.

10. At a restaurant a waiter accidentally spills some soup on your jacket. While he is apologizing, the manager intervenes and threatens to fire him for being so careless.
   a. You assure both manager and waiter that the jacket has not been damaged and the incident is unimportant.
   b. Recalling mistakes you've made yourself, you reassure the manager that no great harm has been done.
   c. You convince the manager he should excuse the accident if the waiter will pay for dry-cleaning your jacket.
   d. You make light of the incident and joke about it with your companions.

11. A new neighbor has asked you for a recommendation to your em-

ployer for a position that is available. You don't know the individual well enough to give a competent recommendation but you

    a. Are pleased to have the neighbor know you have influence, so you agree to the request.

    b. Agree to ask your employer to interview the neighbor.

    c. Have a feeling he or she wouldn't be right for the position, so you refrain from arranging any meeting.

    d. Do as asked so you won't hurt the feelings of the newcomer.

12. You are in line at a supermarket with about nine items in your basket, when someone with a full shopping cart asks to go ahead of you so as not to be late for an appointment. You have ample time. You

    a. Perceive that the person is always late, so invent an excuse for refusing.

    b. Are happy to be of assistance, so exchange places and start a conversation with the person.

    c. Know what it's like to be late, so agree to change places.

    d. Realize the other couldn't save that much time by going first, so invent an excuse for refusing.

13. On a television show you are offered the choice between taking a stated sum of money or gambling on what is behind a curtain. You decide

    a. To follow your impulses, since whatever you receive will be best for you.

    b. According to whether you need the money or can risk losing it for something that may be worthless to you.

    c. To gamble on the prize behind the curtain because you're enjoying being on the show and want to prolong the fun.

    d. On the basis of your success or failure in guessing correctly in the past.

14. Everyone is taking a turn at telling stories at a gathering. You choose the content of your story on the basis of

    a. What you believe is most suited to the backgrounds and interests of those present.

    b. Some possible future incident of a science-fiction nature that would intrigue your listeners.

    c. Whatever seems most important to you at the moment.

      d. The inherent fascination of the topic, so you can tell one of the most memorable stories.

15. Though you are happy in your present position and expect advancement, you are offered an immediate promotion in another part of the country. You decide

      a. You will refuse the offer rather than leave your family, friends, and current business associates.

      b. That while you have considered the situation, no clear alternative seems preferable, so on the basis of a hunch you decide it is or isn't right for you.

      c. After carefully considering the pros and cons of the offer.

      d. That what is in your best interest will happen without any strenuous effort on your part.

When all blanks are filled, you are ready to interpret your profile. On the next page you will find the key. Locate the letter you have assigned to number 1 and mark the appropriate square. If you have chosen c for the first question, for instance, you should place your mark in the sensation column; if d, mark the intuition column. Repeat the procedure for all questions.

When you have counted the number of marks, you will find you have the largest sum in one column and a second largest number in another column. You may, for instance, have six marks under sensation and five under feeling.

Answers

1 _____	6 _____	11_____
2 _____	7 _____	12_____
3 _____	8 _____	13_____
4 _____	9 _____	14_____
5 _____	10_____	15_____

Question No.	Thought		Intuition		Feeling		Sensation		Centered	
1			d		a		c		b	
2	a				b		d		c	
3	c		b		a				d	
4	b		c		d		a			
5	d		b				c		a	
6	c		a		b		d			
7	a		d				c		b	
8			b		c		a		d	
9	b		d		a				c	
10	c				b		d		a	
11			c		d		a		b	
12	d		a		c		b			
13	b				d		c		a	
14	a		b				d		c	
15	c		b		a				d	
Total Number										

Thought

If your number is largest in the first column, you are a thought-oriented individual. This means that you perceive and interpret your world mainly through thinking and drawing logical conclusions. You rely on your world mainly through thinking and drawing conclusions. You rely on your thought processes to help you adapt to the world. Thinking tells you what exists and helps you to understand what you have perceived about the world through your other senses. In short, it helps you to interpret experience. You are interested in the past, but your interest is unlike that of a feeling-oriented individual; yours is a historical past that affects everybody rather than a personal one. You place great store on principles derived from the past and on planning for the future by working on sound, logical guidelines. You fear letting your emotions run away with your head, and for you this could be dangerous. Because you value thought, you are sometimes accused of being cold and unfeeling, but this is because your psychological makeup is geared to thought, and this is the opposite of feeling, your suppressed function. Thinking or intellectual types will usually have as their secondary or auxiliary function either sensation or intuition. If you have a strong secondary type of sensation (a score of six on thinking and five on sensation, for example), you will base your thought on direct experience and be what is called an empirical thinker. If you lean toward intuition, with your secondary function being strongest here, you will be a speculative thinker. Of course, most of us are not pure types, and we must judge the influence of our secondary function by the extent to which it differs from the dominant.

Intuition

If your largest number of marks fall under the second column, you react to your world intuitively. You perceive experience less through the senses than through an inherent knowledge and are apt to be disturbed by the reality of things. You base your decisions on hunches, flashes of insight, and your immediate awareness of relationships. You are concerned primarily with the future, and what will happen is more real to you than what is occurring now or has occurred in the past. If your secondary function is thinking, you think speculatively, and if it is feeling, you operate on intuitive feeling. Because your suppressed function is most likely to be sensation, those who are sensation-oriented may feel you are impractical, unrealistic, or frivolous, though this is not the case. You merely perceive the world differently.

Feeling

If your score is highest in the third column, you are feeling-oriented. You judge experiences as being pleasant or unpleasant, favorable or harmful. You prefer the stronger emotions, which will be remembered even if they are unpleasant, rather than the weaker. You have a personal stake in the present and are apt to intensify a situation so that others become either happier or more dissatisfied as a result of your efforts. You value your emotional past, however, because it helps you to interpret present experiences in the light of the former. If your secondary function is intuition, you feel intuitively, but if you lean toward sensation, you combine feeling with sensory stimuli. Your suppressed function is probably thought, and you do not like to engage in logical thinking. This does not imply that you are incapable of thinking or are less valuable than an "intellectual," but that you perceive the world differently from thinkers.

Sensation

If you have scored highest in the fourth column, you are sensation-oriented. You interpret the world through the senses in order to perceive things as they are. You know reality, you experience the present in depth, and you are action-oriented. Because you have such a highly developed notion of what is "real," you interpret situations as they *are*, not as they have been or will be. Chance and possibilities are foreign to your way of thinking, for the here and now is all. If you have a strong feeling secondary function, you will interpret your experiences through sensory feeling, but if you have a strong thinking auxiliary function, you will use your senses in connection with thinking. Your suppressed function is probably intuition, and you may find it more difficult than other types to believe that some of the matters we discuss in this work are not only possible but probable.

Centered

Those of you who have scored your greatest number of points in the last column, on the other hand, will find the subsequent chapters easiest, for you are already on the path to realization. Even those who have a few marks in the centered column are to be congratulated, for your answers indicate you are sometimes able to perceive a better and totally different way of life. In either case, we urge you to continue reading so that you may use your abilities to the best advantage.

If you have not marked any of the "centered" answers, do not be disheartened. You will have ample time to change, if you so desire.

As we have explained, few of us have pure thinking, intuitive, feeling, or sensation orientations, so we are apt to fall somewhere between any two points. Of course every individual uses all four functions (thinking, intuition, feeling, and sensation), but only one is dominant, and an adjacent one is (usually) the auxiliary. This means that you will react the same way despite varying circumstances, so you do not respond as a thinking type in one situation and as a feeling type in another, similar case *unless* you have become psychologically well-advanced.

Each of these orientations is right. All are equally valid, and your recognition of your own type can be helpful in understanding those who are your "opposites" in that they think and react differently from you.

Much more will be said about the various functions in the closing chapters of this work, but for the present it is best to file your results away in a safe place so you will have them to compare with the results of a later test. Then you will understand more fully why the pretest is advisable, as well as its relationship to your development.

3

Detachment

Bring out the lists of fears and joys that you compiled after reading the closing paragraphs of Chapter 1. Look them over, and then inquire of some friends or relatives about the things that make *them* happy or unhappy. Do not tell them why you are requesting such information if you do not wish them to know about your meditation work, but simply say that you are curious about their reactions to life. Ask at least ten people, so you will have a good sampling for comparison, then check their responses against yours. Note how many of you have listed the same fears and joys, and how in some cases the items are so different. Discuss your findings with your friends.

The lists of unhappy thoughts are apt to be formidable. Yet they shouldn't be. Whatever your experiences in the past, you were not meant to be unhappy, or fearful, or anxious. Even if you cannot accept this statement at present, ask yourself what is worse—the fear of what might happen to you or the actual happening? Most of us find the fear more frightening than the actuality.

Now recall a specific instance when something you feared came to pass. You were able to handle it, weren't you? And even if you didn't cope as satisfactorily as you believe you should have, you survived the experience, didn't you? But perhaps the incident left a bitter taste in your mouth. If so, you can and will do something about it—though not quite yet. We will deal with recollections of the past later.

Check your lists once more and think about all those things you feared that *never* came to pass. Think of all the time and energy you wasted on dire events that never materialized. Take a few moments and recall the numerous fears that were groundless and the relatively few that merited an investment on your part. Then ask yourself if it is worth living in a constant state of agony just to be prepared for a few isolated instances. Fear is a paralyzing, absolutely senseless and useless emotion. As Franklin Delano Roosevelt said in 1933, "the only thing we have to fear is fear itself."

Hard Times

His words came at a time when the United States was in dire straits. The depression was in full swing. Uncounted numbers of people were out of work. Breadlines and soup kitchens were commonly set up in the cities, and the lines of the needy stretched for blocks. Those fortunate individuals who were employed were not well off, either. Salaries were low and covered little more than the necessities of life for the majority of Americans. Entire families were being dispossessed from their homes because they could not afford to pay their mortgages or their taxes, while others lived on steady diets of bread and potatoes. If ever there is a time to fear, it is during such a depression. Yet Roosevelt knew that fear would paralyze the people of the country into inaction when they needed to forge ahead and meet the challenges on a day-to-day level.

But we have seen an even more personal example of the debilitating effect of fear. During the first weeks of the initial teaching of this course at our college, a student announced that he could not permit himself to make any friends because he feared the results. Subsequent consultation with Robert revealed that he believed himself responsible for the deaths of several relatives and friends. At first we thought he was joking. Obviously he was not, for he began to enumerate the relatives and friends who had died suddenly, in car accidents or from illnesses. Believing himself to be the harbinger of death, he had closed himself off from contact with others. He had consulted psychologists and psychiatrists, and they were unable to help him. Further questioning revealed that his friends were all reckless drivers who, like himself, were addicted to speeding in old, beaten-up vehicles. We pointed out this fact, along with asking him why he thought he was important enough to be a "carrier of death" when in fact he was a normal, healthy young man who was being warned to change his driving habits. We asked whether this overwhelming fear wasn't truly a big ego trip, something he had convinced himself of in order to feel important.

How serious Robert was about his foreboding we shall never know, but the following day he met us in the hall and when we inquired about his problem, he said, "Oh, that's okay. I see that now. But I have a real difficulty that I want to talk to you about." The new issue turned out to be excessive smoking. We worked on that, and within a couple of weeks, Robert was able through meditation to cut his smoking from three packs per day to one cigarette. He could have eliminated the habit, but he hung on to that one cigarette, so he eventually worked back up to three packs per day.

Fortunately he was more successful with his first project, the elimination of fear. And so must we be in our lives. We are strong, resilient, capable of handling the great crises in life. We need not confront them all at once, either, but take them as they arise, one at a time.

Setting Time Aside for Worrying

Perhaps you don't feel capable of dealing with a crisis. Maybe you've encountered one in the past and feel that you didn't measure up. That's a concern we shall talk about shortly, but at this point in your development we shall ask you to set aside a "worry time." If you find yourself beset by fear during your waking hours, tell yourself that you do not have the time or energy to do justice to the worry and that you will handle it just before meditation. No matter what your fear is, or how pressing it might seem, postpone it.

Before you begin your meditation, open your box of postponed fears and wallow in them. Explore them to their fullest. Imagine them in their complete horror. Really let them out. What you will discover when you take the exercise far enough is that you will "crash through" the fear and it will dissolve, never to bother you again. If you don't achieve peace of mind, resume the work at your next meditation and continue it until you have completely demolished the fear.

Naturally there is a risk in working with any deep emotion, and that is that we attract disasters by dwelling on them. Then we literally bring them down around our heads. But the risk is substantially minimized in the "crash" handling of them, because we are ridding ourselves of them and can then proceed to a peaceful and positive meditation. Moment-to-moment fear is far more dangerous, for by keeping the thought constantly before us, uppermost in our minds, we draw the actualization of it to us like a magnet. Remember, whatever is going to happen to you will happen and nothing will prevent it, at this stage of your development. Within a short time you will learn how to attract only positive experiences, but for the present you are required to do nothing more than accept the slings and arrows of life and use your energy to cope with them.

A passage from the New Testament applies to Christian and non-Christian alike. Luke 12:31–32 cites Christ's words: " . . . seek ye the kingdom of God; and all these things shall be added unto you. Fear not, little flock, for it is your Father's good pleasure to give you the kingdom." Observe the "fear not." Then recall one of the nicest things that ever happened to you. It may have been winning money or some other prize, or receiving an unexpected gift, but it would have been something you didn't really expect or work your heart out for in order for you to recall it with such pleasure. Surprises of this sort can be the norm if you will simply open yourself to the possibility of ridding yourself of worry. Impossible, you think? Not a bit. Hundreds of people are successful, happy, well-adjusted. Look around you and you will find them. Should you ask, you would discover they have problems, too. Everyone does. But they impress you as being more fortunate than you because they don't permit the obstacles they encounter to spoil their appreciation of life. An admittedly rare but still existent few won't even permit themselves to entertain such negativities as worry.

Using Energy Productively

You can utilize your energy in a much more constructive way than by frittering it away with worry. Whatever happens to you is meant to teach you an important lesson, or is otherwise meant to be for your eventual good, and no amount of preinvested emotion will change that—at this moment. In fact, just the opposite will occur. Your fears will be magnets that draw misfortune to you, and you will create your own "Room 101," as does the lead character of George Orwell's novel *1984*. In the story, Winston has defied the government by having an affair with Julia. The government, known as The Party, has captured the lovers and sent Winston to prison, where he and others have been tortured. During his incarceration, he sees a skullfaced man dragged off to Room 101, the place of ultimate horror. When his own turn comes to be led to the Room, he asks his captor what is in it and is informed that he knows the answer already, that everyone knows it, and that Room 101 contains the worst thing in the world. Later the jailer tells him that in his case, the worst thing in the world is rats, and since he has a terrible fear of rats, Winston is doomed to have a cage fastened to his head and starving rats let into the cage so they can attack him. The implication is that the tortures of Room 101 vary, depending on the greatest fears of those to be punished. So it is in actual life. We bring our worst fears to pass if we continue to dwell upon them.

But it's useless to *advise* anyone to stop worrying. The habit is ingrained in all of us. It's the sort of cultural conditioning that takes work to root out, plus the desire to replace it with something more conducive to our well-being. Our work will begin with an exercise in detaching ourselves from every situation, feeling, and emotion. This is not as impossible as it may seem at first. The reason is that each of us is a composite of three parts: body, mind, spirit (or soul, if you prefer that term).

Exercise in Detachment

The concept of the three is an ancient one, going back as far as the Egyptians, who spoke of the Akh, the Ba, and the Ka, three parts of the soul or body of man, at least one of which survived death. While these are not synonymous with the body, mind, and spirit as we know them, they are the first account of triple parts which can be divided, so the idea carries the weight of history. You need not be thoroughly convinced that the body, mind, and spirit can be separated in order to observe their actions, but we do ask that you keep an open mind and make an honest effort to follow the suggestions below:

1. Wait until you are at a meeting or in church or in some place where there are people around you. Glance about the room and notice your fellow beings. Check your surroundings. Also notice that YOU ARE THERE. See yourself not as an individual, but as part of the whole group. Take a complete inventory of the surroundings. Notice the furniture in the room, the atmosphere, the clothes others are wearing, the way they are seated, the expressions on their faces, or anything else about them that is noteworthy. Also notice that YOU ARE THERE. See yourself seated in your chair and a part of the total environment.

Now think a moment. While you were doing this exercise, you didn't exist for yourself—not if you were really concentrating on following the instructions. You were too absorbed in remembering the steps and observing to be fully aware of YOU. But when you added yourself to the picture, you began to experience a sense of self. You strengthened this when you perceived yourself as part of the total environment. During your meditation you will further strengthen your sense of self by paying attention to your body and its reactions. Ignore what is happening in the group while you go through the following practice:

2. Close your eyes and visualize the other people and yourself seated among them. See yourself in whatever position you've assumed, wearing whatever clothing you've chosen for the day. Notice your hairstyle or anything else that distinguishes you from others in the group. Do not be concerned if you draw a blank when it comes to

imagining your face. Seeing one's own face is most difficult, and you will be able to accomplish this later if you don't succeed this time. However, you should try.

3. With this general image of yourself in mind, notice what that separate you is feeling. Are you comfortable? Anxious about a situation? Worried over a problem? Maybe finding it difficult to visualize the scene? Whatever your reaction, relax, and you will be able to observe your feelings.

4. Next, suspend judgment on your feeling and simply notice it, as disinterestedly and dispassionately as if someone else were telling you about how he or she feels.

5. Now slip back into yourself and work up a strong emotion. Be happy. Be fearful. Or be in love. Or jealous. Whatever emotion you choose, let it out to the fullest and push it to its limits.

6. With your eyes still closed, see yourself in your chair undergoing this emotion. Observe your face, if possible, and your kinesics as your body acts out your emotion. Watch the emotion you've chosen flow through your body. Stand aside and watch what is happening. Do not judge either yourself for choosing such an emotion or the feeling itself as being good or bad, but let it pass through unobstructed.

7. Slip back into your body and react again to the emotion as you normally would. Relax for a couple of seconds. Then ask yourself whether there is a difference between simply observing what you feel, as you'd observe someone else in an emotional state, or letting it affect you. Are you the emotion? Is the emotion you? Or are you something separate that can stand aside and watch? When you reach the point where you can answer YES to that last question, you have succeeded in detaching.

This is the most difficult task you will be required to undertake in this course of study. Some of you may be able to detach easily, while others may require more practice. If you feel you haven't been successful, relax and try again. Tension and anxiety can hold you back, but only temporarily, for every one of you can do this exercise. The reason is that you are *not* your body and *not* your emotions, and whatever pain or pleasure you experience can be separated from your mind and spirit in order for you to observe it. If you think about it, you will be able to recall several instances when you have done this spontaneously. When you have been in the midst of an argument, for example, you may recall having said or done something you wouldn't normally do or even wish to do—almost as if you had done so in spite of yourself. No doubt there were other times when you could "hear yourself'" or "see yourself" in action, as though you were a stranger observing yourself. In these cases you were naturally detached.

That you can separate mind from body in order to detach is easily proven. Let us suppose you have a toothache. You go to bed and finally fall asleep. When you awake, you have the same pain in the same tooth. But you didn't feel the ache while you slept. This toothache represents a malfunction of your body, but you were not conscious of it while you slept. Neither were you cognizant of the rest of your body during the sleep period. This being so, the body is separable from the mind during the unconscious state and therefore can be separated in the conscious period.

Conscious "Split"

Let us examine a *conscious* "split" by supposing you have a bad headache. Your head is really throbbing and you have no aspirin, so you decide to go to the drugstore for some. As you're leaving, the phone rings. You answer and find it is one of your friends, who has the most interesting news to tell you. The two of you converse for ten minutes, and when you hang up the phone, your head begins to pound again. But you weren't aware of having a headache while you were speaking to your friend. What happened to the pain? The answer, simply, is that in the excitement of the conversation, the pain of your head and your body was separated from your mind, so that while you were fully conscious, you were naturally detached.

Since conscious detachment is possible when your attention is directed elsewhere, such accidental detachments offer clues for deliberate and planned ones. All one must do to detach is to direct the attention someplace else, as we have done in the current exercise. But this time, choose a positive frame of mind and relive some happy moment.

8. Select a joyous occasion, such as a holiday or a celebration with your family or friends. Relive it as fully as possible: seeing, hearing, touching, smelling, and feeling the reenactment. Give it your complete attention.

9. Stand aside and watch yourself as you are seated in your chair in the midst of your surroundings, experiencing your recalled moment of bliss. As though you were watching a film of yourself, taken at the delightful moment and now replayed for your enjoyment,

observe your bodily reactions. Do not judge, criticize, or congratulate yourself for any reason. Simply observe the scene.

Open your eyes and continue to watch yourself. Keep up the watching for the remainder of the day. Pretend you are standing slightly behind
your right shoulder in order to observe everything that happens to you and
in you. Be sure to watch, exclusively. Do not judge yourself—or anyone
else—no matter what occurs.

As you progress, you will find that you will be able to mentally stand
aside and see yourself moving, feeling, living, as the day wears on. Doubt-
less there will be times when you slip back into yourself and forget about
watching or withholding judgment. Old ideas are hard to change, and our
cultural conditioning inclines us to believe that a human being is an in-
dissoluble whole. Yet we are not all of one piece, and after we surmount
the apparent foolishness of trying to separate body, mind, and spirit in order
to "catch ourselves in action," we begin to realize that each of the parts
can operate independently but join to form a "mystic three" that functions
as a whole.

Any of the three parts can dominate the remaining two while giving
the illusion that everything is one. The body, for instance, can be engaged
in such intense physical activity that one is conscious of only the exertion.
The mind and spirit take a back seat, and little real thinking or spiritual
evaluation takes place.

The mind can take over, as it frequently does when we are engaged in
an interesting conversation or in reading some fascinating book, so that
the body is entirely forgotten and the spirit (or soul) is likewise ignored,
since it is not called upon to evaluate the information on a higher level.

Spiritual Dominance

Few of us are accustomed to spiritual dominance in which body and mind
are subservient. In fact, the spiritual element in our makeup is grossly un-
der-developed and our body and mind grossly overdeveloped, when they
should be in equal balance. Because of this inequality, we are led astray,
particularly when we find ourselves in disagreement with others. Then we
are certain we are right and the opponent is wrong, when in reality we are
working on the more immediate body and mind principles that delude us,
ignoring the spirit, which would tell us how to operate at a higher level of
consciousness. When, on the other hand, body, mind, and spirit are exercised harmoniously, the spirit elevates the body and mind consciousness

above the level of the selfish and egotistical and enables us to function as a true whole.

While you experiment with separating the three parts of yourself, remember you are dealing with a natural function of the mind. Moreover, it's a healthy exercise. You need never fear adverse mental effects, for you are in complete control of what is happening. The awareness of yourself, your motives, your habits, and your attitudes toward the world will strengthen you in every aspect of existence whether physical, mental, or spiritual.

After you have finished your day of detaching, don't stop. Continue your conscious detachment for three days, or as long as it takes to realize you can separate these parts of you and observe the results.

Also, include the detachment exercises in your meditations, adding them to the meditation framework previously outlined. Continue working with detachment during meditations for one week at least, longer if necessary. Only when you feel you have mastered detachment and can be comfortable with it should you drop it from your program.

Do not attempt to rush this stage of your meditation schedule. You did not build your old world overnight and must adjust to the new you gradually. You will save time and gain the abilities you seek more quickly if you build a solid foundation.

4

Body, Mind, and Spirit

In the discussion of detachment, we have emphasized the body, mind, and spirit. These we shall call the "mystic three." In order to reach our full potentials as human beings, we must work with this interior "three" as opposed to the physical world and its symbol, four. As you know, we perceive the world as having four directions: North, South, East, and West. We also speak of the four winds that blow from the four corners, although civilizations other than ours identified the world by the symbolic *four*— the Egyptian and the Babylonian-Assyrian cultures before the Christian era being the first to do so. But humanity has traditionally been associated with the number seven, which comes from the four parts of the world that influence human life, and the three—body, mind, and spirit—that react to the external stimuli of the world. In the Middle Ages, the four and three became seven, the symbol of humanity, and the number seven has retained its symbolic importance to this day.

Furthermore, three was frequently depicted as a triangle, and four as a square. Another important geometrical configuration was the circle, symbolizing wholeness and completeness, and this was represented by the number ten. In the alchemical tradition of the Middle Ages and the Renaissance, the human figure was surrounded by a triangle, a square, and a circle to represent the ability to function as a whole person, but apart from alchemy, the earthly man was distinguished by seven.

Seven as a Magic Number

As a magic number, seven is nothing new to history. In Western civilization, it first became known to us from the inhabitants of the Tigris-Euphrates valley called the Sumerians (4000–3000 B.C.E.). This ancient culture identified seven planets and twelve signs of the zodiac. Jupiter, the creator planet, and the Moon and Sun were the prime three, and Mercury, Venus, Mars, and Saturn completed the sum. The descendants of the Sumerians, the Babylonians, believed that the soul had to pass through the atmosphere of each of the seven planets and assume the qualities of each planet in turn as it made its way to earth and the last step, assuming the earthly body so it could be born as human. One who died completed the process in reverse, shedding the fleshly body first and then the attributes of each planet as the soul made its way out to the last, Saturn. A similar concept was used by the Egyptians, for in their ancient religion there were seven mysteries the initiates had to master; these began with the Earth and moved out to Saturn.

So important was the number seven to the ancients that the Chaldeans of the Tigris-Euphrates region erected their Tower of Babel with seven steps, one for each of the planets. The base of the structure, furthermore, represented the four corners of the world.

The Bible and the Number Seven

Nor was the tradition ignored by the Hebrews and Christians. From first to last, the Bible deals with sevens. Genesis records that seven days were needed to create the world (including the seventh day on which God rested), while the Book of Revelation piles sevens upon sevens. Notable Christians like St. Augustine, St. Thomas Aquinas, and St. Teresa of Avila also categorized in sevens, Augustine and Aquinas dealing with the seven deadly sins and the seven mansions that one must pass through on the way to God.

Today seven is known as a magical number and in some circles stands for the mystic, retirement, inner work, and seclusion. So it comes as no surprise that detachment requires the same number of steps, seven, and the pattern becomes clearest when we begin with the quadruple segment.

Though we are accustomed to speaking of five senses, there are actually just four that originate from localized, specific organs: the eyes, ears, nose, and mouth. These account for the major stimulations we receive from the world. The so-called fifth sense, feeling, is unlike the other four because it is generalized, and it is not confined to the body or exterior stimulation per se. It can be subjective and can work with the body, mind, or spirit separately. Thus we can classify the five senses as the four involved with the specific organs that gather sense impressions from the world *four* (sight, hearing, smell, and taste receiving their stimuli from the world square) and one sense, feeling, which is triple rather than single.

The Sense of Touch

When feeling operates in conjunction with the body, the sense is tactile and we refer to it as the sense of touch. But touch is merely a partial description. The mind feels, as well as the body. It observes stimuli conveyed to it by the four localized receptors, analyzes the data, and makes a decision on what it "feels" is consonant with the whole. In this manner we pass judgment on a new dish we encounter at dinner. We employ sight, smell, taste, and even sound when necessary, to judge crispness and then decide whether or not we like the new food. Our decision is mental, so we use a different "feel" from the tactile.

Still another type of feeling affects the soul. This aspect of a human being can be described as an abstract condition that gives rise to the spirit, just as a rose exudes its fragrance. As the soul's aroma, the spirit's feelings differ from corporeal or mental feelings, thus accounting for such reactions as those termed "heavy-hearted" or "light-hearted." We all understand that these reactions have nothing to do with the physical organs; rather, they are descriptions of spiritual responses to given conditions. (However, the spiritual responses must be of a positive nature in order to truly reflect the soul, which is perfection. A heavy-hearted feeling, therefore, is a denial of the soul, whereas a light-hearted feeling is in accord.)

Our classification can thus be seen as sevenfold. We employ four receptors that are open to worldly stimuli and three having to do with feeling. Of the three, touch originates with the physical body in the world, but the other two feeling phenomena stem from the mind and spirit. The distinction is important, for it is the mind and spirit feelings that we detach from the sight, sound, smell, taste, and tactile feelings in order to stand aside and watch ourselves in action.

We can see, then, that the five bodily senses are not the total of ourselves. Nor are the emotions. Body and emotion can be set aside and observed. We reiterate this point because in some future meditational moment, you may encounter the stillness at the core of your being and unless you realize that you are NOT your emotions and DO NOT REQUIRE emotional content to exist, you may be panic-stricken by the feeling that you've reached the center of yourself and found no one home. Fortunately this is not the case. Once we dispense with superfluous stimuli and pare ourselves to the core, we reach the true meaning of life.

For the last few centuries we have looked to the world for the answers to our most pressing problems, notably war, famine, pestilence, death, and our inhumanity to one another. During the Middle Ages, some people believed the dilemma would be solved if everyone had the opportunity to be educated. But we know education has not succeeded, for in our country at least it is available to all. From the beginning of the twentieth century, we have looked to science for the answers. Our technological advancements have been mind-bending; we have progressed almost from the horse-and-cart stage to a manwalk on the moon. But despite the fact that 90 percent of all scientists who have ever existed are alive today, we have made little progress toward improving the essential quality of life.

Answers Within Us

Clearly the answers do not lie in the world outside. They are hidden within us—the last place we have thought to search. So we must begin to attend to our inner selves, and the way to start is to watch. See precisely how we've been living. Notice how foolish it is to become excited over matters that are either trivial or transitory. Why, for instance, should we become upset over hard-boiled eggs for breakfast when both soft-boiled and hard-boiled have the same nutritional value? Instead, let us give thanks for at least having eggs when so many others in the world are denied proper sustenance. And what is so important about missing a bus when another will be along shortly? Why do we permit ourselves to become disturbed over the slightest events of the day? Why should so many niggling concerns irritate us at all? Events are outside us, and what does not touch the inner self is trivial, fleeting, and scarcely worth an emotional investment.

Benefits of Detachment

The benefits you will derive from detachment are immediate. First of all, a keen appraisal of yourself will permit you to identify your faults so you can begin to work on improving your attitudes, personality, and character. Second, detachment will prevent you from continuing to be one of the weak people who live by alternately attacking and defending—or, if you are not one of these, it will protect you against those who are. By word or action and sometimes by physical assault, the weak strike—and when their victims attempt to retaliate, the weak have their guard up. Now you can free yourself of this deplorable habit or protect yourself from others who exhibit such behavior. The principle is that used in the noncombative martial art called aikido: one permits the opponent to attack or defend, to strike or recoil. All takes place without effect, since *resistance is required for an injury to take place.* The air cannot be harmed. Neither can we if we refuse to satisfy an aggressor's emotional need to attack, for the aggressor will thereafter ignore us and seek satisfaction elsewhere. The secret of self-protection against weak people of this sort is exactly that of aikido, although both require retraining of the mind. Detachment is our initial lesson in retraining.

All the same, our real purpose in this study is to improve ourselves. We are the only individuals we can change, and if we encounter those who would attack us, we recognize that the problem is theirs—not ours—and we have enough to do with remaking our own lives without trying to change the entire world.

Energy-Sappers

Another bonus of detachment is that it can prevent us from continuing to sap the energy of others and will protect us from those who launch a similar attack upon us. Energy-sappers are individuals who tire others out, both physically and mentally. We start off feeling refreshed until we meet them, and then we leave feeling exhausted. It isn't necessarily the subject matter of the conversations that is at fault. We've encountered some persons who wear us down by constant complaint, a whining voice, clutching at our clothing, or any of the other ploys by which the temporarily weak and insecure attempt to hold the attention of their prey. They, on the other hand, thrive on our depletion. They go away feeling great.

To avoid energy-sappers is often impossible. They are members of our households, close relatives, neighbors, or colleagues at work. Even worse, they are ourselves, for we are often guilty of this fault. But we needn't continue to drain the energies of others or permit anyone to drain ours. We can detach. We can watch ourselves in action, observe our techniques, and learn what havoc we are causing, just as we can watch others, observe them, and wait patiently for them to finish.

The principle is identical to that of electricity. A current will flow unimpeded through open wires. But when resistance is set up—as in the form of a clamp midway on the wire—the current will continue to flow up the clamp while the current beyond it will drain away rapidly and not be replaced. Any resentment of our resistance to an energy-sapper creates a blockage in the energy flow. Detachment keeps the wires open and the energy coursing through. As rapidly as one uses energy, it is replaced, for nature abhors a vacuum. Later we shall explain how to build your energy without trying to drain it from others, but first you must learn to control your own life and to play by your *new* rules, not anyone else's. Of course, you may feel you came into the game after the rules were established, but that doesn't mean you can't change them once you realize they are wrong. And it is always wrong to permit others to control you negatively.

Let us suppose you awaken in the morning feeling refreshed and reasonably content. Then someone picks an argument at the breakfast table or while you're on your way to work. That fight, or even one cross word, can start a chain reaction that will make your day miserable, for you got off on the wrong foot and the results will echo and reecho through your waking moments. But they shouldn't have. And they won't, once you refuse to accept the negativities of yourself and others.

Needing People

You make a similar error when you permit others to say what is right or wrong for you to do, how to dress to keep in fashion, how to act so people will like you. Of course, we are not talking about young children being instructed by their parents, but about adults who should know better. Why is it so vital to have friendship, love, success, power—whatever? Certainly these intangibles are advantageous, but are they really worth the sacrifice of our higher selves? And do they really depend upon the advice of others? Aren't there times when you—like all of us—have tied yourself in knots trying to satisfy another person, and it hasn't worked? Do our true friends, or those who really love us, demand that we pander to them constantly? If they do, there's something wrong with the way we're approaching the world.

Despite anything any of us does or refuses to do, if people are going to like us, love us, give us a raise, or elect us to office, they'll do it anyway, as long as we don't hinder our progress by being phonies, hypocrites, vacillators, or doormats.

In short, if you are true to yourself, and that means being AN HONEST AND WORTHWHILE HUMAN BEING, you don't need a solitary thing in addition. Far from being lonely, you'll have more friends than you can find time for. You will achieve success beyond your wildest imagining. Power, too, will be granted to you if it is in your best interest to have it. But you should not want it for personal gain or to compensate for some inadequacy you may feel, because then you wouldn't be able to use it for the general good.

Wanting Power

If you have been ambitious for power or position, this might be a good time to examine your motives. Sit down and list the reasons for wanting this exalted status. You may be attempting to cover some hidden "lack" in yourself. However, there is nothing you require from life that you don't already possess. You are a unique individual—as unique as your set of fingerprints or any snowflake of the billions that float to earth during a winter storm. You have a particular set of talents, a genius in one or several areas. You have your particular niche in the scheme of life that no one else can fill, and you have only to uncover this area of expertise, to discover your individual mission, in order to be free. And you must never compare yourself unfavorably with others. Their abilities, their talents may exceed yours in some areas, but you are just as important as they in the design of life. You will find this is so as you progress in your meditation work. The detachment exercises should give you the first clues to the truth of the statement.

Suspending Judgment

Another aspect of detachment that you should observe is the willing suspension of judgment. Like the "willing suspension of disbelief" which Coleridge claimed an audience must adopt to enjoy a poetic work, the willing suspension of judgment is temporary. Try it for one day. Then extend your trial period to three days. By then you may discover that it's such a valuable technique you may want to use it forever. In any case, begin with other people. No matter how terrible they are, or how admirable in terms of your former assessment, do not see them in this light. Simply note what they do or say without drawing conclusions. Even if they direct emotion toward you, they can do nothing to you unless you grant them the power. The old cliché is true: "Sticks and stones can break your bones, but names will never hurt you." Only the *belief* that names, other words, or emotions felt by others can injure you, will do you harm. But when you detach and suspend judgment, you will be in a position to see how influential others *really* are. Why allow yourself to play by anyone else's rules when you can find better ways of serving the world?

One caution, however. Some of us at the start of our meditational work fall prey to self-pride. Because we have set foot upon the path leading to a higher consciousness, we may begin to criticize those we consider beneath us or to envy those who are advanced. It is well to remember that we are each at our own stage of development and that we are not engaged in a contest. We are where we should be, just as others are, and we are not entitled to feel superior or inferior. Detachment can save us from this pitfall.

Once you've practiced a bit on other people, you can begin the more difficult part of this assignment: the suspension of judgment on yourself. Before you can transform yourself into a bright, shiny, new individual who can leap tall buildings at a single bound, you must pass through this period of apprenticeship. And it isn't easy. The fact is, we are all our own worst enemies. We forgive others their transgressions and mistakes and lie awake far into the night berating ourselves for sins of omission or commission. The tune is the same for everyone; only the words differ. They can run something like this: "How could I be so stupid as to tell my girlfriend she's an ugly, inconsiderate blob?" or "My boss really needed help and what did I do? Selfish idiot that I am, I told him to solve his own problems," or "I had no business losing my temper, no matter what the provocation. I made myself look like a real fool."

Naturally, we should recognize when we have made a grievous error and resolve to do better in the future, but we must be willing to release ourselves and others from the past so we can start our personal reformations.

Haunting, Past Sins

Even when we haven't made any recent *faux pas,* old sins can come back to haunt us—sins we may have committed years ago, sins we'd prefer to forget that creep up on us in the silent, lonely hours when the rest of humanity abandons us to our private reckonings. And how we punish ourselves for them—even after a glorious success when the initial excitement dies down and we begin to realize we shall have to pay the price for such glory, since we are, after all, unworthy and imperfect human beings.

But you will have to put these destructive attitudes behind you and start afresh if you're ever to break the circle of blame and recrimination. Forgive others completely. Then forgive yourself. You are now on the threshold of a new life. Nothing of the old will carry over if you are sincere about improving yourself.

God's Forgiveness

We hope you are eager to take advantage of this new condition, but perhaps you think that God, or whoever you believe operates this orderly universe, won't permit you to get off that easily. Let's analyze this misconception. Suppose you're a parent whose child has misbehaved, perhaps by stealing some candy and eating so much as to become ill. You punish the child for the misdeed, and the child apologizes and promises to change. The child is sincere in wanting to reform. After that, could you hold the incident against your child? Will you punish the child forever for what is past and done and apologized for? If you'd forgive your child, as any rational human being would, how much more will the power that we call God forgive us? The New Testament has a message for everyone: ". . . what man is there of you, whom if his son ask bread, will he give him a stone? Or if he ask a fish, will he give him a serpent? If ye, then, being evil, know how to give good gifts unto your children, how much more will your Father which is in heaven give good things to them that ask him?" (Matt. 7:9–11).

The pain and suffering we experience from our transgressions do not come from outside. They are within us, and rightly so, for they keep us from making worse mistakes. But particularly when we've repented, pain and suffering do not come from God, who is too fair and too busy to hold grudges. We hang onto our sufferings ourselves, and we can, if we will, let them go so we can start afresh. Let us start by forgiving others and conclude by erasing our own errors.

Even extreme cases will yield to a new attitude. Suppose someone has been released from prison after serving a sentence. He may wish to begin a new life, but feel that society will not provide the opportunity to work or offer the respect to which every decent human being is entitled. This individual must do what each of us is required to do—change his or her attitude and think and act like a decent and respectable person. In a brief time others will come to accept this evaluation. We know ourselves best, and if *we* do not believe we are worthy, how can we expect others to believe it?

Steps Toward a New Life

Let us begin a new life together. Today. This moment. We shall start by practicing detachment and the willing suspension of judgment. These are not new or radical concepts, of course, merely ones that we must remind ourselves to put into practice. As we do so, we must be careful to avoid the false pride that comes from thinking we are better than others. In truth, we are no better or worse but merely at a different level of development, so we have no right to make invidious comparisons. The problems that we encounter on *any* level are not confined to a single circumstance or individual, either. They're universal. But we can begin to change the universe if we start with the only thing we *can* change—ourselves. Let us put these concepts into use. Now. This very moment. As you meditate, decide to forgive others their transgressions. Then forgive yourself your own transgressions, and be reborn as a sincere and worthwhile human being.

Do not expect any earthquakes or bolts of lightning to punctuate your decision. In fact, you probably won't feel any different at first and may conclude nothing has changed. Later you will wonder why it took you so long to learn such a vital lesson about life—but that will be after the "new you" has adjusted to the change.

The following exercise may be used to hasten your adjustment. Turn back to page 7 in Chapter 1 and follow the basic meditation procedure through step 2c. At that point, run through the detachment exercises outlined in this chapter, and then return to your mental film screen.

When the random thoughts have flashed across your screen and been erased, visualize a "transgression" or some other incident in your life that has caused you anguish. Then follow these steps:

1. See yourself on your mental film screen reliving that moment, and feeling all the pain and suffering it caused you. Now detach by pretending that you are another person watching the incident, and you will be able to see the occurrence for what it really is: something that happened to a stranger who has no earthly connection with this new person you have decided to become.

2. Repeat the visualization for any two other major transgressions that bother you still. If you have more "sins," crowd them together on your mental film screen and then detach yourself from the total by pretending you are a bystander who is watching the show.

3. Say the following prayer:

   "This is the beginning of a new day. The Lord has given me this day to use as I will. I can waste it, or I can use it for good. What I do today is important because I am exchanging a day of my life for it. When tomorrow comes, this day will be gone forever, leaving in its place something I have traded for it. I want it to be gain, not loss; good, not evil; success, not failure; In order that I shall not regret the price I paid for it."

4. Know that you have been forgiven and are ready to be reborn in the light and will have no connection with the old, former you.

5. Use Step 2 of the original basic meditation. While focusing on your

blank screen, seek the silence and let it heal you of old hurts and injuries. Remember always to stand in the light, for the light will hasten your healing. Complete the remainder of your basic meditation, and bring yourself back up to the conscious level.

The preceding prayer, written by the brothers of the Abbey of the Genesee in Piffard, New York, and printed on the wrappers of their bread, is perfect for your new condition. We recommend you use this beautiful invocation, which the brothers gave us permission to share, to begin all your meditations.

Resurrecting Yourself

What you have accomplished in this exercise can be compared to the legend of Dumuzi, told by the ancient Babylonians. Each year Dumuzi died and descended to the underground. Each spring he was resurrected by the goddess he married. You, too, have descended to the depths and have shed your old life in order to be born again. Just as the Christians believe Jesus died for the sins of mankind and was resurrected, know that the old you has been sacrificed so the reborn you will be freed of the past. But as with Christ rather than Dumuzi, your "resurrection" will happen just once, instead of being an annual occurrence.

In this exercise you have also completed one of the most important symbolic figures—the circle. You have gone down into yourself and come back out to start a new and better cycle. Further, you have achieved in each meditation what is called a catabasis—a descent to the depths in order to emerge with greater insight or knowledge.

Naturally you may have difficulty at the outset in accepting the permanence of your rebirth and begin to backslide. If so, do not become discouraged. If you work on detachment and the willing suspension of judgment for three days of conscious time and seven days of meditational time, you should need no further reinforcement.

Be patient with others and yourself. Old habits are hard to break, but you can succeed if you persevere. The procedures will become easier and your meditations longer as you continue. In a few weeks you will begin to reap the benefits of your work.

5

Emotions

If you have persisted in your detachment exercises, you may have experienced some interesting situations. First of all, your behavior will have puzzled others. Your relatives and close friends may have become quite upset by what they perceive as your "indifference" to them or their needs, or as your "coldness" towards them. If so, they probably have reacted angrily, tried to pick a fight with you, or in some other manner attempted to "bring you to your senses."

One of the signs that detachment is working for you is this "psychic storm" that arises when you begin to practice it. The reason is not hard to fathom. Your family, friends, and business associates have learned how to get along with the old you. They know exactly how much pressure to apply and when to capitulate—in short, exactly how to keep your association on an even keel. That is not to say that their behavior is wrong. We do the same in all of our relationships with people, and we must not criticize others for doing what is required. And we can't condemn them for reacting when, virtually overnight, we change our patterns of behavior. Alterations in personality are confusing. Others aren't prepared for the change, and they certainly don't want someone they love to change for the worse—and detachment could well give this impression to start with. So they may ask if you're ill, because you're not "acting like yourself." When that doesn't work and you continue with what they regard as indifference, they may accuse you of being selfish and concerned only with yourself.

Please be patient with others during this time, for it is normal for them to be upset. And they are correct when they accuse you of being selfish. However, it is vital that you are, for you must learn what is best for you before you become involved again with normal living. Detachment is not meant to estrange you, only to shock you out of the rut of habit so you can see what you are doing right or wrong in life and make the required adjustments. When your learning period is over, you will have ample time to make amends, and your newfound insights will help you to be a more valuable associate, friend, or relative. And if, during the period of trial, others become disturbed and manifest negativities, remember you have no right to judge or to feel the least bit superior. Self-pride is the worst of the possible feelings towards others, and our goal is to be more understanding and loving individuals rather than insufferable egotists concerned only about ourselves.

The Dark Period of Detachment

But whatever reactions you get from those about you, do not abandon your position of temporary indifference that we call detachment. Ride out the psychic storms of this period, no matter how difficult they might seem, for the important successes do not come easily. Consider yourself as undergoing a required period of alteration, and remember that reform is always upsetting and frequently tumultuous. Do not despair if in every facet of your life, things seem to go wrong. They well might for a brief time. The mystic St. John of the Cross called this period "the dark night of the soul." For most of us, he is correct, for we all have accumulated the effects of bad habits (often known as karma), which must be cleared away before we can start fresh. So this period of readjustment when people strive to "bring you back to normal" could be the most disruptive. Nevertheless, once you have cleared out the harmful energy patterns that cling to you like barnacles on a ship and slow your progress, matters will smooth themselves out. The storms will pass. You will emerge from your self-centered detachment with a more tolerant attitude toward humanity and a deeper appreciation of the problems of living that will put you at one with others instead of in opposition to them.

Love, Hate, and Emotions

During this period when you've been divorcing yourself from your former ways, you may have discovered something about emotion. Whether love or hate is involved, you sustain it by holding onto the other person. This is clear enough when we talk of *our* love or *our* hate for someone else—the emotion originates with us and we can visualize it as a hold we are exerting. But the same applies to the love or hate others may feel *towards* us, even if we don't reciprocate. We recognize the emotion, of course. But we also contribute to it by that recognition. We become convinced it is they who clutch at us and fasten the love or hate onto us, while in reality it is we who refuse to let them go. It is one thing for any of us to love or hate, and these emotions are more closely associated than we normally credit them as being. But your love, your hate, your envy—or whatever else you feel for others—is *your* burden, *your* business, the problem you have to deal with and understand if you are to grow spiritually and psychically. The emotions others direct toward you, however, are not your concern. The love, hate, or jealousy—whatever form it takes—is theirs. They generate it. They must pay the price for it, and that includes the attack it makes on their bodies. It has nothing to do with you *unless* you recognize it and, in doing so, accept it. Then *you* hold your persecutors as surely as if you were the direct cause. But if you detach and let go, the emotions of others fade or your antagonists move out of your life. Here is the meaning of Shakespeare's phrase to "kill with kindness." The "kill" injunction is not a physical command and has nothing to do with revenge; it simply means that when you stop accepting an enmity, it will fade, alter, or be directed elsewhere.

If this concept is difficult for you to believe, try a simple experiment. Pretend that a person who hates you is a flaming stick. You hold this stick in your hands, knowing that the longer you hold it, the greater your danger, for it will burn its way out and scorch your flesh. Of course you are too sensible to let this happen. You will drop the stick and walk away from it, letting it burn or fizzle out as it likes. This is precisely what happens with the negative emotions others feel toward you. *Unless* you accept them and hold onto them, they cannot affect you in any manner. If you believe that your antagonists will pursue you, think again of the stick. If the flaming brand is used to attack you in any fashion, you still have your mobility and can move out of its path.

The Burden of Hate

The hate or any other negative emotion someone feels toward you is that person's burden and responsibility, not yours. In fact, it may not have anything to do with you. It may spring from the other's recognition of some quality in you that he or she is trying to either repress or create in the self. In either case, it is a compliment of sorts. Something about you is important enough to cause another human being who is indulging in hatred, to fear you, and this fear erupts in enmity. This may wound your self-esteem, for you believe that you have done nothing to merit this reaction. Whether you have or not, it makes no difference. So long as you hold onto this negative emotion projected by another person, you are permitting the other to tell you how you should feel about yourself. That is ridiculous. *You are you, unique and important to the universe, and you should assess your own worth instead of letting others do it for you.*

Whatever individual dislikes you or seeks to harm you for any reason, release that person now. In the meditation exercises that follow, you will be given a statement of release. Use it. Let go of the destructive emotion harbored by another, and you will be set free, for every person you hold will keep you in chains forever.

Temporary Detachment from Love

While pleasant, the happier emotions, such as love, can also enthrall. In fact, the world *thrall* originally referred to a slave, one held in bondage. If you are to advance, you must free yourself of love's bondage in order to observe its effects. We are not asking you to begin an emotional divorce, by any means. You can return to your usual state in a couple of days and need only—during the detachment period—cease being affected by the other person's moods and whims. Why, for example, should you be happy if he smiles? Or miserable if she is angry with you? Why should you permit anyone else in the entire world to dictate your feelings? Why should you play someone else's game, no matter how fond you are of him or her? Let the other come or go, frown or smile—those are not your problems. If it is right for you to be loved by this individual, nothing will be able to prevent it. If it is wrong, nothing you can do will change that, so you are better off releasing yourself in order to accept a higher good. And that is what always happens. Nothing is taken from you without something better replacing it.

Besides, love cannot tolerate restraint. You hold this precious quality as you do when you wish to drink from a spring but lack a glass. Your cupped hands will retain all the need for refreshment, but clench your fists and the water—or love—slips away.

To be reborn you must be free. Release others from the emotions they feel for you, and yourself from whatever you feel for others, and you will be released from dependence on every person or thing in this world.

When the period of detaching and watching is over, you will have learned some important things about emotions and can resume the more positive ones, such as love. The exercise is merely temporary.

Keeping Responsibilities

This does not mean you can abandon your responsibilities, however. You must continue to do your duty toward family, employers, teachers, friends, and acquaintances. All you do is stop seeking returns from any of them.

If you bring home your wages, for instance, do not expect a reward. That is your duty. If you give a gift to a friend, do not expect one in return. Do not even expect a thank-you. If you do receive recognition, fine. If not, it was still your pleasure to give the gift, and it should not make the slightest difference to you whether the recipient is pleased or not. If you are kind to someone who returns the kindness, you receive a bonus. But if you are kind to someone who returns an unkindness, you have a real opportunity to flex your spiritual muscles. Ingratitude is his or her problem, not yours. You do what you must, what you ought to do in order to fulfil your purpose in life, without considering reciprocities. You should expect nothing in return for your goodwill—neither smiles nor gifts nor friendship.

At first it may appear the height of egocentricity to be concerned only with your own reactions. Admittedly, you are being selfish for a time, though the sacrifice is necessary. WHAT IS GOOD FOR YOU IS GOOD FOR YOUR WORLD, and that includes every person in it. If you are not reasonably happy and content, others around you cannot be. Happiness begins with you.

Certainly others may misunderstand your actions at first But do not let that deter you. Your job is to disentangle yourself from all relationships for as long as it takes to learn what is truly right or wrong for you. Once you learn, you will find that your responsibilities to others have increased rather than lessened and that it is considerably more difficult to do what is *really* right for you and your world, yet ultimately easier because you will be capable of handling any task. Whatever is wrong with your world will become right when you approach it correctly. Remember also that the detachment exercise is not permanent.

Good and Evil

Some concepts need to be completely eliminated, however. One of these is society's dichotomies: right-wrong, good-evil, and so on. The natural order does not contain these contradictions. There are no absolutes, merely varying shades of gray that depend on how any situation is perceived by an individual. In order for society as a whole to recognize opposites, humanity had to split itself Into warring camps. This division occurred centuries ago in Western civilization in the area of religion, when our ancestors decided that what was not of God, or good, had to be a direct opposite— the Devil, or (to drop the D) *evil*. Having made that decision, human beings proceeded to set up rules and regulations to which people could conform.

We have accepted these imposed rules as part of our cultural conditioning. Now it is time to become realistic about them. The fact is that THERE IS NOTHING WHICH CAN BE TERMED GOOD OR BAD EXCEPT ON A PERSONAL BASIS.

Food, for instance, is required by all creatures. A lion needs food to exist; thus its actions in securing food are neither good nor bad. It kills to live, not for pleasure. We humans likewise require food, but our case is more complicated. We frequently kill for pure sport. We might justify our action if we consumed our own prey, but often the carcass is left to rot. And many people harm creatures of the lower species simply because they have the power to do so. An ant in its natural habitat normally doesn't pose a threat to a person, but many people—adults as well as children—will deliberately crush an ant, a spider, or a beetle underfoot. Though these creatures are performing some specific function of which we may not be aware, each is a part of the universe and thereby entitled to continued existence.

"One Man's Meat . . ."

Furthermore, everything that we put into our mouths is not cosmically beneficial. Of itself, food is benign, blameless. It is misused when we eat too much, too little, or the wrong combinations. And even what is salutary for the masses may be poison to a specific person, such as an ulcer patient or a diabetic. To use a more extreme example, babies afflicted with PKU (phenylketonuria) have faulty metabolisms and cannot properly deal with the protein that most of us need. These babies have to be kept to a strict diet formula or they may suffer brain damage. Food itself is never at fault. Whether it is "good" or "bad" must be determined on an individual basis.

Alcohol is another benign substance. If taken judiciously it can be used to relax tensions. For those with certain chemical imbalances that make them potential alcoholics, it can do harm. Use or abuse is an individual decision, and even occasional abusers have reason to regret their intemperance. The mildest form of punishment is the hangover, but many who indulge themselves to the point of drunkenness have committed acts and made statements for which they are sorry afterwards. Yet one cannot blame alcohol. It is the individual who is so foolish, as the old English saying goes, as "to put into his mouth what will steal away his brains."

Drugs other than alcohol are neutral, as well. They can be used to alleviate pain when taken as medication, or they can cause untold pain and suffering, lifetime complications for both the abusers and those members of society who are somehow associated with them.

But use or abuse extends beyond what is ingested by humankind. Every substance, force, or emotion is governed by an identical law. Money, for example, can be a dangerous weapon in the hands of one human being or act as a blessing in the hands of another. Money is not good or bad. The way it is used by the possessor determines its effect.

The rule applies to power, success, education—the list is infinite. What we use wisely for ourselves, we employ for our own good and the good of the world. When we go to extremes, we create trouble.

Even abstract qualities fall under the rule. Honesty, for instance, is considered a virtue. Too little of it will cause one to mistrust Joe Smith, and too much of it can be disastrous—if Joe Smith prides himself on being "honest" and thus excuses his deliberate attempts to hurt others. Any virtue can become a vice when taken to extremes, a fact that our pagan ancestors well knew. They believed that measure is best, and that one should do everything in moderation, a concept that the Roman writer Horace later called the Golden Mean. The rule still holds. Each of us bears the responsibility for carrying nothing to excess. Perhaps this is another way of describing free will, for the choice must be made by you and you alone as to how you will utilize whatever emotions, talents, or material possessions have been entrusted to you.

While we are on the subjects of emotion, drugs, and money, let us explore them a bit further and determine whether the attitudes we have adopted toward them need to be altered.

As we have emphasized, you are responsible for *your* emotions, and yours alone. At the present moment you are being asked to observe them as they pass through you and not judge whether they are good or bad. When you finish these detachment exercises, however, you will be faced with a new set of problems: whether to allow your emotions full play or suppress them, how to deal with emotional flareups, or whether to accept or avoid other people who exhibit emotions you consider harmful.

Emotions Placing Strains on the Body

Emotions are transient and should be treated as you would any guest: with courtesy and consideration. Nevertheless, they are powerful psychic charges while they last, and to suppress them over any length of time might cause them to build up such pressure that they will explode. Yet to give vent to any emotion is to place a strain on the body, in the form of higher blood pressure or released adrenalin, to mention but a couple of the possible results. Objectively speaking, the alternative is equally bad. Anyone who exhibits no emotion may as well be a zombie, for he or she doesn't care enough about himself and others to respond.

How, then, are we to come to grips with this problem? As rational human beings, we must ask ourselves a few questions. First, is the situation important enough to become excited about? Be honest with yourself as you answer. If you have low blood pressure, you can indulge in an emotional outburst more readily than someone with high blood pressure or heart trouble, though in either case the outburst will exact its toll on your body. Do you believe the momentary satisfaction of "blowing your cool" is really justified? Do you wish to subject your physical body to such a strain?

Any emotion effects your body. The positive ones such as love and happiness are soothing and healing, but the negative ones like hate, envy, and malice erode the vessel that contains them—your body. Over time they can manifest as ulcers, heart attacks, cancer, or any other of the debilitating diseases. Do you really need to punish yourself this way?

Soul-Searching

Other questions you should ask yourself are these: "Why have I become emotional about this situation? Is this really a threatening experience, or are there some hidden, subconscious reasons why I have been aroused?" As the yogis say, DOES IT REALLY MATTER? Don't accept the first answers that pop into your head. Do some soul-searching. And don't let up on the self-questioning until you are satisfied you have the entire story. Each time you allow your emotions to run unchecked, you establish a precedent. The situation that arouses you will occur not just once but over and over, and it behoves you to uncover your real reasons for reacting in such a dramatic fashion. Only then can you determine whether your reaction has been in proportion to the stimulus.

As you have noticed, the preceding discussion has been couched in negative terms. This is because the emotions that harm us the most are the negative kinds. Love, happiness, sympathy for others are emotional states as well, but these soothe the body rather than inflame it. Positive emotions can be indulged at will, but even then we should observe moderation. You can determine how far to go for yourself, and you will know instinctively what is right. If you feel you cannot rely on your instincts, take heart. Your meditations will sharpen your abilities in these areas.

Problems with Drugs

One of the most pressing problems of modern society stems from drugs. There are numerous forms. Caffeine is a drug. Alcohol is a drug. Marijuana and LSD are others. Sedatives and sleeping pills alter the mind. Aspirin affects the nervous system. That some are in common use makes no difference. They all change some part of the body and are drugs. As we have stated before, you will have to determine for yourself whether you will use such substances and, if so, when and how. Naturally, if you are under a doctor's care, you would be foolhardy to ignore medical advice and dispense with your prescriptions. Further along in your study, when you have become centered, you may be able to discard some medicines you now need. For the present, work with medication and meditation. If you need sleeping pills, you will eventually learn to relax and sleep soundly without their aid. Sedatives will not be required for you to be calm. Even aspirin will become a thing of the past, for you will know how to prevent headaches or other bodily pains currently relieved by aspirin or its derivatives. But we must caution again: this is in the future.

Most individuals who are serious about meditation find drugs a hindrance. This is particularly the case with drug abusers. Many individuals in our society have attempted to expand their minds and force the doors of perception with drugs. Once they become interested in meditation, they learn that it is easier and infinitely safer to achieve a natural high and that continued drug abuse keeps them from making progress.

For the lesser drugs like alcohol and coffee or tea, there is no set rule for everyone. Many meditators dispense entirely with alcohol because it impedes their meditations, but if you enjoy drinking moderately, there is no reason to stop. Each person must become aware of his or her own inner signals, and if the time comes when you should stop ingesting alcoholic beverages, you will know it.

We are among those whose meditations are hampered by the common drug coffee and who discovered it was no problem to switch from twenty cups of black coffee per day to a few cups of decaffeinated beverages a day, or even hot water for weekly fasting days. Let us add that none of these changes came about overnight. Aspirin was the first to go. A year or so later, we began omitting the social drink and replaced it with iced water with a twist of lemon to cut out the chlorine taste. Another year and a half elapsed before the end of the coffee-drinking, and we began experimenting with weekly fasts a few months later. In each instance, our body alerted us to the need for change. Yours will, too, if and when you reach the point where it will be beneficial to you.

Fasting and Restriction Diets

Don't try to force your advancement. And don't be concerned about what others are doing. Fasting is not for everybody. Neither is vegetarianism, although some natural-foods promoters would have you believe it is. Perhaps your body requires meat, so unless you lose your taste for it, you should continue your normal diet and eat meat in moderation. Some advanced psychics are vegetarians and some are meat-eaters, just as some are non-smokers and others chain-smoke Each of us react differently to the commoner drugs such as coffee, to generally accepted foods like meat, and to smoking. There are no set rules for all. What's more, THERE IS NO PSYCHIC PATTERN. The use or nonuse of these milder stimulants will not make you a better meditator or increase your psychic abilities—which come as you advance spiritually—though drug abuse will definitely halt you in your tracks.

While we are on the subject of what is right or wrong for the individual, we must discuss the role of money in our lives. Nowhere are there more conflicting arguments than on the subject of wealth and poverty. In this country, great emphasis is put on money. It is stressed that worthy and hard-working people become rich. At the same time many people suffer guilt stemming from such biblical injunctions as "It is easier for a camel to go through the eye of a needle, than for a rich man to enter into the kingdom of God" (Matt. 19:24). Since money is so important in this material world, we are confused about what we should believe and how we should use our assets.

Love of Money

Money, like food and drugs, is neutral. It is neither good nor bad. The way it is employed by the individual determines its effects, and even then, it is the individual who is responsible rather than the means of exchange. If you take this thought into your meditations and dwell on it, you will discover it is true. Allot a few moments to thinking about money during your meditations this week. To do so will ease the pangs of the affluent who feel they work hard and deserve the rewards of their labors, yet possess more than they have a right to when so many others must do without. But the *love* of money is the root of evil; the emphasis on it for its own sake is wrong. The way it is used determines whether it is good or evil. The love of and hoarding of possessions bought by money is wrong. What one possesses can hold one in chains just as surely as the emotion of hate. But the person who can enjoy his or her belongings without being enslaved by them, without being owned by them instead of the other way around, can rest easy.

Concentration on the subject during a meditation can do even greater wonders for those who feel they are poor. Most individuals who lack basic essentials have a deep-rooted, subconscious belief that money is the root of all evil and that as long as they remain poor they are safe. The assumption is ridiculous, of course. As we've said before, money is neither good nor bad. At the risk of sounding materialistic, we must say that this attitude should be changed. Meditation is not meant to be a get-rich scheme, but once any individual places himself or herself in the right frame of mind and begins to live as a worthwhile human being, anything and everything needed for comfort and advancement will arrive. This includes money and material possessions. If you are poor, debt-ridden, or even destitute, you need only change your inner convictions to change your circumstances.

Positive Attributes

We shall discuss the love of money further when we come to renewing and reprogramming, and in order to prepare you for these lessons, we shall ask that you compile a list of all the positive attributes you possess. Do not be modest. Your list will be private, for your eyes only, so no one else will have the opportunity to challenge your claims. Right now, this very moment, jot down all those things you feel make you a good person. Do not list them as negatives. If you are destitute, for example, you might write, "I want to be financially comfortable." A desire of this sort is a positive one, though we are certain you can think of better examples.

When your positive list is done, write down three—and only three—faults of the "old you." Examine these carefully and see how you can change them into positive attributes. During your meditations this week, dwell on your positives and determine that the "new you" can transform the former, worst faults into virtues. Keep your list handy and review it on a daily basis.

We have covered many topics in this chapter, which you should work on during your meditations. For this week, include the following:

1. A release of every individual you may have disliked or differed with. You may change the following sample release if you like, or use it verbatim:

   _____ is a child of the light, even as I am a child of the light. The light guides each of us to our highest good. I freely release _____ to the light so he may find his highest good. There are peace, understanding, and divine love between us._____ walks in the light.

2. Detachment exercises, if you still require them.

3. The "beginning of a new day" prayer on page 39, or another that you consider suitable.

4. An examination of your emotions.

5. An examination of your attitudes about food, meditation, money, and so on.

In adding the above, do not neglect the most important part of the meditation work—the stilling of the mind or the keeping of the silence. Of course this is difficult, and we have been using a blank mental film screen to help you accomplish the task. Now we suggest another way of gaining the silence. That is to use a mantra (a sound pattern), which will assist in banishing the thoughts that race around our minds like squirrels in a circular cage.

Mantras

A traditional Eastern mantra is *Aum*. To use it, you inhale deeply and on the exhale sing "Ahh . . . ooo . . . mmm" until your breath is completely expelled. Inhale again and expel with *Aum,* repeating the sacred sound until you are able to visualize your mental film screen as a blank.

There is nothing magical about *Aum*. Any positive sound can replace it, though it should be a one-syllable word of an inspirational nature. If *Aum* offends you, try *God, Lord,* or *Christ,* or invent a sound of your own.

Experiment with the mantra for a few meditations. Thereafter you may find you do not require it or can get better results with the basic meditation. Do whatever seems right for you at the moment. We wish only to introduce you to various techniques so you will know what other meditational disciplines use and can adopt those which fit your needs.

By now you should be meditating at least once a day. Twice daily, once in the morning and again at night, is recommended by many groups, but your disposition or circumstances might prevent your holding double sessions. Again, it is up to you to determine your procedure, though we hope you will try to use the same location and approximately the same time for all meditational work.

Do not feel guilty about taking this time for yourself if you have other obligations—as we all do. You can find the time for whatever is important. Furthermore, WHAT IS GOOD FOR YOU IS GOOD FOR YOUR WORLD, for your world cannot be happy unless you are. Alert your family and friends to your needs, and insist on keeping your meditation appointments. At this stage in your growth, nothing is more important than the time required to improve yourself. Your work will be waiting when you finish. Your self-improvement will not and cannot wait. Indulge yourself. You are worth it. If you aren't already convinced of that fact, you shall be within a few weeks. Then even the most confident among you will be astounded by the wonders of the new you.

6

Light vs. Darkness

Evil exists. Make no mistake about that. You can feel it in certain situations as it emanates from individuals. The vibrations may be so powerful that they remain in the atmosphere long after the person responsible for them has departed. The more sensitive among us can feel them—in a room where some violent crime has taken place, for instance—for thoughts take forms that are as real as chairs and tables. They can manifest as ghosts, or, more often, give a particular location an evil atmosphere.

Yet evil isn't confined to the violent, the criminal, or those who oppose us. It is present in every sentient creature. It exists in each of us. And it must, for we are beings endowed with free will, and unless we contain the powers of darkness we are denied the strength of light. They are part of the same spectrum.

The choice, then, is yours and mine. We can employ the destructive forces of darkness to wreak havoc in the lives of others and possibly succeed—for a time. But such victories are short-lived. Whatever we send out is returned doubled and redoubled, and once we become involved with the psychic world, we learn that what we launch returns swiftly, like a boomerang, to injure us rather than our target. The law of immediate return applies, moreover, to any attempt to change the lives of others and so infringe on their free will. As you progress you will discover how to help others overcome their problems, but at the moment you must observe a hands-off policy no matter how good your intentions. The only person you can change is yourself. If your world is disjointed, the old you is responsible for that—not any other person or any other circumstance.

All intelligent humans realize that they must pay the price for their actions. To choose evil is, therefore, self-defeating. However, most of us understand we are not all good and are inclined to worry about whether our choices are right. We are particularly anxious once we determine to be reborn, for the societal rules of right and wrong no longer apply. We are on our own, it seems.

Of course this is not true. We couldn't begin to count those in what we call the past and the present who join us in our search for a better world. In fact, most people are good most of the time, and if we ask ourselves how many evil persons we have encountered in our lives, we will find they are rare. We as individuals are good, and you have only to review your list of positive attributes to prove that you are one of them. Now if the old self could contain that many positives, think what the reborn self can do!

Walking in the Light

Our agonizing over decisions can and will change as we learn to walk in the light. In your first meditation you were asked to visualize yourself stepping out of your elevator into a pool of light that shines down on you from above. At the start, this light must be imagined. If you still find it difficult to see, picture a flashlight or a spotlight suspended above your head and following you wherever you move. From there you can extend the visualization and see the light emanating from a cloudbank and focusing on you alone. Whatever else you omit from the meditation instructions, be certain you place yourself in the light. It will illumine, surround, and protect you, for it is the source of all good. From the beginnings of Western civilization human beings have used it. The Egyptians recognized its power and worshiped it, calling it a sun god, although in that country, as in any desert land, the relentless, constant sun with its devastating effects might be considered a deadly enemy rather than a benefactor. But as in most formative cultures throughout time and the world, the Egyptians understood that the sun, rather than the shade or the fruitful, life-giving rain, was their source of greatest good. Today we perceive the sun as a natural force created by an all-powerful force and use it as a symbol of the Supreme Power.

Light and Creation

The ancient Hebrews also thought of light in terms of a Creator. In Genesis, they reported "God said, Let there be light: and there was light. And God saw the light, that it was good: and God divided the light from the darkness. And God called the light Day, and the darkness he called Night" (Gen. 1:3–5).

The early Christians continued the association. John 12:35–36 states, "Then Jesus said unto them, Yet a little while is the light with you. Walk while ye have the light, lest darkness come upon you: for he that walketh in the darkness knoweth not whither he goeth. While ye have light, believe in the light, that ye may be children of light."

In Ephesians 5:8–14, Paul advises, "Ye were sometimes darkness, but now are ye light in the Lord: walk as children of light: . . . . And have no fellowship with the unfruitful works of darkness, but rather reprove them. . . . But all things that are reproved are made manifest by the light: for whatsoever doth make manifest is light. Wherefore he saith, Awake thou that sleepest, and arise from the dead, and Christ shall give thee light."

Regardless of your faith, light is equated with a higher force. It is also used to refer to intellectual accomplishments in such terms as "I see the light" or "In the light of this information" or "It was an enlightening experience."

Whatever your reason for accepting it, surround yourself with the light during your alpha or meditational experiences. In the exercise at the end of this chapter you will be shown how to use it for your protection, both in and out of meditation, so you will "walk in the light" always. Whenever you encounter evil thereafter, you will be safe from attack. Those individuals or situations you once feared cannot survive the light. The decisions you reach when you place yourself in the light will be the right ones, and you need worry no longer about choosing wrong.

To provide a rite of passage to your rebirth as a creature of the light, we shall add another exercise at the end of this chapter, although such an initiation isn't really required for those of you who have chosen to be reborn.

One additional light reference from the Bible must be mentioned in connection with our earliest forebears, because they identified it as an important symbol. Matt. 6:22–23 states, "The light of the body is the eye: if therefore thine eye be single, thy whole body shall be full of light. But if thine eye be evil, thy whole body shall be full of darkness. If therefore the light that is in thee be darkness, how great is that darkness!"

Opening the Third Eye

This cryptic message makes sense if we recall that Horus, the Egyptian god of light and heaven who had his eye gouged out by his evil uncle, regained the organ and donated it to his father Osiris, whose name meant "seat of the eye." Matthew testifies to its continuance as a symbol in the Christian era, and even the founding fathers of America considered it important enough to incorporate in the Great Seal of the United States. Other civilizations respect it as well. From the yogis and other holy men of the Eastern faiths comes information about an organ that has prompted mystics of all eras to refer to it as the third eye. It is located between the two physical eyes, at the root of the nose; it is reputedly based in the pituitary gland and it must be activated for a person to become enlightened—literally lit from within.

If the theory stretches your credulity to breaking point, please be patient. The mystical third eye may have a rational, biological explanation, and we shall discuss it when we study the glands of the body. For the present, consider its importance as a symbol used from the Egyptian era to our own, and for its connection with the light that enters our consciousness through the physical structure of the eye.

Unlike the light, the mental film screen you've been asked to imagine is not a symbol. But it will help you to focus your attention and assist you in practicing detachment while you are in meditation. However, if you don't require mechanical apparatus of this sort later on to detach or focus, by all means eliminate it. Most people find it a valuable tool at first, but eventually every meditator dispenses with it.

Similarly, most of you will find it helpful to use the relaxation exercises for a few sessions. Once you learn to relax without them, drop them from your basic meditation program or substitute a simpler instruction such as "Relax, body."

None of the techniques for entering into or emerging from meditation are sacrosanct, and none should be considered permanent. Be prepared to abandon unnecessary methods, to change, to be open to new experiences so your mind can expand at the fastest possible rate. And this is all mind work you're dealing with. There is nothing weird or occult in the mental process. We merely do not understand it. Nonetheless, it is wisest to adopt an attitude of guarded skepticism. Try to keep an open mind, but question any claims others may make about having supernatural abilities. Believe only what comes to you experientially, and don't be too fast to jump to conclusions about your own experiences, either. As you progress, you will learn to evaluate correctly and interpret phenomena without deluding yourself. This knowledge will come through your meditations, so seat yourself in a comfortable position, with spine erect, head up, and prepare to begin the basic instructions.

Initiation into the Light

For a formal initiation into the light, the following adaptation of Plato's allegory of the cave is recommended. You can ask some sympathetic person to read it to you as you meditate, but if you prefer to work alone, tape it and play it back during your meditation. If neither of the above is possible, familiarize yourself with the details and visualize them while you meditate.

In all cases, let the action Plato describes flash across your mental film screen. See it as though it were happening to you today, rather than centuries ago when Plato put the words into the mouth of Socrates in Book VII of *The Republic*.

Proceed first in your basic meditation to the point where you step out of your elevator. Seat yourself in a dim light and listen to the following:

Along with other human beings, you are living in a cave with an opening leading into a tunnel that connects the cave and the world of light. Like the others, you are a prisoner who, since childhood, has had your legs and neck chained so you cannot move and can only see straight ahead because the chains prevent your turning. The tunnel leading to the light is behind you and you are not aware of its existence. Also behind you is a fire, and between the fire and you and your fellow prisoners there is a raised walk with a low wall built along it, forming a sort of primitive projection booth.

People pass along this wall carrying all kinds of objects, statues, and figures, and these are raised above the wall. Some of the people speak. Some remain silent.

You do not see the people or the objects, only the shadows of them which the fire throws on your screen in front of you. Thus they are perceived as shadows, and if you and the other prisoners were able to talk to each other, you would describe the shadows as the true things.

If the cave had an echo, when the people spoke, you would think the shadows were talking.

Now imagine you are set free from your chains and forced to stand up and turn around to look at the fire and at the light shining outside the entrance to the cave. What pain you would suffer. What distress you would endure from seeing the flames of the fire and the light, however dim, that comes down through the tunnel. How you would try to look away and avoid the brilliance to which you are not accustomed.

No longer would you be permitted to view the shadows. Instead, you would be forced up the steep and stony incline of the tunnel, protesting each step of the way because the increasing light from the entrance assails your eyes. Finally you would be thrust to the mouth of the cave, where the sun would beat full upon you. What pain that would cause. How dazzled your eyes would be, and what a time it would take for your eyes to adjust to the light. But soon you would be able to make out the shadows of objects in the light. Later you would be able to see reflections in water, and at last to view your surroundings themselves. As your eyes grew stronger, you would lift them to the heavens to gaze at the stars and the moon. Eventually you would see the world in sunlight and look at clouds washed by the sun.

When you accomplished all this, and remembered your life in the cave and your fellow prisoners, would you not pity them and want to share your discovery?

How much more eager you would be if the prisoners of the cave held contests to find who observed most carefully the movements of the shadow people and could foretell with some accuracy what the shadows would do next. Wouldn't you want to return to the cave and gain the greatest honor by showing the prisoners their shadows were false?

And when you returned, your eyes would have to reaccustom themselves to the dimness. Then, wouldn't those who remain imprisoned consider you mad because you cannot see the shadow-show yet rave about what you perceived in the world of light? Wouldn't they believe you had lost both eyes and reason and resist your attempts to make them ascend to the mouth of the cave? Might they not attempt to kill you or anyone else who would force them to leave the familiar and safe world of the cave?

Reality and the Real World

The cave is the world that we call reality, and the light of the fire is the sun, the visible sun of the real world. The ascent to the mouth of the cave is the journey of the spirit into the intellectual realm. In this world of knowledge, good is seen only with an effort, but when it is, it is recognized as the source of light and the lord of light in the visible world and the source of reason and truth in the intellectual.

You have now been reborn in the light and need never return to the cave of half-truths and ignorance. Plato's allegory has been your formal initiation and need not be repeated. From this day forth, you will walk in the light.

Join all your fellow light-bearers of the world now by reciting the "beginning of a new day" prayer on page 39.

Follow the prayer with the exercise of release. See yourself on your mental film screen as you were before your illumination. See all the faults, the problems, the sins of the old you. Erase that picture and see yourself as you are now, a new and shiny individual, surrounded by the light, protected by the light, transformed by the light into a being that bears no relationship to the old self.

Now, visualize the light coming down from above your head, and let it form itself into a ring or a hoop large enough to pass over every part of your body.

Protecting Yourself with Light

Let the ring descend over your head and illuminate every part of your head. Bring it down past your shoulders, your torso, your hips, your thighs, the calves of your legs, and your feet. Stop it seven inches below your feet and watch it shrink to a pinpoint of light.

Expand the pinpoint until the circle of light resumes its former dimensions. Then let it drift up over your feet, filling your feet with light inside as well as out so it penetrates every pore. Feel it rise past your calves, thighs, and hips, filling your entire lower body. As it progresses up over your torso and arms, you will begin to see it and to experience the lightness of your body, and when it passes over your head, it will fill your head with its brilliance. Let it stop seven inches above your head and then ask it to shrink to a pinpoint, sealing itself off so you will be encased in an envelope of light. This envelope will extend seven inches from the widest points of your body and will be smooth and egg-shaped on the outer edges.

You will carry this seal of light wherever you go, sleeping or waking. It will be your protection against harm, and when you encounter anyone or any circumstance that might alarm you, visualize your light. Recall it to your conscious mind and it will shield you. Strengthen this shield by repeating the light exercise in meditation until you know you can rely upon it.

Do not, however, tempt fate by placing yourself in situations that are dangerous. Your *light* is infallible, but *you* might forget to use it in a tight spot, or permit others to penetrate it at some weak point. Similarly, for the present at least, do not linger when you encounter someone who is projecting negative thoughts or engaging in dubious activities. In short, proceed with your customary caution until you have assimilated all these concepts we have discussed, plus those we shall cover in future chapters.

By now your meditational pattern should be set and you should be able to take advantage of the deeper insights that the practice brings. After your customary period of silence, you may wish to test those insights by concentrating on Plato's allegory. You will know then, if you do not already, why this particular work was chosen for your formal initiation. When you have solved this mystery, consider the plight of the prisoner who returned to the cave to enlighten others, and apply your conclusions to your own advancement.

One of the greatest benefits you may have discovered is that meditation helps you to relax. Some individuals find they cannot sleep well if they have omitted their alpha breaks. Others will require less sleep than they formerly did because meditation leaves them so refreshed. However, you must not expect these benefits; what you gain may be entirely different, though equally rewarding.

Overcoming Insomnia

If your problem is insomnia, meditation plus an adaptation of the exercises will earn you a full night's sleep. When you feel you cannot rest because your thoughts are running their customary treadmill, begin the relaxation exercises. Lie prone on your bed, eyes closed, and start with the tightening and relaxing of all your muscles in your feet. Work your way up to your head, then tighten and relax all the muscles at once. Next, open your eyes as wide as possible and stare into the darkness. Sleep is guaranteed for even the worst insomniacs.

During your early meditation sessions, you may encounter a difficulty with heightened sensory responses. As you recall, we said the descent to the alpha level screens out stimuli originating from the five senses. Paradoxically, alpha can heighten one of those senses. For example, the sound of traffic outside your window could become extremely irritating, though you normally wouldn't hear it. So many individuals have encountered this phenomenon that it merits discussion.

Accept any sound, smell, or other stimulus. Do not attempt to ignore it. To do so makes it more persistent. Recognize it, accept it as the sensory intrusion that it is, then wrap it up in a mental box and place it aside. This is to say that you perceive it as an annoyance, you realize you cannot screen out all the distractions in the world, you know you are not required to do anything about it, so you devote full attention to what is happening within.

Some practice may be required, but it's necessary. There are moments when your senses may become so acute you will feel the blood coursing through your veins or hear your nasal passages dripping, but even in these cases you are not required to pay attention. Keep working. You'll discover that your meditation sessions will grow longer and deeper and that you will receive innumerable other benefits to aid you in your future development.

7

The Concept of Time

Congratulations. You are now, officially, a child of the light. As a child, you must learn to adjust to your new world by adopting customs, beliefs, and habits that will enable you to live comfortably. This means you must avoid all the mistakes of your previous self. The task is easier than you might think, and in order to help you accomplish it, we offer the following exercise to RENEW:

R — Relax. (Enter the meditational state.)

E — Expect. (Be alert and eager for change to occur.)

N— Note or name the change. (Decide what changes you require in your attitudes, thought processes, even exterior life.)

E — Envision a desired change. (See it on your mental film screen as having come to pass.)

W—Withdraw the thought picture. (Watch and wait for the results of your efforts to manifest in your life.)

At the conclusion of this chapter we shall detail a revised meditational procedure, but first let us discuss the steps of RENEWing.

The R step needs no further explanation, for you understand the necessity of relaxing the body so the mind can begin its work on the subconscious.

For "E" you need only be alert and expect positive results. Your alertness and expectation keep you from falling asleep and also enable you to reach your goals. Everything you have in the physical world is the actualization of your thoughts, and unless you *expect* or *believe in* what you want, it cannot come to fruition.

Positive Thinking

Before you begin your meditation, you must decide what you want to accomplish. Choose *one* project now, and prepare to repeat it during subsequent meditations until you have accomplished it or feel you've sufficiently impressed your subconsious with its importance. Then phrase your desire simply and clearly. Use as few words as possible and make them all positive. Avoid negative terms. For instance, you should say "I got the job today" rather than "They will not turn me down." Phrase your desire as though it had already come true. Avoid being too specific, however. This may limit the benefits, because your reward may be even greater than you anticipated if you permit your subconscious to do what it is capable of.

The E for envisioning is what brings your desire to pass. Of course, you must be certain that what you envision applies only to you and that you are not forcing others into circumstances that are detrimental to their welfare. You must not, for instance, see another person fired from a position so you may have it. What you can do is visualize yourself employed in that business or industry and being highly successful. Here you take advantage of the way your mind works, for it uses pictures rather than words. At the E point, then, FORESEE YOURSELF AS HAVING ACHIEVED AND POSSESSING YOUR GOAL. Do not picture yourself working for it, or worrying about it; just see yourself on your mental film screen as BEING THERE. Then invest your picture with all the emotion of which you are capable. See yourself, feel yourself luxuriating in your success. Experience it in all its glory. Invest the scene with all the positive emotional content possible. Picture people congratulating you as you rejoice. Feel it. Bring every sense organ into play as you visualize: smell the fragrance of the perfumes, hair tonics, or soaps your well-wishers have used; hear the words as they congratulate you; see the colors of their clothes and the details of your surroundings; feel the kiss of relatives or close friends and the warm handshake of acquaintances. Take all the time you require to do a complete job of visualizing. Next, withdraw every ounce of emotion. Continue to visualize yourself experiencing your triumph, but view the incident as though you were watching a film of it happening to you. Be certain to include both the expending of emotion while you are involved and the withdrawing of it. Be sure to vision as well as visualize, for as Florence Scovel Shinn explains in *The Game of Life and How to Play It,* visualizing "is a mental process governed by intuition, or the superconscious mind." In doing both you prepare yourself to watch and wait and act on the leads that come to you through intuition.

Preventing Negative Thoughts

W requires releasing. Let your project go. Consider your achievement as having come to pass and think no more about it until your next meditation, when you will repeat the RENEWing. Meanwhile, do not worry about whether it will happen, or how, or when. To do so sets up blocks and causes confusion in your subconscious. You are programming your subconscious to achieve a goal. If your program is clearly stated—as it should be, because your subconscious is literal—and if you envision clearly, your desire will materialize. But you must not interfere by worrying about it during your conscious moments. Most important, do not discuss it with anyone. Keep all RENEWals to yourself. Give your subconscious the chance to build the tension required to accomplish the goal, and then forget it so the subconscious can work unhindered. If you happen to think about the project during the day, tell yourself that any thought of it must wait for your meditation time. In the cold light of day, doubts and fears can arise to work against you. But doubts and fears are the products of the conscious mind, and if you do not permit the conscious mind to dwell on your project, these doubts and fears will fade.

Like other meditation exercises, RENEWing requires practice. It is best to start, therefore, with a simple project or to simplify an extremely urgent one. Use this technique seriously, however. Your subconscious has no sense of humor and will do precisely what you instruct it to do. Remember also to check carefully to insure you are not transgressing on the rights of others. If any portion of your success is at another's expense, or limits that person's freedom to do what is for his or her good, then you will suffer the consequences. RENEWing is for you and you alone. Later we will offer programs to help others regain their health or achieve their goals, but these will come after you have developed further.

Replace your original meditation program with the one at the end of this chapter that includes RENEWal. It will help you put on your new self, to affirm the New Year's Day in your life. Only in this fashion can you separate yourself from the past. And if you're going to live at all well, remember Shakespeare's line "What's past is prologue." So forget the past. It doesn't exist. Nothing exists but the present moment, the here and now. The playwright Luigi Pirandello recognized this in Act III of *Six Characters in Search of an Author*. He shows us two characters onstage: the Father of a family and a Stage Manager who asks if the Father understands what he is saying. The Father responds:

> . . . only in order to know if you, as you really are now, see yourself as you once were with all the illusions that were yours then, with all the things both inside and outside of you as they seemed to you—as they were then indeed for you. Well, sir, if you think of all those illusions that mean nothing to you now, of all those things which don't

even *seem* to you to exist any more, while once they *were* for you, don't you feel that . . . the very earth under your feet is sinking away from you when you reflect that in the same way this *you* as you feel it today—all this present reality of yours—is fated to seem a mere illusion to you tomorrow?

The past is precisely what Pirandello described: ILLUSION. The you who agonized over a school football game, or about what you should wear on your first date, is not the you of today. You've changed. You're a completely new person, or at least enough of you is new to make the old appear ridiculous and immature. Further, what you experienced back then wasn't a *fact*. It was a circumstance, an event that you perceived in a certain way only because of your development at that moment. But stop and analyze that experience. Most likely it was an unhappy one, since we tend to remember painful experiences more than the pleasurable. Then ask yourself whom it was unhappy for. Was it you alone? Or did it cause grief to others as well?

Coping with Death

Let us consider a typical unhappy incident: the death of a grandmother. Ask yourself who felt the unhappiness then. No doubt it was your parents. You also, if you were close enough to have spent much time with her. But if you loved her, your memories of your grandmother were happy, so you can recall experiences some people have never enjoyed. And you must remember what you had: happy memories of times spent with a loved one—memories many people miss entirely in their lives. Why then do you count your loss? Isn't it because you've been left behind and are feeling sorry for yourself? The dead, particularly the aged who suffer from prolonged illnesses, are well rid of their pain and suffering. And your grandmother, though she may have been well up to the last, could have suffered had she continued to live. Death is part of the natural process. Do you have the right to deny it and possibly cause others lingering pain so you can avoid feeling sorry for yourself?

But—you may object—we're talking about the elderly. What about the death of babies, children, adolescents, or anyone else who hasn't run a full race? Why should these deaths occur? And isn't it heartless to accept their passing without feeling sorrow? We are not expected to be heartless—just to be human. And it's human nature to weep on occasion and to sympathize with those who do. Death is often inexplicable, and the deaths of the young are generally beyond our comprehension. But the choice is not ours. Death is as much a part of life as birth, and every life has its purpose. Who are we to say when the purpose has been accomplished? Nevertheless, every experience teaches us something, and if our encounter with the death of a young person has helped us to be better, more understanding, or more loving individuals, then it must have served a positive purpose. Think about it. All that happens is for our eventual good, and whatever your attitude toward the past, you can change it. See the past for what it is—a learning situation. As such, it can prevent you from making worse mistakes in your present.

When you change your attitude towards a past situation or event, you change the event itself. This is not self-delusion but a lesson in values. If you have lost something and deeply feel the loss, it is because you had something valuable. Learn to count what you had and be grateful. Not everyone is that fortunate.

History as a Personal View

You may argue that history is a record of the past. One might better say it's a record or account, generally written in chronological order, of events of the past as they were *interpreted* by an individual. The key lies in those last words: as they were interpreted! In short, history is nothing more than a collection of interpretations of past events. The American Civil War is a good example. To the Northerners, particularly those who weren't involved in the fighting, it was a victory of right over tyranny. To those soldiers who spent years in Andersonville or other prisons, or suffered wounds that troubled them for the remainder of their lives, the war was totally different. And the defeat, according to the Southerners, set humanity back a millenium. For the blacks it was a third experience, and Americans are learning the views of their black citizens only now, more than a hundred years after the war's end.

History as we know it from the books is an interpretation of an experience, and the person recounting the experience in the best possible manner becomes the recognized authority. But even history books can be changed, and when attitudes of people change—about the present or the past—the events themselves change.

Examine your own experiences and see what you can alter from the past. But whether you retain your original conclusion or accept new ones makes little difference. The past is prologue still.

And the future is a delusion.

In his book *Meditation,* Bradford Smith speaks of the futility of living in the future:

> We keep putting off the day when we shall have time to be happy, when we shall have time for the important things, when we can have our work done and all our little duties attended to. Then, we promise ourselves, we shall really live. But so long as we go on telling ourselves that we shall do it tomorrow, we are really seeing to it that there shall be no such tomorrow. And in truth, there may not be. Let us do it now!

A retired couple we met in Paris learned about the future the hard way. For years they'd dreamed about a trip abroad, and when the man sold his bar in Pittsburgh, Pennsylvania, they finally left for Europe. Their first stop was Paris. As they disembarked at Orly airport, the wife fell and broke her ankle. They tried to continue their sightseeing, but it was pitiful to watch a couple in their late sixties or early seventies trying to enjoy what they'd scraped and planned for all their lives while she, in agonizing pain, hobbled about on an enormous cast.

But you needn't take another's word that the future is a delusion. Prove it to yourself. Remember how, as a child, you became so excited over a coming event—Christmas, for instance. You looked forward to it for weeks, perhaps even months. Somehow it was going to be a magical time; it would alter your life and you would live happily ever after. Then the great moment arrived, with all its joy. But how long did the joy last? Until Christmas afternoon when all the packages had been opened and all those marvelous gifts you had asked for and received had somehow lost their glamour? Did that experience teach you about the future, or, like many of us, were you already planning some new request, seeking some future date that would bring you everlasting happiness?

The future is a delusion. All there is is the present. TODAY IS THE TOMORROW YOU DREAMED ABOUT YESTERDAY. It's all any of us have, all we can depend on. "Time" may halt or our lives terminate abruptly—the future is a concept based on a cultural illusion. We can't *count* on living one second, one minute, or one hour, day, or week longer.

Precious Minutes

Yet "now" is not as fleeting or ephemeral as we are apt to believe. In fact, we have distorted time by measuring it in increasingly smaller segments.

While our ancestors thought in terms of seasons (the time for harvest) or days (the day to mend the nets or the harnesses) we think in terms of minutes. Clocks run our lives, warning us to wake on schedule so we can catch the train or bus that will get us to work on time. And the clocks hurry us through the day with so many minutes for lunch and ten-minute coffee breaks, until we become so accustomed to the tyranny of minutes that they rule even our leisure. Minutes are precious, we contend, though we proceed to squander them by killing time until the next class or the next television program. Yet, however deplorable our situation, it is likely to become worse, and in the future our children may be sectioning off their lives in what science-fiction writers term disecs.

This narrow view is unwarranted. The present is longer than the split second we smile at a friend or gasp at the latest headline; it is possible to widen our view to cover a present time of a day, a week, or perhaps a month. People who have advanced in their meditations to the point where they acquire some of the abilities we term psychic can see even further.

Our constricted view of time is analogous to a man riding a train. From his train window he cannot see very far ahead, and his view of a bridge the train is approaching is thereby limited. He can see part of the bridge as the train nears, get a better view during the crossing, and only a little of it again when it is behind him. And even if he cranes his neck out of the window, he can't see the entire train on which he rides if it is a long one, but perhaps a few cars ahead and behind.

A Wider View of Time

But let us suppose our man is standing a mile or so away from the track when the train passes. How many of the cars would he see? How much of the bridge would be visible to him? Suppose that he could climb a hill or fly over the area in a helicopter or a plane. Would he not be able to see the entire bridge, the complete train—indeed, farther and in more detail than when he was on the ground?

On the ground our vision is obscured by buildings and trees, and we are rooted in the moment. Fortunately we can learn to "rise above" the earth, to perceive that time is a delusion. It is a cultural conditioning that is worse in this country than it would be in a more agrarian and slower-paced nation such as Spain, and worse in a Spanish city than in the countryside, where people deal with the seasons.

People who are not time-oriented—beyond that consciousness demanded by our culture—are capable of moving up and away from the moment and of getting a panoramic view. Those who learn to do this can read the future, just as the early Christians did who were rooted in the present yet were sufficiently disinterested in it to be able to achieve the distance required for prophecy. And what your ancestors have done, you too can accomplish.

The Pride of Youth

If you wish to see or become a seer, you must be willing to consider time an artificial concept and search for an alternative. If you are young, for example, you are possibly both conscious of and proud of your youth. Unfortunately, your joy will be limited, for as you grow older the same media that created this pride of youth by catering to the young market aren't going to change, and there may be traumas in store for some. Witness those people who panic on reaching the age of thirty! Also, if you are inordinately impressed by your youth, you may be estranging yourself from many interesting and worthwhile human beings. Even if you're eighteen and your next-door neighbor is eighty, you and your neighbor are contemporaries. You have no more guarantee that you will live another day, week, year than your neighbor does. Statistically the odds are in your favor, but your futures are equally nonexistent.

Of course there are noticeable differences in your appearances. You're young, strong, and healthy, and your neighbor may be a walking assortment of spare parts: teeth, glasses, hairpiece, hearing aid, or any other of the "merit badges" earned from living. Yet in outlook the other *may* be younger than you. Some people are old at twenty. Others remain young all their lives. And at the core of each human being there is a spirit that remains unchanged from birth to death. It has no concept of time. It never changes, never ages. The reason bodies do is that the species would not truly benefit by everyone's appearance remaining the same throughout life. Older people might more frequently marry those much younger, while it is usually in nature's best interest for partners to choose each other from their own chronological time span. Without such controls, the situation could become chaotic.

Nonetheless, aging is primarily mental. No body is truly old. Cells die and are replaced by new ones at a constant rate, and each physical body is completely renewed every eleven months. People age quickly because they choose more sedentary occupations and don't keep themselves in the same shape they did when they were young, and because they are culturally conditioned to *believe* the body deteriorates with time.

Living for the Present

In every respect, time is a snare and a delusion. This present is all there is, but the present can be days or weeks, depending on one's vantage point and how successful one becomes in detaching from the moment or situation. Still, the only time you can do anything about, the only time you can live, is NOW.

DON'T LET THE BEST DAYS OF YOUR LIFE HAPPEN WITHOUT YOU. Those days are now; the hours are now.

TODAY IS THE TOMORROW YOU DREAMED ABOUT YESTERDAY. Don't let it happen without you. Live in the NOW. BE HERE NOW.

In this week's meditation, feel yourself being present. Be acutely aware of what happens to you every moment of your revised meditation, every moment of your consciousness when you are out of meditation. Do not permit yourself to dwell on the past or the future, except your RENEWing exercises when you rearrange your life so it will conform to your ideal. Root yourself in the HERE AND NOW. Paradoxically, this living in the present will enable you later to achieve the distance necessary to see greater segments of time, as did the Hebrew prophets, the early Christians, and numerous other seers throughout the ages.

To help yourself achieve these goals, use the revised meditation that follows:

1. Close your eyes and relax.
2. Step onto your private elevator (if you still require it) and descend to B, descending as you exhale, and assisting your descent by visualizing and saying the number of the floor to which you are descending.
3. Let your elevator door open, and step into the shaft of light that shines down on you from above.
4. Say, "I am now in the healthiest possible state of being. I and I alone will control my mind. No one else or nothing else can or ever will be able to control my mind but me."
5. Recite your "This is the beginning of a new day" prayer.
6. Visualize your mental film screen and spend several minutes focusing on the blankness of the screen.
7. RENEW. Relax; Expect positive results; Note or name your goal; Envision yourself as having achieved your goal and charge the scene with emotion; Withdraw the emotion and watch the screen. Wrap

up the screen, place it aside, and prepare yourself to watch and wait for the visualization to manifest.

8. BE HERE NOW. Attend to your body. Listen to your breathing, your blood circulating, your food digesting, or whatever else is happening within.

9. Add your circle of light exercise or any others of your choice.

To bring yourself up to the conscious level, begin your ascent as follows:

10. Say, "I am now in the healthiest possible state of being."

11. Say, "In this healthiest possible state of being I am completely relaxed." (Pause.) "If any part of me was tense, it is relaxed now."

12. Say, "In this healthiest possible state of being, I am absorbing energy." (Pause.) "When I bring myself out of this state, I will be thoroughly refreshed—as refreshed as though I'd just awakened from a night of deep and restful sleep after a month's holiday at my favorite spot."

13. Say, "My body is in perfect condition and feels as though it were new-made."

14. Say, "My mind is open to learning. Whatever I hear, whatever I see, whatever I experience I will understand and use. Subjects or courses or business details that may have been difficult in the past are now clear and understandable to me, and I will master them easily."

15. Say, "I am filled with energy. I overflow with energy."

16. Say, "I am suffused with joy, a joy that will last for days."

17. Now step into your elevator, close the doors, and ascend as you inhale. Assist yourself by visualizing and saying the numbers of the floors to which you rise. When you reach floor level 4, open the doors, step out, snap your fingers, and come out wide awake and feeling great.

Continue to practice the presence of NOW in your waking moments. BE HERE NOW. TODAY IS THE TOMORROW YOU DREAMED ABOUT YESTERDAY. BE HERE NOW TO LIVE IT.

8

Dealing with Negativities

Living for the moment demands that each of us comes to grips with our fundamental nature. As we know, free will implies choice, and each of us must continually select what is right for us, as in the case of what to eat or what to drink. Our ability to choose was attributed to the *daimon* by the ancient Greeks, who believed, as Bergen Evans explains in his *Dictionary of Mythology,* that it was the gift of the god Zeus. This *daimon* acted like a guardian angel that watched over the individual throughout life, but it was not the kind of guardian angel who would always protect a person. Inasmuch as the word *daimon* came from the Greek *dai,* to divide, from which two modern opposites, *demon* and *divinity,* are derived, it could help or could harm its owner. The more modern definition of the psychiatrist Rollo May is perhaps clearer. In his book *Love and Will,* May describes the *daimon* (or demon) as "any natural function which has the power to take over the whole person" and adds that it "is obviously not an entity but refers to a fundamental . . . function of human experience . . . " found in each person. How it is employed by the individual determines whether the results will be good or evil.

But "good or evil," "God or devil" are terms that may have gone out of fashion, and today we are more apt to think of them as positive or negative attitudes. Nonetheless, the daimonic opposites remain, and we can't *renew* ourselves and have the renewal last until we eliminate the negative choices. This is not to say we deny them. They exist and will always do so as long as we have free will—we are neither all good nor all bad and must continually strive to overcome the darker side of our natures. Still, we can conquer our negativities by programming ourselves or, in other words, by instructing our subconscious to choose the positives. This must be done with care. The subconscious is LITERAL and will do precisely as instructed—no more, no less—and we must avoid confusing it with negative commands.

Effects of Negative Thoughts

We make such commands when we signal our subconscious with any of the following physical instructions:

He gives me a pain in the neck.
Get off my back.
Oh, my aching back.
Stop riding me.
That drives me crazy.
I need to get ahead.
I can't swallow that argument.
You're breaking my heart.
The experience was a real heartbreaker.
It makes my blood boil.
I can't stand this any more.

What happens when you use such phrases is that you signal your body to react in the way mentioned. People who persist in finding other human beings or situations a "pain in the neck" always end up with stiffness or pain in that part of the anatomy. Those who refer to their backs or to being ridden will eventually develop back troubles. Those who repeat "drives me crazy" or "can't get ahead" signal their bodies that it is acceptable to be confused, disoriented, or empty-headed. The "can't swallow" order closes the throat and produces hiatal hernias. Constant negative references to the heart will trigger heart abnormalities, "blood boiling," or high blood pressure. Repetition of "can't stand" will result in foot or ankle troubles.

Such instructions need not be voiced, however. All one has to do is *think* in such terms often enough, and the body will react to the repeated commands. We must, therefore, weed such phrases out of our speech and our thoughts if we are to avoid these kinds of bodily reactions.

Other and more abstract signals are equally dangerous. How often have you heard people say "I can't remember dates" or "I can't remember faces"? They could, of course, remember anything of importance, but they are instructing themselves that dates or faces needn't be recalled, and their minds obey the commands. People who declare they have memories like a sieve do *not* remember anything because they have deliberately told themselves that it's acceptable to forget. Such instructions are deadly. So are suggestions such as "I'm dumb," "I'm no genius," "Teachers expect too much," or "My boss works me to death." What we do when we use phrases like these is tell our subconscious that it should react in a specific manner. Repetition reinforces the commands, so the subconscious believes the signals and therefore produces the physical result or refuses to produce names, memory of faces, or facts, even when the person desperately *wants* to recall them.

Other verbal or thought forms are a bit more general though equally harmful: "If I get my feet wet I'll catch cold." "If I sit in a draft I'll catch cold." "I get cranky (or get a headache) when I'm hungry." "I require at least eight hours of sleep each night."

Training your Body for Illness

If you are convinced of the "wet feet" notion, consider the numerous times you have had wet feet and have *not* caught cold—for example, after you have been swimming or have taken a bath or shower. If wet feet invariably cause colds, why don't they do so under these circumstances? The reason is that you've mentally qualified the conditions—wet feet have to be accidental. Nonetheless, the order given to your subconscious is silly. If you *know* that you won't catch cold and reinforce your belief with the positive command that you will always be well, you can eliminate the problem.

The notion that one must eat at a certain time to avoid being cranky or getting a headache is just as ridiculous for the majority of people. Excluding those with diabetes or some other long-standing ailment, many people are able to skip meals without any adverse effects. They do so when they are intensely interested in something else, such as an exciting sports event, and the crankiness or headache is more the result of mental conditioning than physical hunger.

If you feel you must have at least eight hours of sleep each night, consider all those days when you existed on less. They would have been days when you were happily intent on more important matters than sleep, days when you were on holiday perhaps, and your desire to participate in leisure activities outweighed your need for sleep. Then ask yourself what is so important about eight hours. Why not nine or six? Isn't eight hours a norm imposed on you by culture—a generally accepted belief that everyone should have at least that much rest? Perhaps this length of time is not in your best interest. Why not let your body decide rather than conditioning yourself in this manner?

Listening to Yourself

Whenever you program yourself to act in a certain way, you indulge in negativities. Stop and listen to your speech and monitor your thoughts for an hour, and you will recognize such negativities. Then, for two days, keep a list of every negativity you utter or think. Write each one on a card you can carry around with you. As soon as you've recorded the negativity, cross it out and write a more positive thought on the card. If, for instance, you've said, "His attitude makes my blood boil," draw a line through the instruction and write, "He is as entitled to his attitude as I am to mine." If you say or think you can't remember a name, cancel the sentence and write, "The name has slipped my mind for a second, but I will remember it shortly." Then forget about it. Because you've trained your subconscious over a long period of time to react to negativities, it will take time to sort itself out before the results become evident. But they will. Within a day or so you will find yourself remembering in a second. When that happens, congratulate your subconscious. Thank it. Let it know it's appreciated.

Illnesses are too often the result of faulty programming of your subconscious. Ninety percent of our ailments are mentally induced. If you fear having to give a speech or to attend some function where you may have to talk to others, you may bring on a case of laryngitis, thus giving you an excuse to turn in a poor performance or even miss the event. Your body did not cause the inflammation of your throat. Your mental attitude did. You do not need to "catch" any illness unless you program your body to do so by negative thinking. Eliminate the negatives, and you can be healthy. A young neighbor of ours recognized this fact after many years of recurring illnesses and accidents.

A Case History

John, as we shall call him, was a sickly child. As a preschooler, he came down with every ailment imaginable. If a child three streets away developed measles, John broke out in a rash, even if he had no contact with the ailing youngster. In kindergarten he was the first to get chicken pox and whooping cough, which he promptly passed on to his classmates, and he was often the last to recuperate. His nose ran constantly, his glands swelled, and recurring earaches forced him to wear a cap to ward off the slightest breeze of a summer day.

He was operated on for the removal of his tonsils and adenoids the year he turned six and forfeited his appendix at the tender age of nine.

Accidents, too, were the rule rather than the exception. In his first years at school, he fell off some steps and developed a Baker's cyst, which ballooned his left leg to four times its normal size and required him to be hospitalized for several weeks. About the third year in grammar school, he broke his right arm sliding into home base during a baseball game. Numerous cuts requiring stitches made him a regular visitor at the emergency room of the hospital, and recurrent high fevers earned him the enmity of the pediatricians in the area, since he could be counted on to become delirious during the small hours of the night when the doctors were trying to recuperate from their day's work. In high school he started to run track and developed blood poisoning from blisters on his left foot on one occasion. He was afflicted with headaches and with a tight nervous throat, which prevented him from swallowing anything that remotely resembled a pill.

Doctors had tested him for epilepsy, brain disturbances, and other bodily malfunctions that would explain his proneness to accidents and illness and found that he was normal. Yet John continued to collect broken bones and bruises until a school psychologist took an interest in his case.

After a couple of months of retraining, the psychologist was able to announce that John was cured. The young man has been healthy ever since, for he discovered that he was expecting disaster and indulging in the kind of negative emotions that would bring them to pass.

All in the Mind

When asked about his experience, John confided, "I was pretty mad when the teacher sent me down to the school shrink. I'd had this cough and I was sure I was getting TB or something because every time the teachers called on me, I'd start hacking. I was even madder when the shrink told me it was all mental and to forget it, but he kept after me until he convinced me he was right. And he explained my accidents, too. It seemed every time I became upset over a situation—like the time my parents refused to buy me a new bike—I'd have an accident. That's pretty dumb, isn't it? Well, I know better now and I don't allow my anger or disappointment or any other bad feelings to get the best of me. My body and mind work as a team, and I'm planning to keep well."

John's realization that the body and mind are a team was a tremendous breakthrough; though these functions are separate, the mind does exert a tremendous influence on the flesh. What it thinks has a definite impact, and thoughts that are either visualized or verbalized will most quickly be brought to pass. There is only one way to avoid catastrophe, as John has discovered: Think positive. Negative thoughts can maim or kill, the principal victim being you. The only method of avoiding poisoning your body with poisonous thoughts is to eliminate every last one and to substitute positive thoughts.

This is why you must release every person for whom you formerly felt hate, jealousy, or contempt, or who directed such harmful emotions toward you. This is why you must think and speak good thoughts—the loving, kind, creative, decent thoughts the new you will be proud to claim.

Freedom from Negative Emotions

Once you erase your negativities, you will free yourself from anxiety in all its forms: worry, grief, envy, resentment, greed, and so on. This means you must live in the present. It means you must accept others as they are, not as you want them or expect them to be for your personal sake. Remember that you have detached yourself temporarily from others; you have released them, friends and foe alike, and no longer need to dance to their tunes because in freeing them, you have freed yourself. For the same reason, you must not expect anyone else to live according to your standards. If *you* live up to them, you'll have enough work to last for ever. No matter what anyone else says or does, he or she is a creation of God. You must not meddle. Offer support or help if it's requested, but remember that God knows what is right for every individual in every moment of time, so you've no business interfering. And you've no right to judge, either. People are never at identical stages of spiritual development any more than they are equal in particular talents, appearance, or wordly possessions. Wherever you stand in the scheme of things, there are others above you whom you may not be able to appreciate as yet and those below whom you must not criticize. It is not their fault if they are onions instead of roses, and you should not pick a bouquet of the former as a centerpiece for your dining room table. Accept the onions for what they are, the poison ivies for what they are, just as you accept yourself, knowing that God can and will in his good time transform them and you into more highly evolved beings. See everyone as standing in various positions on a spiritual escalator. Only be certain you're headed in the right direction—up.

You may ask about those who are on the down escalator. Somehow these are always our "enemies," either long-standing ones or the temporary ones who are doing something of which we disapprove. Again, we must not judge. Each of us is a child of the highest creative force of the universe. The sun shines on each of us alike, without discrimination. The other has a particular place in the world and a special duty to perform, even as you. He or she has a particular genius; you have yours. And you needn't struggle to find it or display it. All that is required is to become attuned to the infinite, the natural law, and it will flow. It is as Christ claimed in Luke 12:22–26: "Take no thought for your life, what ye shall eat; neither for the body, what ye shall put on. The life is more than meat, and the body is more than raiment. Consider the ravens: for they neither sow nor reap; which neither have storehouse nor barn; and God feedeth them: how much more are ye better than the fowls? And which of ye with taking thought can add to his stature one cubit? If ye then be not able to do that thing which is least, why take ye thought for the rest?" The message transcends Christianity to speak to everyone. When you work in the light, when you live as a decent, upstanding, worthwhile individual, all that you need for your development will be given to you.

Separating from Anxiety

Other people or circumstances cannot keep your good from you. They never have, and they never will. Negativities, however, can and do. They are our worst enemies. They manifest themselves as anxieties that rob us of peace of mind, prevent us from coping with the exigencies of life, and waste our energies. If you're now going through life half alive, weary, and tired, anxiety stemming from negative attitudes is the reason. Separate yourself from anxiety by replacing fearful thoughts or other negative concepts with positives. Keep your list of negativities on three-by-five cards, and as they occur, cross them out and substitute simple, constructive thoughts in their place.

It is vital to eliminate the dark thoughts. You cannot grow, either spiritually or psychically, until you do. When you have begun to identify them, add a technique devised by Walter Germain and detailed in his book *The Magic Power of Your Mind*. This technique involves making "radar trap" checks four times a day.

Begin when you awaken in the morning. Ask yourself if you feel good, if you're ready to face the day and are looking forward to the new opportunities the day has to offer. No matter what your circumstances, you can't afford to be anything but positive. Thinking negatively only worsens health, finances, and happiness, and you must break the lockstep forever. Each day is a new beginning, a chance to remake your world to your taste.

Your second checkpoint comes at noon. Stop then and ask yourself whether you thought and reacted positively all morning. If you did not, write your negative responses on a card and replace them with positives. Never permit what is past to influence the present. Life should be treated like a game of golf, in which the professionals learn not to permit one bad shot to ruin their scores. The morning is over. Any errors you may have made are over. If something did not go well for you, change your attitude toward that circumstance and see it positively—perhaps as a learning experience. Clear any negativities from your consciousness of the morning so you can enjoy your lunch and permit the food to benefit your body.

Make your third check at the end of your work or study day. Before heading for home, ask yourself how the afternoon went. Were you able to meet all the challenges? Did you respond to every individual with loving kindness, knowing that each, like you, is a child of God? Did you enjoy this new day granted to the new you? If there are any negativities you did not deal with as they occurred, cancel them out at this point.

Using Opportunities

Your last check is at bedtime, just before falling asleep. Reflect on your day, canceling any negativities that may have accumulated during the evening hours. Erase the slate so only positives remain. Then ask yourself a vital question: "Am I eagerly anticipating tomorrow?" If you can't respond with a resounding YES, prop yourself up in bed and consider your situation. You are being given the gift of a new day. And what a wondrous gift it is. You have twenty-four more hours to be kind, loving, and positive—to contribute to your work and your world. Not everyone has this opportunity, this second chance to put matters right. Furthermore, there aren't as many chances as one might think. Those who live to be seventy, for example, can count on a total of 25,500 days, but if you're twenty years old, you've already used 7,300 and have only 18,200 left. And who knows whether there are actually 18,200 days, or 18,200 hours, or 18,200 seconds left? Can you afford to let the best day of your life happen without you? And a new day is precisely that: the best day of your life. It is a day to live, to work without reservation, to enjoy to the fullest, and you will accomplish these objectives by surrendering yourself to the natural force, the natural pace of life by living as a positive human being in the present.

Nonetheless, this does not excuse you from planning. You must work to the best of your ability, moment to moment, but plan for the future as though you were going to live forever. Minus the fear, the doubt, the uncertainty, you will plan wisely and choose the best way as a matter of course even though you know each *present* moment is the sole time available.

Taking Positive Action

Furthermore, you can and must take positive action and hold the ideas and opinions that are right for you even if they differ from those of everybody else in the world. You must stop judging others, though this does not mean you should become wishy-washy. You can legitimately entertain positive thoughts without experiencing negative emotions toward those who disagree with you. In fact, you must learn to differentiate between individuals and their deeds. There is a vast gulf between opposition to actions, thoughts, or intentions of other people and opposition to the people themselves. The concept or deed must be opposed, never the person who commits it. If the temptation to succumb to animosity toward another assails you, remind yourself, "_____ is a child of God, even as I am a child of God. God guides that person's development, and if _____ is wrong, God will correct him in due time, just as he corrects me when I err. _____ walks in the light."

There are occasions when we must fight an opposing thought or deed with every fiber of our being. If we see Joe Smith, for example, about to commit some crime, we cannot stand by and watch. Instead, we must do everything in our power to prevent him from harming others and eventually himself. But not every circumstance is that urgent. If Joe Smith maintains that the grass is gray, and we *know* it to be green, why do we persist in the argument? If Joe is color blind, to him the grass *is* gray or brown, and who are we to say it is otherwise? Maybe both Joe and we are correct; possibly neither of us is. Maybe the truth is greater than we realize and we are perceiving just a small part of it.

The Sufis tell a story that illustrates the point. Blind men were asked to describe an elephant, and some described the creature as a rope. A few said it was like a tree trunk. Others claimed it was like a wall, and one group persisted it was similar to a snake. Each was correct in his own limited way, for those who felt the tail, the leg, the side, or the trunk recognized the similarity of the part to the object to which they were comparing it. Yet none of the men adequately described the entire animal because their experience was limited. How often we fall into this trap by insisting we alone have the answers when the truth is greater than either disputant realizes.

Differing Opinions

Furthermore, not everybody is at the same stage of development, so you cannot expect others to agree with you about everything. What a dull world it would be if they did. And whether you or they are right doesn't matter. Your entire concern is whether you are abiding by what is *right for you.* This presupposes a lack of restrictions for you, but in fact this nonrestrictive condition must be granted to everyone else in every circumstance. Each difference of opinion comes under this rule. Believe what feels right for you and stop worrying about opposing concepts. When you must oppose, be certain you deal only with the concept and not the personality. Live and let live. You have been endowed with a *daimon* that permits you to choose for yourself. Grant that right to others. Unless you do, you restrict your own free will. But know that with this privilege to choose for yourself come certain responsibilities. Whatever your desires or deeds, you are accountable for them. You can no longer look to the rules and regulations established by society—they may be totally inadequate for you. You must formulate your own. If the prospect sounds risky, let us assure you it is not. You have only to be certain you are thinking positively and applying your code to yourself. Then pay close attention to your inner signals. Any step in the wrong direction will be brought to your attention at once by your subconscious. You'll *know* when you're about to make a mistake and have ample time to correct yourself.

Other People's Reactions

Individuals who strike out on their own in this fashion may be misunderstood by those who follow the herd. So long as you do not indulge in false pride and consider yourself better or more advanced than your fellow humans, pay no attention to such reactions. Persevere in your efforts and people will soon learn, as you have, that *what is right for you is right for your world.* But give them time. Adjusting to the new you will take a considerable effort, and they might not be prepared to make it, but when the period of shock is over, they will appreciate the improvement and regard you more highly than ever. Some individuals may fade out of your life, however. Do not be dismayed if this happens, for you will attract others who will be more attuned to your new state of consciousness. As you rid yourself of negative thoughts, negative people will disappear as well, so resist the temptation to lapse back into your old attitudes and habits. The new, positive ones are far more healthy. They stand for progress, and life is meaningless unless you improve steadily.

Again, we must caution against the negativity of pride. Often individuals become impressed with their achievements when, in reality, the credit belongs entirely to the higher power that guides them. False pride can halt progress, so be on guard.

Eliminating Negativities

In this week's meditations you may want to use a program that will help you eliminate your negativities more quickly. Start by jotting down what you wish to achieve—perhaps a positive attitude toward life, plus whatever specifics will contribute to that goal.

Check your writing. Be certain your goals are reasonable, constructive, and pertain only to yourself. Foolish suggestions can harm you by confusing your subconscious and making later corrections difficult. Remember that your subconscious is literal, has no sense of humor, and will perform exactly as ordered, so make your orders simple and clear.

Reword your orders so that they are stated positively. To use "no" or "not" could confuse your subconscious. Phrase your commands positively. Eliminate all unnecessary words so that the order is as brief and clear as possible. The ideal is a slogan of ten words or less, but don't despair if you can't write a slogan-type order on the first try. Any wording will do as long as it fulfils the requirements and is easily remembered so you can incorporate it in your RENEWing exercises when you meditate. Of course, you must visualize the results of your instructions as having come to pass, rather than being in the works, but you should do this for all visualizations.

A typical program could sound something like this:

1. I enjoy whatever I do today.
2. Enjoyment is a habit I cultivate.
3. I am free of tension and anxiety and thus enjoy every moment.

Use the three steps for a couple of meditations. Thereafter a simple "I enjoy whatever I do" should suffice.

Another tool you may wish to use during meditation is a yantra. In some meditation disciplines, yantras are mandalas, ornate geometrical figures, which help to still the mind. Use one if you are inclined, but it is not necessary to go out of your way to find a mandala. A circle, a square, or interpenetrating triangles are simple yantras that will work as well. You may prop such a figure up before you and concentrate on it, or visualize it while you meditate, remembering always to pay attention only to the yantra and let whatever thoughts that do not pertain to it drift by and vanish.

Neither mantras or yantras should replace the seeking of the silence, however, as we shall explain in the next chapter.

9

Breath Control and Posture in Meditation

Christ instructed his disciples, "Except ye be converted, and become as little children, ye shall not enter into the kingdom of heaven" (Matt. 18:3).

You have been converted, and thus have fulfilled the first part of the command. This is not to say that you have changed your faith in the religious sense of the word or are required to become a Christian if you are one of the millions of people in the world who believe in Islam, Confucianism, Hinduism, Judaism, Buddhism, Sikhism, Taoism, Zoroastrianism, Jainism, or Shinto. Any member of the eleven great religions or the numerous smaller ones must certainly have equal claim to God, for he is a just and loving force that would not permit various religions to exist if they did not lead to the salvation of his creatures. His light shines upon each of us, without discrimination, and in matters of the faith we are apt to be like the blind men who attempted to describe the elephant.

Certainly we each are positive our particular faith is the only true one. That is as it should be, for what is right for us is right for our world. However, conversion is not confined to one creed. We have a wonderful friend who is a Roman Catholic priest. As a missionary in the Philippines, Father P. encounters devout Muslims who assure him they are praying for his conversion to their belief. Like him, they are decent, sincere people who wish to save the world. Yet the only person one can save is oneself, and that is accomplished by following whatever creed one is convinced is the most valid.

Our conversion, then, has been to the light, and whoever turns toward the light and heads in that direction will walk in the light of God. That person will walk with God and so discover that heaven is now—not out there beyond the sun, but here on earth, within him or her, waking and sleeping. As a child of light, he or she cannot err in thought, deed, or action.

Returning to Your Childhood

Thus we must learn what it means to become a child again, and we ask you to recall your own childhood for a few moments. If you feel this is impossible, observe a youngster of your acquaintance who is between the ages of four and eight. A child is complete. As a child you perceived yourself as the center of the world and everything in the world as existing for your benefit. But as you moved toward adolescence your self-centeredness disappeared. In fact, an increasingly painful awareness that you were not the center, and that someone or someplace else might have been, often made your life extremely difficult. During adolescence, changes were swift and constant. You can recall them for yourself. This was the period in your development when you stopped learning so easily. Now we know that this shift in learning patterns was part of your physiological development and that your dominant alpha waves, at which one learns quickly, were being replaced by the faster betas, though this is scant consolation when one considers the loss. In addition, your family-based loyalties began to wither, and you sought the companionship and approval of a group of individuals of the same age and tastes as yourself. The complete happiness that characterizes youngsters in the second and sometimes third years of school disappeared without a trace. Whether you describe the period as one when you "grew up," or in Freud's terms as the period when the superego began to assume the function of the parents, or as Jung does in his autobiography as a "splitting of myself," and a "disunion with myself, and uncertainty in the world at large" when he reached the age of ten, the effect was devastating. This occurence is very common; in fact, it is universal, a part of natural growth. As Arthur Koestler explains so well in his *Roots of Coincidence,* "The universe is focused on the self, and the self *is* the universe." Yet the child exists in a self-centered world that is too limited to continue, and he must break out of this tiny circle into a greater consciousness of his surroundings and of other people in order to realize that the real centeredness must be in the enormous circle of the globe.

Becoming Whole

The injunction to become as little children, therefore, means that we must regain the sense of wholeness, of completeness—only this time on a global basis. In short, we must attune ourselves to the *natural* rhythm of the world and see ourselves as a valuable part of the great whole so that we become what is termed holistic. When this happens we will know beyond any doubts that heaven is here now, with us and in us.

Your decision to be reborn in the light entitles you to be a child of the universe. Your meditations permit you to enjoy the fruits of this childhood, for they keep you attuned to the great circle of humanity and nature.

But the word *meditation* is often misused. We ourselves, in order not to confuse the issues at the start of the course, have used it loosely. Now that you have progressed in your exercises, you should know that it is not synonymous with *alpha*. It occurs in the alpha state when one reaches the deepest levels, but it can be preceded by what we call concentration and contemplation.

You have been given exercises in all three. For concentration, one focuses the slitted eyes on a candle flame or the geometrical figure called a yantra, or directs the attention to an intoned mantra, the sound pattern that aids breath control and thereby leads one into meditation. The aim of concentration is to merge with the "seed" object or sound so that the full attention is directed to it. The altered state of consciousness is not strictly meditation, however, but the first step towards it. Disciplines that deal only with concentration are thereby insufficient.

Some so-called meditative techniques proceed to the second step, contemplation. The student can become one with the object studied, or can arrive at the period of study with no preconceived ideas and let the subconscious suggest a thought or visualization, with which he or she "merges." Contemplation requires a yielding of self in order to experience the object or thought to its fullest, but it still falls short of the desired effect.

The third step, true meditation, requires an emptying of the self. One closes the eyes, goes down to alpha level, and seeks the silence rather than something within or outside the self—in short, exhausting the mind as thoroughly as possible so that ideas, sounds, and sights are eliminated. Only by emptying a glass can we obtain a complete refill, and since both concentration and contemplation methods must eventually yield to this—the emptying of the self to seek the silence—it is this approach which has been selected for you. The stilling of the mind is the goal. We are not meditating in the true sense until we have reached this point. Admittedly it is not easy. Our bodies fight it first, our minds next, and finally our emotions resist by telling us that if we do not "feel anything" we are not living. Still we must clear away the debris, clean the slate, penetrate to the core of the self where all *appears* empty and still at first. Then into the vacuum will come new thoughts, new visions, and new ideas, for nature cannot tolerate a vacuum. At this point we must be careful to let the contents "drift past" instead of trying to hold onto them and, after we have done this long enough, our minds become truly still and the minutes or the hours pass unnoticed. In this stillness we advance spiritually and psychically. Some benefits are earned through concentration or contemplation, but none can compare with the benefits of true meditation.

Posture in Meditation

Some disciplines claim that posture can assist in these respects. Those who favor the lotus position believe that entwined legs and arms permit the vibrations to move in a figure eight. If you are comfortable in the lotus position and feel that it helps, by all means use it, though we have found it no more beneficial than the pharaoh's posture (i.e., sitting upright on a chair with feet firmly on the floor and hands placed on the thighs).

Almost all meditative techniques employ relaxation and breath control. Here the oriental practices can be of incalculable benefit to Westerners. We are too tense and our physical exercises are most often calculated to build muscle tone rather than relax the body. Our most popular participatory sports—baseball, football, golf, and tennis—exercise muscles not used in ordinary occupations. Only swimming relaxes, and this is a seasonal activity in many locales. Thus, we moderns must use whatever exercises we can master that emphasize muscle relaxation, and the most noted form is yoga. This is a meditative technique, which in its entirety requires years of study and is unsuited to a culture like ours, which requires rapid adjustments, but its preliminaries, the asanas (body exercises), are recommended for those who can find a teacher.

Respiration

Breath control is more important for achieving an altered state of consciousness, and once we assume a suitable position that will leave the body erect, with the rib cage free for deep breathing, we are ready to observe the benefits of decreased respiration. On an average, we breathe sixteen to eighteen times per minute. When we become excited, our respirations increase. When we use our minds, they decrease. And what happens naturally can also be controlled, although it must be remembered that breathing is a natural, easy, involuntary process, which shouldn't be forced. When this rule is violated, as critics of hatha yoga are quick to point out, the abuser can do himself incalculable harm. However, it must be noted that hatha yoga nowhere recommends force. The emphasis is on the gentle retraining of the breath, and any difficulties arise from people trying to compress a process designed for years of study into a space of a few weeks. In both the asanas (body exercises) and the pranayamas (breathing exercises), the rule of moderation applies.

Yet you *should* learn how to alter your respiration enough to use it for your own protection. Begin by closing the mouth and breathing through the nostrils. Place your hand on your diaphragm and take deep breaths, so your hand will move out and back as you inflate or deflate your lungs. Your shoulders should not lift but remain stationary. Now pay attention to what happens, letting your breath come or go as it will. If you become excited or nervous about your breathing, relax and think of something pleasant for a moment, and when your breathing has slowed down to normal, resume the exercise.

Next, open your mouth and take twenty-five or so gasping, shallow breaths. Do this just once. Quick, shallow breathing may be used for emergencies such as striking your funny-bone or bracing yourself for the stab of a doctor's needle. It temporarily suspends the pain of an injury, though it is a stopgap method that should not be continued. People who overbreathe through sustained excitement or frequent sighing are likely to suffer from hyperventilation, with its accompanying symptoms of lightheadedness and fainting spells.

Slowing Down Respiration

Over-breathing should NEVER be used for heart pain. In fact, for heart ailments the opposite applies. One must slow the breathing as much as possible. We know many individuals who have averted incipient heart attacks or halted those already in progress by controlling their hearts through reduced respiration. The secret is to relax as completely as possible under the circumstances and breathe slowly and steadily from the diaphragm. Everyone should practice this simple, do-it-yourself life-saving method, but particularly those with heart problems.

Another reason for learning to breathe slowly is that it prevents one from remaining angry or annoyed. Those conditions tense the body and increase respiration. Most of us have been advised to count to ten to overcome anger, but it is more direct to deliberately hold the breath to ten or twelve deep inhalation-exhalations per minute. This dissipates the emotion. We cannot retain it when the body relaxes.

Stage fright or other fears can be similarly disposed of by slowing the breathing. What happens in a fearful situation is that our muscles tense, and this tensing restricts the flow of blood and inhibits breathing. The tightness causes greater tension and in extreme cases can even close the throat so we cannot swallow or speak. The body often tries to combat the effect by yawning. All fears that prevent us from taking appropriate action can be overcome by breathing slowly and deeply.

Reducing the rate to ten or twelve breaths per minute is also the best preparation for mental activity. Some people never get into the proper mood for study or thought because they breathe too rapidly. Just a few minutes devoted to slow, from-the-diaphragm breathing will accustom the body to the desirable thought-producing state. This is precisely what we do when we begin to meditate. We relax the body and use our breath to start the "countdown." As we descend into ourselves, our rate of respiration slows— as it must if we are sufficiently relaxed and desirous of achieving the alpha state—and it remains slowed for the greater part of our meditations. It can accelerate a bit during certain exercises, such as the visualization with emotion when we do our RENEWing, but it invariably decelerates when we withdraw the emotion.

When respiration increases, we may find ourselves rising from the alpha level. If so, all we have to do is take a deep breath and tell ourselves that as we exhale we shall find the right level. Slower breathing and its accompanying relaxation are two reasons why we emerge from a period of either concentration or contemplation feeling so refreshed and invigorated. Meditation (that is, seeking the silence) also does this, of course, but adds additional benefits.

Reducing Respiration

During your meditational work this week, listen to your breathing. Do not attempt to slow it down or speed it up at first. Just listen. Feel how natural, how easy it is. If focusing your attention on it causes you to speed it up, relax a moment and think of a pleasant experience. Breath is automatic. It is your natural exchange with the universe, and you need do nothing but observe it for a time. Later, when you become familiar with this natural rhythm, count your breaths for each minute. Then, with your eyes on the second hand of your watch, reduce the rate by one breath per minute. If your normal rate is sixteen breaths, practice breathing fifteen times per minute for one week or until you feel comfortable with fifteen. Do not rush it. A reduction of one breath per week suffices. The second week, work on reducing to fourteen. Take another week to get to the thirteen, and keep reducing the breaths until you can produce *easily and without strain* ten breaths per minute. Stop there. Under no circumstances should you attempt to go below ten. When you progress to the point where fewer than ten are required, you will do so naturally. The brain requires oxygen, and you must not cut off an adequate supply. Remember, you are not in competition with anyone in the world, and this applies particularly to meditation work. You do what is best for you and let others advance or remain stationary as they will. If someone else wants to brag about breathing once or twice per minute, let it go. It's the other person's brain, not yours, that is apt to suffer the damage.

You may help yourself to breathe slower by sitting before a lighted candle. Hold your face close to the flame and respire until you can breathe through your nostrils without disturbing the flame.

Practice with a candle and time your respirations until they are slow and steady. You will find this a relaxing experience as well as one that will assist you in overcoming emotional outbursts or coping with physical pain.

Do not forget to observe the rule of moderation in your work with breathing: *Nothing to excess.*

New Psychic Abilities

The dictum applies to all aspects of your development. As you read on and learn about others who possess psychic powers, you may become impatient with your progress. You shouldn't. You are already on the path to new awareness, and it does not matter that some individuals have advanced further or more rapidly. You are not in contest with them. There should be no contests. You do what is right for you and refuse to worry about anyone else's gifts. The powers of telepathy, clairvoyance, psychokinesis, or the rest may already be manifesting themselves in your life, but if they are not, they will. You cannot hurry them by forcing or being anxious. Moreover, when they do appear, do not become overly impressed by their importance. The Orientals call them *siddhis,* inconsequential powers, and they should not distract you from your goal of becoming a complete individual who can live at ease in the world. They are not a cause for pride or a subject for boasting. Quite the contrary. When they manifest, you should keep the knowledge to yourself while you use them to benefit yourself and everyone around you. But they are not evidence of your "arrival" at the desired goal, merely signposts to be observed along the way. Overemphasizing them can sidetrack you at best and halt your growth completely at the worst, for many individuals have been so enamored of their psychic powers that they stop at this stage and therefore fail to reach the true goal.

Let your psychic abilities come and go as they will. As you continue to grow they will become stronger and more reliable, and what's more, you will earn greater rewards than you can imagine at this moment.

Filling Your Body with Light

During this week's meditations, work with your breath. When you have succeeded in reducing it by a breath per minute, add another exercise. This will require you to seat yourself in the light. Repeat your circle-of-light exercise until you are surrounded by and filled with the light, but when you bring your circle back up over your head, do not close it off. Instead, inhale it right down to your feet and saturate your feet with the light. The circle exercise has already filled your feet, but perhaps it has not done a complete job. Inhale the light, pulling it in until your feet feel light in weight. Then exhale, and as you do so exhaust or throw off any aches, pains, tensions, or other negativities in your feet or the calves of your legs with the light. Exhale, and get rid of anything in your calves or thighs that would prevent you from filling your thighs with light. Inhale the light and pull it into your thighs. Exhale and dispose of the toxins in your hips. Inhale and fill yourself with the light to your waist. Exhale to exhaust anything that might prevent you filling your chest with light. Inhale the light and direct it into your chest. Repeat for your arms and your neck, and feel your entire lower body becoming lighter in weight. Now work on your head until it becomes so filled with light that it spills out of the top of your head and you begin to envisage, with your eyes closed, your head becoming brighter.

At first you may have to take more than one breath to fill a particular part of you. Do whatever you require. If it takes ten breaths to fill your chest with light, do not skimp. Take as many breaths or as long as you need to complete your work, but do a thorough job.

Psychic Energy

This light with which you have been bathing the interior of your body is what we shall call, for lack of a better term, psychic energy. It will provide you with physical energy if you are tired in body, mental energy if you are intellectually exhausted, and emotional energy of the positive kind. Do not hesitate to use it. Also, do not worry about getting more than your share. There is no such thing as getting too much, and it is available to all. Psychic energy abounds in every living thing—especially in vegetation and running water. It packs the walls of your room and the chair on which you sit, but it is found in its purest and most helpful forms in nature. Seat yourself under an oak or a fir tree or beside the cataracts of a mighty river and draw it into your body through breathing, but if you cannot take yourself to such a spot, use the bricks or stones or wood of your house or apartment to supply your energy. Use things like leathers and natural wools to build it, but seek it always in things, not people, for in people it might be contaminated by individual negativities that you do not desire or need.

If you are sensitive enough, you will feel the energy flowing into you. Do not be alarmed if you don't, however. Psychic energy is a high, fine vibration, which takes some getting used to, and you may well experience the benefits of your infusion before you learn recognize it.

Later we shall discuss methods of using this psychic energy for your RENEWing and for helping others, but first we must explore some important aspects of the human personality that will guide you in its correct application.

10

Foreseeing the Future and Reading the Aura

•◆◆◆•

The agonies of your childhood need no longer affect you, for you are a child of the light. But before we discuss your new vision, we must examine the effects of your former ways of seeing.

One of your most difficult hurdles may concern your expectations of the future. The bulk of humanity expects disaster. Fortunately, once you attuned yourself to the natural process through the elimination of negativities, you programmed yourself for good. Your world is your creation, and you will create what is in the best interest of yourself and all others. Everything you now own or have about you is the result of your past expectations. You would not have a car unless you had built a desire for one, and if the color of the vehicle is not to your taste, it is only because you imagined something more important than the color, such as immediate delivery or price. Your dwelling and your clothes are the end products of what you *thought you* should have or what you believed you deserved. And herein lies an important secret. If you are living in substandard housing or are wearing cheap and unattractive clothes, you are reaping the harvest of your negative thought in the past. You have what you have because you've led yourself to believe, no doubt unconsciously, that poor housing or ugly clothes are all you are entitled to. Your innermost thoughts were seeds, and you reaped what you sowed. Now if you desire better conditions, start visualizing yourself as having achieved them. Do not see yourself owning something that belongs to another person, but envision your possessions as yours, and in your grasp this very moment. Eliminate the negativities that have prevented you from receiving better.

Foreseeing Circumstances

This advice further applies to circumstances. If you think about disasters, you actually FORESEE them occuring to you. Pause a moment and think of some disaster that might befall you. Now analyze what happened. You FORESAW the trouble, didn't you? It unrolled before you like a mental film. You pictured yourself in trouble, perhaps suffering great pain. Now close your eyes and erase that mental catastrophe completely, seeing yourself as having averted the disaster and being well, happy, prosperous. When you live with the light, you must FORESEE only good, because you are programming your subconscious for positive results. Otherwise you will foresee disasters and attract them to you. Remember, only your *present* situation is the result of past thoughts; your future depends on how positively you visualize your world and your circumstances. When we say this, we are not contradicting ourselves but merely trying to explain in simple terms. The present IS all we have. We must live in the here and now. Nonetheless, what you shall have in the future is in your current subconscious. It EXISTS NOW, only waiting to manifest, so you must strike out all thoughts of trouble and insufficiency and RENEW your subconscious with positives. Tell it what you want, desire it with all your heart, know you have *already* obtained it—at this moment—and it becomes yours.

College students have often asked how this is possible. One young man, Rick, wants to be a doctor, and he could not understand at first how it was possible to see himself NOW as a medical practitioner when he had several years of study before he could reach the goal. He soon learned that unless he SAW IT NOW, BELIEVED IT NOW, it might not happen at all, and that his subconscious has no sense of time as we perceive time. He now knows himself to be a doctor, though it will be several years before he will treat his first patient.

He also knows that he must not verbalize his accomplishment, and we should remember this also. Confine your RENEWings to meditation sessions only. Between sessions, do not dwell on your progress. Don't think of your goal in any way, because to do so permits doubt to creep in. Don't talk about your ambitions, because talking will destroy your progress quickly. Have faith that the process works. Believe that it does. More so, believe in yourself and the higher power we call God. Attract the good things in life to you by thinking positively. You'll find that "them that has, gets" and you can be among the fortunate who *have*.

Doubting Intellectuals

Admittedly, faith is difficult for some people, particularly those of an intellectual bent. This type of person requires hard evidence, which simply isn't available at the start of the psychic journey. Like others, the intellectual may even doubt the advisability of such a self-development process. Yet progress won't be halted in the twentieth century, any more than it was in medieval times when some hopefuls believed the world would improve when there was universal education and others were convinced that mass education was too dangerous for society, since evil people would use it for evil purposes.

Like education, this foreseeing technique can be misused. It is, after all, a product of the mind, and the mind can be used or abused to produce positive or negative results that will benefit or harm the user and his or her world. That argument will not stop the process, however. Wrongdoers will continue to function at the dark end of the *daimon,* and it makes no sense to deny those who will use the light. This is an idea whose moment has come, and when we winnow the charlatans and the self-seekers from the healthy crop, we will reap a bountiful harvest.

To date, education has not yielded the required fruits. Robert S. DeRopp, in *The Master Game,* declares:

> A materialistic, spiritually impoverished culture can offer no instructions to the aspirant. The huge, highly specialized training centers that call themselves universities are obviously lacking in universality. They do not put the emphasis on expansion of consciousness first and acquisition of specialized knowledge second. They educate only a small part of a man's totality. They cram the intellectual brain with facts, pay some lip service to the education of the physical body . . . But true education, in the sense of expansion of consciousness and the harmonious development of man's latent powers, they do not offer.

Education should expose students to varying disciplines, diverse concepts, so they can reasonably and logically choose. But certain psychologists are so imbued with their own theories that they refuse to consider any that would expand the mind. Those who *do* accept such possibilities are designated as neo-humanists, and some of the greatest thinkers among the psychologists and psychiatrists of our era promulgate holistic theories of humankind. Such theories deserve a hearing.

Learning from Experience

We ask you, therefore, to keep an open mind but to avoid being too trusting. If you believe all that is in the newspapers, magazines, or on TV about individuals who are making names for themselves as psychics, you could become bitterly disillusioned. Many reputations will be destroyed and many charlatans unmasked before we arrive at the truth of our mental abilities to move objects via thought or to perform any of the other psychic phenomena. And even some of those committing fraud may be deceiving themselves, for the mind can be suborned by the will to please an audience. Psychics don't always know when they're "on" and must test constantly. And the honest ones will admit they oftentimes cannot tell whether they are receiving information clairvoyantly, precognitively, or telepathically when they read for a subject. So learn to trust only what you experience for yourself, be careful that you are not deceiving yourself in your desire to believe, and keep an open mind about the rest.

As you eliminate negativities, you will find yourself progressing. Eventually you will come to a point where you do not need someone else to tell you what is going to happen, for you will be your own psychic. And you won't need to worry about misusing any powers you acquire, for you cannot abuse them when you are working in the light. If you lapse momentarily into a negativity, furthermore, your subconscious will alert you to the error. Practise FORESEEing in the light and you will receive what you desire.

SEEing isn't limited to the future, however. It is something you can take advantage of right at this moment and, at the same time, prove to yourself that the light exercises you have been working on are based on fact.

Halos

Light and dark were favorite subjects for the writers and painters of the Middle Ages and the Renaissance, and the more enlightened of these artists were capable of perceptions they incorporated into their works. One example is the aureole. During the Middle Ages the halos around the heads of the deity or the saints were large and brightly colored, as the frescoes of Cimabue and Giotto reveal. The Renaissance artist did not deal with religious subjects exclusively but painted both religious and historical-mythical subjects and differentiated between them by painting nimbuses or halos around the heads of the religious figures. These representations grew fainter or narrower as the Renaissance wore on, until they were reduced to the slim golden lines circling the heads of Raphael's madonnas and infants or were completely eliminated.

Until recent years, most people believed these halos to be a mere stylistic device of the painters of that era. Now it has been proved that such bodies of light exist and, in addition, that every living thing has its own halo, or aura. These have even been photographed. The Kirlians of Russia have perfected equipment that captures the auras of humans and plant life, and numerous Westerners have studied the technique in this country. Further information on the subject can be found in *Psychic Discoveries Behind the Iron Curtain,* by Sheila Ostrander and Lynn Schroeder, or in more recent books about the Kirlian work, although we suggest you postpone reading about auras until you have seen them for yourself. Fortunately, this is one instance in which you need take nothing on hearsay. With a bit of time and non-effort, you can view the phenomena witnessed by artists of the past. You will also realize that your exercises with the light have some foundation in fact.

Seeing the Aura

Before we discuss the method, however, we need to define the word *aura.* Its origin is obscure, but it probably came from the Greek word for breath or air. Today it has been called almost everything from a "subtle, invisible emanation" to a "magnetic field of vibration which surrounds every living thing." Neither definition is adequate. Though subtle, auras *are* visible. Those who have perfected their seeing can view the same person or object and compare their sightings to check their accuracy. And "magnetic" in the second definition misleads, for it implies forces that attract. One must further take into account the background or predisposition of the definer. Psychics claim the aura is an ethereal body, while scientists are reluctant to admit it exists because they lack a logical explanation for both the substance—which could be a vaporous, thermal, or electrical discharge—and its effects. Obviously an interpretation that could be accepted universally is needed, but until one is forthcoming, we shall describe the aura as a subtle emanation surrounding the body that produces it. It is a light that can be recognized by trained observers, and it changes according to the changes that occur in the living body that produces it. This phenomenon is not limited strictly to those with eyes or eyesight, however. An individual who has been blind from childhood demonstrated to a group of over forty people that he can accurately observe and describe an aura.

The Blind "Seeing" Auras

The proof occurred by chance. We had arranged a series of lectures on ESP for the YWCA in Niagara Falls, New York. Over forty people participated in the class, including a young minister and his wife, whom we shall call Mrs. W. Before the start of the second class, Mrs. W. confided to us that she was upset. A relative who was studying medicine had been to dinner at her home that evening and had commented on her pregnant condition, saying she was retaining water and was otherwise in poor health. We were already seated, near the front of the class, when the instructor arrived. With her were a couple of guests, who sat at the rear of the room. The lesson had to do with auras. The instructor mentioned that she and a group of blind people were experimenting with aura training and that one of the experimenters, Mr. Lentine—who was then teaching physics at a local high school—was present and might be willing to answer a question or two.

Immediately after the lecture, we approached Mr. Lentine and asked him to read Mrs. W.'s aura. Our purpose was to distract her into forgetting about her relative's adverse diagnosis. People who heard the request immediately moved back. Everyone turned to watch Mr. Lentine. There was no opportunity for anyone to tell him about Mrs. W.'s pregnancy and no way for him to know it otherwise, for this was his first visit to the class and the students were all strangers to him and generally to each other. Mr. Lentine and Mrs. W. were never introduced, and he came no closer than five feet from her, where he stood frowning and perspiring. He appeared highly upset, and he stammered that he would tell her later, in a few weeks or so. This further alarmed Mrs. W., who was certain something was drastically wrong with her and the unborn child, and we finally had to request our instructor, the psychic Carol Liaros, to tell him it was all right to report on what he saw. She said simply, "It's all right, Sam. Tell what you see." Only then did he describe Mrs. W.'s aura as double, as though she were carrying a large basketball. Later conversation revealed he had hesitated because he didn't know whether she was married and, if so, whether she wished others to know about her pregnancy.

This same seer, who left the area to become a physicist at Rensselaer Polytechnic Institute, invented a machine to help other blind people see auras and colors and generally hone their senses to replace the missing one of sight. Carol Liaros, meanwhile, has initiated "Project Blind Awareness" to continue her work with the blind and is training them to see without mechanical apparatus.

Experimenting Yourself

Fortunately, you do not need equipment; you can begin seeing auras with the naked eye once you learn the technique. The requirements are the same as those for meditation. Relax the body as completely as possible. This time, however, keep your eyes open. Simply go limp, as though your body were made of sawdust and as though tensions in the form of sawdust were leaking out through a hole in your right heel. Now defocus your eyes and stare at the spot directly above the head of a subject. The first attempts should be made in a dimly lit room, with your subject standing against a plain background that can be lighter or darker than the subject. If you cannot arrange for a darkened room, don't postpone the experiment; auras can be seen in bright light as well, and in an emergency a coat can be held up behind the subject to provide a solid background.

Relaxing the Eyes

The secret lies in relaxing and defocusing the eyes. You can observe the changes in the pupils of the eyes when they relax: they enlarge, and the eyelids cease to blink. You are thereby admitting more light into the eyeball and this can be painful at first. If so, close your eyes to a squint and stare at your subject. Stay relaxed, and let your breathing slow. After a few moments, you will probably see an opaqueness around the head of the subject. Whether it is darker or lighter than the background makes no difference, for it will probably be colorless. One of the reasons for having the room dim is that it rules out the possibility of seeing shadows—which is what most "see-ers" immediately attribute the phenomenon to. But if you suspect shadows, you can eliminate them by placing your subject where they can't be cast.

It is best to choose for your first subject some individual who exhibits a great deal of physical energy, but you should also use more than one person for each attempt. Generally, those willing to volunteer are high energy producers. Whatever the circumstances, do not feel you must postpone your experiment until conditions are more favorable. In fact, you don't even need another person. You can seat yourself in a dimly lit room and position your hands before a solid-colored background. Relax your body and stare at the tips of your fingers. Or you can stand before a mirror with a plain backdrop behind you and stare lazily at a point one inch above your head. What you will see is an outline that appears similar to clear food wrap or waxed paper and is lighter or darker than the background. Try to avoid becoming excited when you spot it, for the least tension may cause it to disappear. Sighting auras is a lazy person's game. Stay relaxed.

If an aura appears to come and go during the first trials, do not become discouraged. When you are sufficiently at ease you will be able to study the aura, but when you direct normal attention to it, your eyes will shift into focus and you will perceive just the physical body.

Most of us observe colorless auras at the start. A few individuals, however, can defocus well enough to see the color that exists. The first is a narrow band of golden light that hugs the entire body but is particularly noticeable around the head and other unclothed areas. This band is called the etheric double. You can spot it easily around the heads of uninspiring after-dinner speakers when the background is a solid color, the room is dim, and the speaker's rostrum is illuminated. Perhaps it is the dinners that cause one to relax, rather than the speeches, but many individuals report having seen their first etheric double at a banquet or meeting.

Do not be alarmed if the etheric double eludes you for a time. You are not in a contest with anyone; competition leads to pressure, and pressure will bar you from any psychic advancement. Know that you *will* see the etheric double when you've trained your body and eyes to relax. Don't attempt to force your development. Easy does it.

Noticing Colors

After you locate the etheric body, you will notice colors around the physical structure of your subjects. These colors can range from the darkest shades to the most desirable: an opalescent, shimmering, almost non-color, which is purer than white. The color can hug the figure, as it invariably does when the subject is absorbed in his or her own thoughts or is purposely wrapping the aura close to the body, or it can extend several feet in all directions if the subject is identifying with others or projecting his or her emotions.

Because colors change with the mood or emotion of the projector, they are valuable aids to understanding others. Both color and shade are significant. A black aura, fortunately, is rare and most often indicates the darker emotions: hate, malice, envy, greed, and their like. Yet one must be careful not to jump to conclusions. There may be rare instances when the viewer misinterprets the color or its significance. In general, though, it is best to try to lighten the spirits of those people with dark auras, for the black shades or any of the other dark, muddy shades reveal that the individual is in the grip of despondency or some other bad mood.

Colors and Emotions

There is a poisonous shade of yellow that manifests when people are cowardly. Envy and malice erupt in a sickening shade of green. Any of the dark thoughts or moods can be read in the aura, and the color body is so dominant that it causes individuals to choose similar shades for their normal wearing apparel or the furnishings and walls of their homes when a mood persists for any length of time.

The lighter shades are the desirable ones, of course. A pale blue reveals that its producer is advancing spiritually. A lovely pale green is often the sign of a healer, and we have often approached total strangers to ask if they were doctors or nurses because the green is so evident. Gold or pale yellow indicate intellectual pursuits, and the opalescents signify the most highly evolved in the spiritual realm.

Symbols in the Aura

Recently we have begun to see symbols in auras. From the first we have observed halos around the heads of certain people of a religious bent as well as one or more dark bodies behind the subject. At first we thought the bodies were after-images, but subsequent testing on our own and discussions with other seers lead us to believe that we are viewing the silhouettes of living individuals who influence the subjects and are a sort of mind projection, one of which could be termed the guardian angel of each person. They are not always there, however. Sometimes they come and go, and often they are not present. More advanced seers tell us that these bodies are light and have distinguishable features and, as our seeing develops, we shall be able to describe them more accurately. The symbols are different from these manifestations, and the first time we saw them we were listening to a bishop of the Greek Orthodox Church speak about exorcism. We drew the symbols on paper as they appeared, thinking they might be letters of the Greek alphabet. However, when we checked with one of our group who is an advanced psychic, she informed us that they were the personal symbols of the speaker—thought forms manifested by the speaker in his aura. We asked her to draw the symbols that she saw; and when we compared notes we found them identical. Obviously we have not reached the point where we can interpret them, but if the knowledge is important for our development, it will come.

Uses of Aura Sighting

All of us can take advantage of our aura sightings. They are vital clues to the mood or emotions of everyone we encounter. If we meet a person who appears physically calm, for example, and we see flashes of red shooting through his aura, we will know that he is angry. The degree of emotion can be determined by the shade and the extent of the red. Isolated flashes indicate mild anger or temporary annoyance, but an aura shot with red and muddying its beautiful color reveals deep anger. The term "to see red" is literal. Even if the anger isn't strong enough for the person to see red, as one does sometimes, it can show up in the aura. The same rules apply to the other colors.

Those who perfect their auric sightings have a distinct advantage. They can tell whether those they meet are well in body and emotion or need help. Any indentations in the auric body indicate an ailment in the physical part of the body where the indentation occurs. The other day we perceived such an indentation above the right frontal bone of our clergyman as he was delivering his homily. When we inquired about it, he informed us that he had been fighting off a recurring headache, and we had an opportunity to do some silent healing—about which we shall talk later.

Auric readers can also tell whether others are being honest with themselves and the world, for dishonesty affects the colors. Of course, we must always remember that we must not judge, though we can certainly use the information to avoid being deceived.

The existence of the aura is no longer debatable. Once the phenomena were reproduced on film, the controversy over their existence was—or should have been—settled. The interpretation of colors, on the other hand, is not quite as exact, and only your own experience in viewing and interpreting auras will provide you with the sort of empirical data you need to assess them accurately.

Putting the Technique to Use

Now that you know the technique of studying auras, you can start to look for them. Start by relaxing. Defocus your eyes to what is commonly known as a stare. Direct your attention to a spot just above the head of your subject and observe what happens. Many individuals perceive the opaque envelope within a minute or so; others take longer, but they, too, can see it. Colors will often manifest later, after sufficient practice. If you relax when you practice and allow yourself plenty of time, it won't be long before you will be among those who can check their findings with those of fellow seers.

Using the Aura in Meditation

For this week's meditations, work with your own aura by learning to expand and contract it. Repeat the exercise given in the last chapter for filling yourself with the light. When your entire body is permeated with it, do not close it off at the top. Instead, continue to visualize the light streaming down on you from above.

You will be the center of an egg of light that extends seven inches from the widest parts of your body and is smooth on the outside, like the shell of an egg. Now prepare to expand this light by doing the following:

1. Inhale and draw more light down into your aura. Exhale and push out your circle of light twelve inches in every direction, including below your feet and above your head.

2. Inhale and draw in the light. Exhale and extend it to two feet.

3. Inhale the light. Exhale and expand it to three feet.

4. Inhale, and as you exhale, expand it to four feet.

5. Inhale, and exhale it to five feet.

6. Inhale, and exhale it to six feet.

7. Inhale, and exhale it to seven feet in every direction from your physical body, still including below and above you.

You are now the center of a huge circle of light that will mingle with the light of anyone else in the room. Breathing easily and retaining your circle, observe what is happening to you, for this is your initial experience with the universal unconscious, and it will prepare you to understand the wonderful things that transpire when you work with the universal unconscious.

If you do not experience any difference at this point, be patient. The subtle emanation of the aura will become stronger as you practice, and you will be rewarded with a feeling of joy, a sense of belonging to the universe.

After a few minutes of experiencing the expanded aura, begin to reduce it to its normal size:

8. Inhale and draw it in to six feet in all directions. Exhale and let it sift into your physical body.

9. Inhale and reduce it to five feet. As you exhale, let the light fill your body.

10. Inhale it to four feet. Exhale and throw off any aches, pains, tensions, or other negativities to make room for the increased light.

11. Inhale it to three feet. Exhale the negativities to make room for the light.

12. Inhale it to two feet. Exhale negativities and bring in the light.

13. Inhale to one foot. Exhale any negativities and bring in the light.

14. Inhale to seven inches from the widest parts of your body. Exhale and close off the top of the light so that you are encased in a dense shield of light that is bright and clear and provides a protective covering for your physical body.

Subsequent chapters will discuss the proper uses of the light, but for the present learn to expand and contract it for your personal benefit.

11

Finding Your True Self

As children of the light, we do not need to be anyone but ourselves. This means that we must discard our various masks. And each of us wears them. In youth we rationalized by telling ourselves that growth and cultural conditioning demanded barriers be erected, so we adopted various masks to suit specific occasions. We have reached the point where we can discard them. Masks are for the unenlightened. Individuals who've come to terms with themselves no longer require such "protection" from the outside world. If they continue to use them in certain circumstances, they should be fully aware of the falseness of the assumed face and of the culture that leads to such duplicity. We cannot live by the dictates of the outer world when the only true one is interior. Further, there is only one person any of us can change—oneself. So let us proceed.

The masks we use are legion. We assume one for our family relationships. Here we adopt the role demanded by our position in the family. If we are a father, we see ourselves as the star of the drama: the breadwinner, the head of the household, the protagonist who fends off all the dragons, keeps the wolves from the door, and defeats the villains so that the other member of the family can thrive.

If we are mothers, we are the lead actresses, the stars, for it is our business to provide the comforts. If a son or daughter, we feel *we* are the reason for the performance. Father and mother have had their day and exist solely to provide the money, food, shelter, clothing, and whatever else is required for our success.

Where does the truth lie when each person believes he or she is the rightful star of his or her life's drama? Paradoxically, each is correct. Everyone should know he or she *is* the center of his universe. Someone who doesn't is apt to have an underdeveloped personality. The starring role is a natural one. However, we must recognize the drama for the game it is and not expect to be both star and director. What we do when we play the part we have been assigned in a family is use a mask. This superficial cover

105

enables our relatives to identify with us in a fashion acceptable to our culture and backgrounds, but we may find that even in the closest-knit family grouping, members describe each other in completely different terms. Masks, then, can be perceived differently.

Different Kinds of Masks

Our needs change when we move outside the family to another group or situation. In school we assume a different role and adopt a mask to fit it. What we hope to project may be an image of a brilliant and personable youth who *deserves* A grades despite not scoring well on tests, or the alert, interested person who sits through entire classes with eyes glued shut in order to concentrate more fully on the lectures. Still other masks are used by those who "refuse to play the educational game"—they intend to convey the message that they are capable but uninterested in such trivia. And the masks can change according to the relationship with the teacher. They also become totally different for one's peers. Then even straight-A students often endeavor to impress their classmates as ordinary people who don't particularly care about knowledge and aren't pushing up the grade curve to obtain it; on the contrary, these masked intellectuals have too many and too varied interests to be academic grinds.

Masks worn with friends outside of school are as numerous as one's combinations of friends. One group may call for a cynical effect; another a fun-loving, devil-may-care projection; while still another a moody, introspective appearance.

We wear different masks for our employers, our fellow workers, and those in our employ, along with whatever other members of the public we encounter, until we may well ask which of our masks represents the true us.

If we're honest, we must admit that none does. Truth is everlasting and unchanging, while masks can be donned or put aside according to the circumstances of the moment. Truth is synonymous with reality, that quality or state of being which is actual. As Bradford Smith explains it in *Meditation: The Inward Art,* "Only that which is permanent and unchanging is real. Everything else is unreal, is appearance, is illusion." Since we change masks for every situation and every person, and even may use several for a single individual, what we reflect cannot be truth or reality, and we therefore are not the sum of disguises that shift with the breeze. One might say these faces we assume are so far from the truth that they are hypocritical manifestations of the immutable self. And even when they are unconscious manifestations, they remain hypocritical. They distort, they cover, they· conceal—often from the consciousness of the wearer—the actual self that neither changes, ages, rests, nor sleeps. If they are necessary as defense mechanisms, there is patently something wrong with the culture that produces them. Shortly you should be able to dispense with your masks. In the meantime, recognize them for what they are: defenses set up by a false ego in its attempt to cope with an alienated society.

Self-Worth

As we said before, a sense of self-worth is necessary. We require it for self-respect—for self-preservation, even. This appreciation of the self we identify with the ego, which starts out as a healthy, normal, functional part of us. But somewhere in the teenage period it runs amok and develops into the kind of self-centeredness that makes some people demand to be king-of-the-hill or they'll go home and sulk. Others may bury their egos and become doormats for the world. Neither extreme is healthy.

Our egos are responsible for many conflicts in our lives. When we become aware that we may not be as wonderful as our ego insists, and thereby not able to measure up to a demanding world, we find ourselves in difficulties. And there are times when our ego is so deflated, our sense of self-esteem so low, that no accomplishment, however great, can rescue us from the ensuing despair. Clearly we must come to terms with this personality facet that causes so much trouble. Indeed, we have already begun to work on the ego with our detachment exercises and are thus able to identify it through standing aside and watching it perform. Our difficulty lies in the fact that it is often hard to separate the healthy ego, which we shall call the essence, from that which is false, although even here separation and observation are possible. The false ego is not the true self, any more than masks are. Unlike the true self, the false ego changes, rests, and sleeps.

The False Ego

The false ego inflates or deflates according to circumstances. Honors bring with them an increase in self-esteem, thereby puffing up the ego. Criticism can deflate it, at least until it atones for the censure by building itself up again. The point is that the false ego can and does change, so it cannot be considered true or real.

It rests often, as well. When we are engrossed in a book, a film, or some similar exterior phenomenon, our egos become quiescent. The awareness of "I" simply isn't there; instead, we are taken out of ourselves and are no longer concerned with our relation to the object of interest.

The most obvious time when the false ego is missing, however, is during sleep. If it were a part of the self that is truly real, we should be aware of it during the hours we are, as the saying goes, unconscious. Instead, we fall into sleep with the ego intact and wake to a period of split seconds to minutes before it reasserts itself and we are aware of it. During the sleep period we dream, but even here our egos are separable from the self—that is, we can stand aside and watch ourselves act and react in our dreams. For the remainder of the sleep period, whether we snore, grit our teeth, talk out loud, thrash around, or lie quietly, the ego doesn't exist. We are unconscious of it in the same way during a faint, or when we are under an anesthetic—we separate from it at the moment of dropping off and gather it to us again when we return to consciousness.

Hypnosis

Another notable time when egos cease to function is when a person is under hypnosis. This condition should be impossible if you have been following the meditation instructions carefully. The instruction that begins with "you and you alone will control your mind . . . " has programmed you against mind control by another person or force. Nevertheless, those who have witnessed demonstrations of hypnotism will know the power of the mind. A subject can be told that the end of a piece of chalk is a burning cigarette, and a blister will rise on his skin where the chalk has touched it. Contrariwise, a burning cigarette can be held against the skin and if the subject has been instructed that it is a piece of chalk, the skin will not blister or change in any fashion. This would be impossible if the ego or "I" were in control. Also, a hypnotist often instructs the subject to forget all that transpired during the hypnotic trance. This, too, would be impossible if the ego were on duty, and for this reason we must be eager to separate ourselves from it.

Hypnotism is never necessary. Some reputable doctors and dentists do, of course, use hypnotism to put their patients at ease while undergoing treatment. But even their services are not required, for anything that they can do in the form of relaxing can be done by you once you learn to separate the body and mind and, further, the real ego from the false. When you reach this step in your development, we can discuss the kinds of bodily monitoring that will prevent you from being burned when you come into direct contact with high heats, permit you to staunch the flow of blood from injuries, and protect your body from ailments of all kinds. Such control over physical processes demonstrated at the Menninger Clinic by people like the American Jack Schwarz and the Indian Swami Rama (which will be discussed in Chapter 13) are achievable by every intelligent human being. Some people learn these controls through biofeedback, although machines are not required. Once the false ego is tamed, physiological techniques for safeguarding the body are possible.

Inasmuch as there are states of existence when the ego goes "on holiday" we can see that it is separable and distinct from the permanent aspects of the human being. It appears, therefore, that we are dealing with three qualities of the psyche: the false ego, which binds itself to the healthy ego; the masks that we shall call the persona (from the Greek word for masks); and the true, eternal, immutable part of a person designated as the essence. The latter differs from its counterpart, substance, in that it is unchanging and everlasting. A man of seventy, for example, looks different from the way he did as an adolescent. Yet his substance alone has changed, for if you ask, he is apt to tell you that apart from the aches and pains of the substance—the flesh—he feels no different from the way he did at sixteen. Although this becomes obvious only over long periods of time, the feeling is universal and natural. What is impervious to time and the aging process, and what we must contact in order to become fully actualized human beings, is this permanency, the essence. You have been working steadily toward it since the beginning of this course, by detaching, by avoiding negativities, and by changing your concepts of time. Now you are ready for one of the last steps, the separation of the false ego, or the "I."

Separating the False Ego

Just as 90 percent of our sensory words refer to the physical eye, so the bulk of our personal references refer to the egotistical "I." The former indicate that sight is the dominant sense; the latter identifies the dominant personality referent. But when we succeed in reducing the false ego or "I" to its proper dimensions, we permit ourselves to function on a higher plane. As R D. Laing explains in *The Politics of Experience,* "True sanity entails in one way or another the dissolution of the normal ego, that false self competently adjusted to our alienated social reality; the emergence of the inner archetypal mediators of divine power, and through this death a rebirth, and the eventual reestablishment of a new kind of ego-functioning, the ego now being the servant of the divine, no longer its betrayer."

This is what is meant by the Gospel passages "He that findeth his life shall lose it: and he that loseth his life for my sake shall find it." (Matthew 10:39) and "Whosoever shall seek to save his life shall lose it; and whosoever shall lose his life shall preserve it" (Luke 17:33). The old self, which lives according to the dictates of the false ego, must be lost before the true self can be found. There is no alternative. Whether the "I" is a psychological appendix or a cultural graft, it must be excised. When this has been accomplished, all those negativities that linger and persist in robbing us of our peace will be laid to rest for all time. Anger, envy, blame, self-recrimination, each fear, and every conceivable anxiety will terminate. You will be transformed by your association with the essence. This essence is already familiar to you, though perhaps you know it by the label of "God," "the Divine Spirit," "the All-Powerful," "the indweller," "the light," "the overself," "the atman," or a similar term. What it is called doesn't matter; its effect is always the same: joy, peace, perfect understanding. When you reach your essence, you come home. You enter your rightful place, the kingdom of God that lies within you. Nothing else you accomplish in this life is as important as finding this essence, this true and beautiful self waiting to reward you with the peace that passes understanding.

The Desire to Change

We have been seeking God, our essence, in meditation. Only in ourselves can we find the answer. However, we can assist ourselves during our conscious moments by noting our modes of behavior and setting snares for the false ego. Before we begin, however, we must want to change with every fiber of our being; we must be so thoroughly disillusioned by our conditions that we risk all in the hope of finding better. We must be prepared to abandon every illusory feeling and attitude we harbor. The game is not for the faint-hearted. The greater the desire, the quicker the change. Given this craving, we are ready to eliminate the false ego. We will accomplish this by combining detachment exercises and the radar-trap technique we used for isolating negativities: we check constantly and review our progress four times a day.

During your waking hours, observe yourself. Start first thing in the morning to monitor your thoughts, emotions, daydreams, and speech, for they provide important clues to overthrowing the false ego. If necessary, keep a running tally on three-by-five cards. Check your thoughts. Realize that they are not you, the essence. Check your emotions. They are not you. Check your desires. They are not you. Neither are daydreams nor, perhaps, your present mode of speech—and speech is perhaps the most important of all to check, for the words you use reveal your most hidden thoughts.

Too many people are afflicted with verbal "my-opia" and other forms of harmful "I-cite." They conduct endless dialogues about "my ideas," "my triumphs," "my appetite." So great is their short-sightedness that they see only to the tips of their noses. They make it apparent that their thinking and planning concern only themselves, for they can often be heard to refer to "my car," "my house," "my money," when the possessions are clearly those of the family rather than strictly personal. "My-opia" is a dreadful disease that prevents one from contacting his or her essence.

Overcoming Self-Centeredness

If you are relatively free of "my-opia," check your "I-cite." This ailment is less obvious, although it reaches epidemic proportions in some social groups. You check for it by listening to yourself. How often do you use the word "I"? Constantly? Occasionally? Sparingly? If you use it often you are being short-sighted and self-centered, and you must refocus by becoming more interested in the rest of humanity. The stage of your development where you thought only of yourself is past. What is right for you is *still* right for your world, but you must now take a longer, harder look at the universe. You must learn to see yourself in perspective, and this means perceiving the entire picture instead of a closeup of you. If you have been following the instructions, you are more than ready for this step.

Certain questions can help you identify your problems. As you proceed through your day, ask yourself who each incident affects: Is it the false ego? Will this incident be important in five days, five months, five years? Does it hurt my sense of pride? Threaten my prestige? If the answer is "yes" to these or similar queries, your ego, the "Big I" is in charge. Your essence requires nothing in the way of pride, prestige, finances; it is beyond time and neither changes, ages, rests, nor sleeps. Nonetheless, your essence provides all the good you could possibly imagine, now and in the future. It is your sole benefactor, and no circumstances, no individual can keep good from you once you begin to heed and become attuned to your essence. Whatever happens will be for your eventual benefit. Those you encounter will either assist you or fade from your life.

The final step in conscious tuning is to dedicate yourself to God. Surrender the false will that is prompted by the false ego and let yourself become a channel of the light. Reaffirm this surrender during every meditation. And maintain your watch for the enemy "I" for a week so you can hasten the process.

Surrendering

Perhaps you are not ready for this last step. If so, do not try to force it. When the proper time arrives, you will know and be ready. Surrender of this sort is not easy for anyone. Every fiber of the being fights against it. In both conscious and meditative states, the body, the mind, the desires, the emotions, the memories, and the very will to live will join the battle against what the mind insists is a loss of identity. As indeed it is, albeit a loss of false identity. Surrender is the giving over of the life in order to find life, as Matthew and Luke recorded in their Gospels.

Whatever your decision about surrendering, check your progress four times each day. Begin on waking. Before you open your eyes fully or stir from the bed, think about your sleep period. Did you dream? Recall your dreams in as much detail as possible, for they reveal significant messages from your essence, which remains on duty while your ego sleeps. Make it a habit to recall your dreams immediately on waking, or they may elude you. Pay particular attention to the symbols incorporated in your dreams, for it is through these symbols that the most significant messages will be relayed. At this stage be careful not to take your dreams literally. A dream of death does not mean you will die, for instance. Much more will be said about dream symbols and their meaning in the closing chapters of this book, but if you begin now to remember them, you will be ready for the last stages of your psychic development and spiritual wholeness. If you do not recall any dreams, tell yourself you will the next night. Again, desire is important. Everyone dreams. And everyone, by programming the self to do so, can remember their contents.

Daily Checks

Your second radar check should be made at noon. Review your morning and decide whether you succeeded in banishing the false ego. If not, forgive yourself and know you will improve. Make your third check before leaving school or your place of business. Think about your afternoon and determine whether you were deeply interested in others and what transpired during the second half of the day, rather than how you reacted or how this or that benefitted the false you. Make your last check just before you fall asleep, and forgive all transgressions committed by others or your false ego, for they are unimportant to your essence. Instruct your essence to aid you by revealing its needs in your dreams, and know you will remember the revelations.

Once you encounter your essence, further instructions will be superfluous. You will possess the joy, the certainty, the peace that surpasses understanding. Everything you need spiritually, mentally, or materially will automatically come to you so that you can develop further. The rewards far exceed the effort required to obtain them. Persist in your efforts.

Your meditation instructions for this week have been designed to help you contact the essence. Begin with your basic meditation, say your prayer, and then seek the silence. Clear your mental screen of whatever thoughts it might reflect, and focus on the blankness. Then ask yourself, "Who am I? Who is the true self that exists within me?" Listen for the answer. Bring your complete attention to bear on the listening.

If you hear only the echo of silence, wait a few minutes and repeat your question. Above all, remain calm and expectant. What often happens is that people panic when they reach what they *believe* is the core of themselves and no one *appears* to be home. The same people probably panicked before, when they first isolated themselves from emotion and felt drained and empty because the volatile contents were gone. This experience need never be yours. Your essence is there, waiting, but it needs to be certain that you are sincere. Be patient and persevere in your efforts, and you will find it within yourself, much as Jacob did his angel.

In fact, the story of Jacob and his angel is an early account of a man coming to grips with his essence. Jacob, as one reads in Genesis 32:24–30, was spending the night alone at the side of a stream "and there wrestled a man with him until the breaking of day." His antagonist touched the hollow of Jacob's thigh and threw it out of joint as they struggled, and then asked to be released since it was nearly daybreak. Jacob refused until the antagonist blessed him, and then "Jacob called the name of the place Peniel: for I have seen God face to face, and my life is preserved."

Finding Your Essence

Before he reached his conclusion about the identity of his opponent, however, Jacob questioned him, just as you and I are apt to do when we first encounter our essences. Some on receiving an answer to "Who am I?" at first believe their minds are playing tricks. When your answer comes, be assured it has originated from your essence. You may find it difficult to believe at the start and may even wonder if there could be harm intended by your answer, but rest assured, if you are working with the light and have followed the instructions—such as seeking positive results and not trying to change the lives or circumstances of others—you have nothing whatever to fear. Your essence is pure good, and you will come to feel at ease with it as Jacob did.

If you experience any panic or doubt before you reach your goal, be patient and continue your efforts. The joy that will come is worth the struggle.

Ask your questions of your essence at each meditation session from this time on, and continue to ask until you are absolutely certain you have reached the innermost being, the God that was within Jacob and is within each of us. Then ask, too, that you be given the help you need during your waking hours to overcome your false ego, for there is nothing so pitiful as a searcher who has reached this crucial point of development and becomes so impressed with his or her accomplishment as to embark on an incredible ego trip. It happens too often—and with good reason, for when we meet our essence, we unleash the power and knowledge of the universe. We understand that the essence *is* God—or whatever higher power we believe is responsible for the order of the universe—and that it is there within us, just as it exists in every other place in the world. The revelation is mind-boggling, but unless we accept it with the understanding that it is *not* the human being who should receive the honor and the glory, but the eternal power, we are apt to take personal credit where none is deserved. We should emerge from the meeting with our essence with assurance, a profound appreciation for being elevated to the ranks of the immortals and an ingrained humility that comes from knowing we are the least of mortals.

St. Paul warned, "Though I speak with the tongues of men and of angels, and have not charity, I am become as sounding brass, or a tinkling cymbal" (1 Cor. 13:1). The centered individual would do well to substitute humility for charity, for without humility the seeker loses the way.

With this caution in mind, you are ready to approach your essence. An affirmation such as the following may be helpful:

> The being within me is a permanent resident. Emotions are fleeting visitors. Thoughts are temporary guests. Bodily impressions are transient. When all depart, only the eternal being remains: constant, pure, divine, this all-powerful Holy Spirit dwells within me. I AM THE I AM.

12

Psychic Energy

Becoming aware of the I AM raises inevitable questions. If everyone possesses this all-powerful essence, why are some people greater than others? What is the difference between those individuals who rise to power and prominence and people with corresponding equipment and talents who remain obscure? Can such differences be isolated? Apparently they can, for we perceive them. We find that successful people invariably exhibit some personality, character, or mental trait which sets them apart from others. They may be more energetic; they may possess charisma; they may be able to slice through a mass of information to come up with viable solutions to problems. However the quality manifests, it is greater than average and sometimes appears in exaggerated form.

The most obvious of these phenomena is what we call physical energy. Star athletes are noted for their physical energy, but every prominent person seems to have more than a normal share. Emotional energy is another type, with painters, sculptors, and television, film, radio, and recording stars being only a few of the noted energizers of emotion. Mental energy is a third form, and its possessors appear infinitely more intelligent than the average person. But sometimes the physical, emotional, and mental activity are within the "normal" range, and the sole trait that sets the favored one apart is the personal appeal we call charisma. Whatever the plus factor, it is part and parcel of the greater phenomenon of psychic energy. This is the vital and magnetic source inherent in every living thing, though it is most noticeable in the human species. Each of us has it, though some in greater abundance.

It peaks when we are in fine health and excited about some undertaking; then we experience it firsthand, acknowledging its presence by saying that we are full of energy. We dissipate it by fretting over the past, being anxious about the present, being fearful of the future. We can fritter it away by time-wasting and nervous habits or have it drained by energy-sappers.

Previous lessons have taught us how to avoid reducing the energy ourselves and prevent others from doing so, but now we must learn to build, store, and expand it for our conscious endeavors.

Psychic Energy

You already know the basic techniques. You deliberately absorb energy when you seat yourself in the light and inhale it with each breath, and then you expand the light to seven feet from your body. The light is *psychic energy*. When you emerge from your meditations, you feel the invigoration that comes from building and storing a supply of it. When you've watched auras, your own or others', you have been looking at the visible proof of it.

Scientific evidence of the existence of psychic energy is harder to come by. To date it has eluded quantitative measurement, although it has been photographed in its aura manifestations by Kirlian photographers, and its presence has been detected in the telepathy, clairvoyance, and other PSI tests conducted in controlled laboratory experiments. But scientific proof is not a condition of its existence. One has only to experience an aura reading and aura painting by someone like Rick Pfarschner of Toronto, who uses his psychic sight to tell his subjects their past, their innermost thoughts and aspirations, and their possible futures, to be convinced of its authenticity. Recall how countless men were convinced that sounds could be transmitted through the ether at least a century prior to the invention of radio and television sending and receiving apparatus. Light and sound, present from the beginning of time, had to wait through the ages for human beings to discover the principles that would enable them to put these forces to use; psychic energy can be utilized immediately, although the laws that govern it are as yet neither understood nor explainable by science.

Finding Proof

Yet more than the basic laws of psychic energy are unknown. Because our technological age has ignored such personal phenomena, we have made no attempt to learn how this energy is generated and/or what organs of the body contribute to its production. Indeed, the very label "psychic energy" places it beyond the pale of serious investigation and often in the pejorative category. What is "psychic" is automatically "weird" and "nonsensical." Fortunately, this attitude is changing. Parapsychology has come of age. The American Association for the Advancement of Science approved it as a bona fide science when it accepted President Douglas Dean's request for membership for the Parapsychology Association in 1969, so it may be possible before too many years elapse for us to have tangible proof of psychic energy and the physical organs that generate it. Until then, we will have to rely on the Orient for terms and explanations.

The force is called *chi* by the Chinese, *prana* by yogis, and *ki* by the practitioners of the martial art of aikido. From yoga we also have the concept of the seven bodily centers through which the prana (energy) passes. These are known as chakras.

In *Meditation—Gateway to Light,* Elsie Sechrist identifies these energizing centers as "the gonads; the lyden (cells of Leydig); the adrenals, the thymus, the thyroid and parathyroids, the pineal and the pituitary glands" and adds that "the proper application of the energies illuminates them, transforming the individual into a light in the world."

The Chakras

The chemically bound chakras are affected by the assimilation of energies, which fill the gonads first and rise in order to the pineal gland, as Orientals and psychics agree. Indeed, it has been claimed that the spine serves as the channel and can be likened to the rod of a caduceus. (See the facing diagram.) The spinal column represents the body, the intertwined snakes of the caduceus being the mind and spirit that start from the bottom of the rod and, when properly stimulated, rise to the top, where the third eye waits to be illumined by the combination of the three. Another explanation is that the energies are similar to a snake, which strikes at the bottom of the spine and flashes upward. This concept is called the kundalini.

Scientists are skeptical of such claims. They haven't located the lyden gland, and those who are inclined to believe it might exist generally admit it isn't distinguishable. But scientists have been wrong in the past. For generation upon generation they considered the atom the smallest particle of divisible matter, whereas psychics as far back as Leibniz in the seventeenth century referred to a smaller particle than the atom, which they called the *monad.* The scientists of the past also erred regarding the thymus and pineal glands, which they thought were vestigial glands no longer required by the body. Scientists now recognize these organs as having their purposes. At present scientists identify the pituitary as the master gland, though psychics are more intrigued with the pineal and associate it with the third eye, which is the seat of psychic vision.

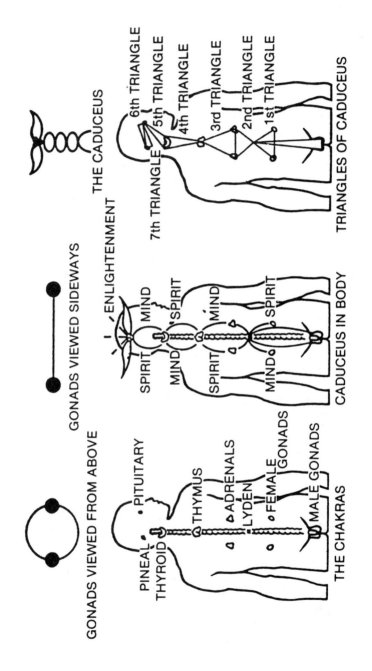

GONADS VIEWED FROM ABOVE

GONADS VIEWED SIDEWAYS

THE CADUCEUS

ENLIGHTENMENT

6th TRIANGLE
5th TRIANGLE
4th TRIANGLE
3rd TRIANGLE
2nd TRIANGLE
1st TRIANGLE
7th TRIANGLE

TRIANGLES OF CADUCEUS

SPIRIT
MIND
SPIRIT
MIND
MIND
SPIRIT
SPIRIT
MIND

CADUCEUS IN BODY

PINEAL
PITUITARY
THYROID
THYMUS
ADRENALS
LYDEN
FEMALE GONADS
MALE GONADS

THE CHAKRAS

The Glands

What we know from medicine, then, is that the gonads, adrenals, thyroid, and pituitary are purely endocrine glands, or ductless glands, which secrete the hormones that regulate the growth, function, and development of certain tissues and assist in regulating body metabolism. Since hormones are affected by mental states as well as other factors such as diet and climate, a connection exists between attitudes and feelings and bodily operations, so even on scientific grounds there is more of a relationship between the chakras and medical knowledge than is customarily acknowledged.

Lack of medical proof should not, however, prevent us from considering the subject. According to tradition, energy assimilation begins with the reproductive organs, the gonads, which are responsible for physical activity. This is why we irradiate the feet with the light first, and fill the lower extremities before we raise the light level to the higher parts. And we must raise it. If all the psychic energy remains in the gonads, the individual will become over-preoccupied with sex. When the energy is raised to the lyden gland, sexual impulses will be purified and the energy vibrations prepared for further elevation. Nevertheless, the lyden is still located in the lower region of the body and is responsive to the emotions, particularly those of a negative type. The individual must desire to lift the prana still further to the adrenals, where a choice can be made between succumbing to the emotions or purifying the self so the life force can ascend to the thymus region, where true balance between the lower and upper glands takes place. The individual must bring the prana up to the thyroid, where creativity resides; raise it again to the pituitary, the vaunted gateway to illumination; and finally bring it across to the pineal gland, where spiritual and psychic fulfilment are to be found.

According to Severin Peterson, in *A Catalog of the Ways People Grow,* devotees of kundalini yoga believe that "one by one the psychic centers, or *chakra,* of his body are brought into functioning activity, as the Goddess [kundalini] awakens . . . at the base of the spinal column, and rises, *chakra* by *chakra,* to meet her *shakta,* the Lord Shiva, who sits enthroned in the seventh *chakra,* in the pericarp of the Thousand Petaled Lotus . . . in the brain centre. Then, from the mystic union of the *shakta* and the *shakti,* is born Enlightenment. . . ." The shakta and shakti are the two snakes, the male and female energies, which we shall discuss in detail later.

Kundalini

Some people describe the kundalini as a single snake that is coiled at the base of the spine. When psychic energy is absorbed and the chakras begin to open from the gonads up, it is said that the kundalini climbs. But there is real danger in activating the chakras in this order, and we refer to the kundalini theory only because it is the clearest method of describing what occurs. When the snake flashes through the chakras, the body comes alive and every inch of it seems to vibrate from the force. The impact is such that it can result in a partial opening of the chakras or an incomplete climb that can leave the energy stuck in the lower half of the torso. Then bodily energy rules, and people who have experienced this can become victims of terrible physical appetites. Also, individuals with various talents who use them for the wrong purposes are suffering from imperfect connections between the chakras, or blockages of the kundalini flow, which divert their energy. The serpent must complete its passage each time in order to attune the body to the higher spheres, or chakras, so that a person can benefit both the self and the race. This is so difficult to do that we have devised a better and safe method that will achieve the same result: the opening of the third eye, and with it the universe.

Opening the Third Eye

No doubt you have already experienced a partial third-eye manifestation. During your meditations when you sit with your eyes closed, you frequently see flashing lights, faces, or scenes. The lights are pictures that are unrolling too quickly on your mental screen. If you wish to view them clearly, instruct your subconscious to slow down the reel, and it will comply. The faces that appear are the same sort of hypnogogic or hypnopompic images that occur when you are falling asleep or waking up, and are unimportant.

For those unfamiliar with the terms, *hypnogogic* refers to those images of faces, landscapes, or lights that drift across the mind in the few seconds before one falls into sleep. The *hypnopompic* images are similar but occur in the moments between sleep and the waking state.

During meditation you may have attributed these visions to your imagination or to partially closed eyelids, but if you blindfold yourself so no light can penetrate, you will still observe lighted pictures, since vision is not restricted to physical sight. In fact, the physical eyes do not actually see; they are merely the apparatus by which a psychomotor process is carried out. True seeing is a function of the mind. This is why the third eye can enjoy vista and vision although the physical eyes are clamped shut, why the mind can picture scenes from the past or future and indulge itself with imaginary pleasures, and why the blind can learn to see auras.

Control of the energies is the mark of the complete or synthesized person. In properly activating the chakras and raising the consciousness, the individual draws together the elements of self and, in the process, employs each of the major symbols recognized by our ancestors.

From the Egyptian and Babylonian-Assyrian beginnings of Western civilization, art and recorded literature have stressed the importance of circles, triangles, and squares. These, along with the caduceus symbol and the catabasis archetype, are rooted in the human psyche (a word used to describe the interaction of the conscious and unconscious). Each symbol plays its part in building psychic energy.

The initial move is catabasic, going downward. One must recognize the importance of descending into the self and be willing to persevere until he or she has worked his way down to the essence. Before this, however, the person should become familiar with the fine, high vibration that is called psychic energy.

Feeling the Effects

As we have said, the exercises with the light are really psychic energy exercises, only now we are ready to feel as well as see the effect. To do so, close your eyes and take yourself down into alpha. Use your breath to help you absorb the energy, bringing it into your body as you inhale, and ridding your body of any stresses, tensions, aches, or pains as you exhale. You will absorb the energy through all the pores of your body, but it will be particularly noticeable on your face and hands, plus any other parts of the body that may be uncovered. Clothing does not hamper the absorption in the least, though it may prevent you from feeling the energy inrush. Breathe easily and pay attention to your uncovered skin. It may feel tight or tingly, warmer or colder, but whatever the sensation it will indicate that you are absorbing psychic energy. When you have worked with it long enough to recognize its presence, you are ready to use it to restore your flagging energies when you begin to feel fatigued, or to build it in preparation for an extended period of work or play.

Some basic exercises for this purpose have been developed by Joseph Weed, who instructs his readers in *Wisdom of the Mystic Masters* as follows:

1. Stand before an open window or out of doors or any place where you can get clear, fresh air.
2. Separate your feet and stretch your arms out horizontally at your sides.
3. Breathe in to the count of five.
4. Then immediately breathe out to the count of ten. Be sure the counting is at the same pace for both in-breathing and out-breathing.
5. Repeat this breathing cycle ten times.
6. This exercise may also be performed with almost equal benefit while sitting erect in a chair or even walking in the open.

Weed recommends this be done at least once a day, preferably two or three times each day, and after a month be replaced with this more sophisticated technique:

1. Sit comfortably in a chair. Hold your back straight and your head erect. Cross your feet at the ankles, not the knees, and hold them touching. Clasp your hands in your lap or, if you prefer, before your breast as if in prayer.
2. Take a deep breath through your nose and count rhythmically to yourself as you do. The intake should cover the period of eight counts. Pace it so, exactly.
3. Now hold your breath in your lungs for exactly twelve counts. Don't speed up and don't slow down. Count rhythmically.
4. Let the air out through your nose. Pace it to cover ten counts. With a little practice this is easy, and after a while the timing will become so natural you won't have to count. As you breathe out, consciously direct the flow of outgoing air to the spot where it enters the nasal passage from the throat. This is about at the root of the palate. Feel the air going past this sensitive spot and accompany the flow of air with a slightly audible vibration like a purring or humming sound. Continue this consciously induced vibration as long as the air continues its outward flow.
5. Repeat the foregoing five times.

When you build energy in this fashion, you refine the parts of your body known as chakras. Always be certain that your intentions are good and that you have rid yourself of all negativities before starting, since you are opening yourself and wish the spaces to be filled with positive energy. Do not worry about getting more than your share of energy. Every existing thing possesses it and there is a great surplus, so the more you draw in and use, the more you'll get. Nature will not tolerate a vacuum. Whatever you expend will be replaced at once. Practice giving it to other people. Let it flow into your system through every pore in your body as you inhale, from the sources mentioned at the end of Chapter 4. Then exhale and let it flow from your solar plexus to people or animals in your vicinity.

Warning

A more specific method of absorbing energy will be detailed as follows. Before we begin, however, we must caution against irresponsible use of breathing exercises that can cause incalculable harm. What is described now is the action of the chakras, in sequence, but is not meant as an exercise. Rather it is an explanation of how the chakras work when fully open. Once we understand their operation, we can proceed to a most effective and safe method of chakra illumination. To attempt to open them in sequence, from the gonads up to the pituitary-pineal, is too dangerous for anyone who has not spent years perfecting the technique, inasmuch as it inflames the lower chakras and can transform anyone using this method into a sex fiend or a glutton. The procedure following the explanation, however, eliminates such risks while allowing the individual to open the chakras to achieve integration.

The human spine is the central rod of the caduceus. Both figuratively and literally, the spine, or rod, is the body. The other elements of the caduceus, the interweaving snakes, are the mind and spirit, but instead of a single snake called the kundalini, they are separate ones that divide and intertwine as they rise through the glands. The rod and the double snakes of the caduceus form the symbol for healing, a symbol that is used by various branches of the medical profession. In the human body the caduceus of body, mind, and spirit performs the same function: healing through unification.

Step by step, the significant patterns described by the chakras and the kundalini are circular and triangular.

Each fully opened chakra, of itself, is an energy circle or wheel and can be seen as such by those skilled in aura-sighting. Imaginative observation of the paired glands, the gonads and adrenals, and the joined glands, the thymus and thyroid (as shown on the diagram on page 123) will indicate the result. Each part would operate in conjunction with its mate, so there would be a sympathetic, constant interchange between each pair that would appear circular. However, the individual glands—the lyden, pituitary, and pineal—also emit their energies in wheels or circles.

Pattern of the Chakras

The triangles are formed as the energies rise. At the lowest point, the energies are coiled at the base of the spine. Then, as mind and spirit begin to rise, they pass separately through the gonads, as shown on the diagram. On reaching the lyden, they intersect and with their circular base at the gonads might be viewed as a tall isosceles triangle in a man, or a shorter, broader-based isosceles triangle in a woman. In each case the triangle is upright.

The forces then change sides, with the mind ascending to the right adrenal while the spirit rises to the left, forming an inverted isosceles triangle, which has its point at the lyden and its base at the adrenals.

Mind and spirit begin their third ascent to peak at the upper tip of the thymus, thus forming triangle three in an upright position.

They crisscross at the thymus and rise to the outer peaks of the thyroid for the fourth, inverted triangle.

The fifth extends from the base of the thyroid to peak at the pituitary for the fifth triangle.

The cycle continues. The pituitary emits fan-shaped energy pulses directed horizontally and back toward the pineal gland, to form the sixth triangle. The pineal, a triangular shape itself (sometimes described as a pinecone shape), emits similar energy pulsations directed forward through the channel between them to the pituitary, for the seventh and final triangle. These interchanging, interlocking pulsations provide the bursts of energy that illumine the third eye, the head, and ultimately the whole body, with the illumination serving the same function as the wings on the caduceus symbol.

But to repeat our warning, the illumination must not be taken for granted. What has been described is the completed cycle with the descent through the rod of the body and the ascent of the mind and spirit through the glands until they have reached the pituitary the second time and have fused. When the exercise is performed by those who are not quite ready—and it takes years of work to arrive at this stage of readiness for the procedure—energies can be unloosed by the gonads and the individual can suffer from heightened sexuality, or at the adrenals or thymus where he will open himself to increased appetite and subsequent gains in weight. Partial success is disastrous. Fortunately, there is no need to take such risks. The recommended exercise is every bit as effective and completely safe.

Yin and Yang

In addition to the caduceus, circles, and triangles, concepts involved in the energy interplay are positive-negative and masculine-feminine. These are best described by the yin-yang of the *I Ching*, where the yang is masculine, bright, strong, positive, and conscious. The mind force is the yang. The yin is female, dark, weak, negative, and unconscious. The spirit of the body-mind-spirit triad is the yin. The terms do not mean that the spirit is inferior, nevertheless. Yang and yin are equally balanced, with each complementing its opposite as the forces rise through the chakras and join to form a perfect circle, the Tao.

Additional information on the yin-yang circle, along with the square, will be given later, since they are the effects of illumination, and here we are more concerned with the methods of achieving it.

Most of us must work persistently on the seven centers in order to open them fully. The seven, as we have noted before, is an ancient concept, and the steps of the chakras and their colors can be traced back to the Tower of Babel, where the seven levels of the ziggurat were assigned to specific planets and painted in the "colors" of those planets. The first level represented Saturn and was black; the second, sacred to Jupiter, was white; the third, Mercury, a brick red; the fourth, Venus, blue; the fifth, Mars, yellow; the sixth, moon, gray or silver; and the seventh, the sun, golden, as Kurt Seligmann tells us in *Magic, Supernaturalism and Religion*.

And just as the ancients believed that the new soul must travel through each of the planets and assume its properties, so the mind and body must travel through each of the chakras in order to reach their full potential. Yet our understanding of the colors has changed over the centuries, and we can describe the lowest chakra, the gonads (the Saturnian region), as a dark red, almost black; the lyden (Jupiter's region) as an orange red; the adrenals (Mercury) as green; the thymus (Venus) as yellow; the throat (Mars) as blue; the pituitary (moon) as silver; and the pineal or crown chakra (sun) as white tinged with gold.

In accordance, then, with our usual exercises of absorbing the light from above, we shall begin with the crown chakra and complete the following steps:

1. Seat yourself in the light that shines down on you from above. See your light as being a brilliant white, flecked with gold, and let this light stream down as through a funnel into the top of your head. While

you are absorbing the light, offer a prayer that you will be freed of all negativities and that you will use the light for the benefit of yourself and the world. Allow yourself all the time you need for your pineal gland to become infused with the brilliant light.

2. Then concentrate on your brow, the point between your eyebrows where the pituitary gland is located. Let the light, which has become a silvery white, irradiate the area and fill vour entire head. Offer a prayer for spiritual awakening. Do not rush the procedure. Just relax and enjoy the benefits.

3. Concentrate next on your throat where the thyroid and parathyroid are located, and let these glands become infused with a brilliant blue light. Ask in prayer that the will of the divine power, not your own, be done. Relax, and let the blue light fill your head to your throat.

What you have done in the first three steps is to bring the higher power of the heavens into your consciousness. When you have completed this part of the exercise to your satisfaction, you are ready to work on the earthly powers. You begin with the lowest of the powers, those of generation, and therefore start at the gonads.

4. Concentrate on your sexual organs and let them fill with a dark red color. Pray that your life force be so illuminated that you may use it for creative efforts that will enhance your own life and assist in enlightening the world. Again, do not rush the exercise. None of the chakras must be forced.

5. Raise your point of concentration to the lyden gland, just below your navel, and see it as being bathed in an orange-red color. Pray that your spirit and body will be refined by the light, so that you may continue your work in the world for good and positive purposes and that your body may be healthy so you can do what is required of you.

6. Concentrate next on your adrenals, which are above the navel and below the rib cage. Let the area be bathed in a green light, and pray that your emotions will be purged by the light so that you will want only good for yourself and your world and will be able to operate always with a positive attitude.

7. Concentrate on your thymus gland just behind and above the heart. Surround it with a yellow light and ask in prayer that you be motivated always by love for others and that you work always for the good of the universe.

8. Return your concentration to your throat, where the white, silver, and blue of the heavenly impetus will join with the dark red, orange-red, green, and yellow of the earthly characteristics to flood your entire body. Relax and enjoy the light as it circulates throughout your body to flush out any impurities and fill you with a sense of buoyancy and the knowledge that comes from being truly enlightened. When you have achieved this result, let your feelings of love, peace, understanding, and joy flow from your solar plexus to all within a radius of a mile around you.

Conclude with a prayer of thanks for your newfound abilities.

A Safe Method

The exercise may be used as often as you wish, although at least once a day, during meditation, is recommended. Unlike the Oriental methods of beginning with the gonads and urging the kundalini to rise, this adapted method is perfectly safe. The Oriental technique is not. As C. W. Leadbeater claims in his excellent book *The Chakras,* the "dangers connected" with working with the kundalini "are very real and terribly serious. Some of them are purely physical. Its uncontrolled movement often produces intense physical pain, and it may readily tear tissues and even destroy physical life. This, however, is the least of the evils of which it is capable, for it may do permanent injury to vehicles higher than the physical." By bringing the light down into the body from a higher source before rousing the lower chakras, one avoids these real and constant dangers. *Never* experiment with the kundalini method. The beneficial results are no different from those of the safe method offered here, and the other results of using it are too often disastrous.

Surrendering the Self

One other important means of opening the chakras is by surrendering the self to the essence, the superior power that rules the universe. Though we have mentioned this possibility before, in Chapter 6, it bears repeating. It is mandatory that we lose this life in order to find life. If you had a choice—as you do—wouldn't you want to know beyond doubt that what is right for you is coming to pass? Or that you no longer need to fret or fume about situations and people, because what transpires is for your own good? Or that you won't have to worry any longer about money, position, status, since all you require for your advancement in the way of material, social, or spiritual benefits will be yours? That you are fulfilling the destiny for which you were born and for which you live? This knowledge and ability can be yours without a shred of anxiety. Even more will be yours if you will hand yourself over to your essence, another term for God, who lives within each of us in the microcosmic body as well as pervading every inch of the macrocosm. In so doing you will make yourself a channel of his will, a clear channel that will assist in opening your chakras and enlighten your body and your world.

Surrender of this sort is not easy. Each of us fights the so-called loss of self, fearing to be deprived of individuality and become nothing in the act of becoming a channel. What transpires is the supreme paradox. We lose the world to gain it. By offering ourselves as channels, we assume we are laying the gift of free will on the sacrificial altar; instead, we find we are more individual than ever before—as separate and distinct as the stars in the firmament or as flakes of snow in a storm, yet merging with all to become a nightly dome of heaven or a soft blanket to shield the warm earth from the deadening blasts of winter. We perceive ourselves as detached from every other human, standing alone and lonely on the terrain of existence. But we are not separate. On the contrary, what we observe is merely the peaks of the mountain range jutting above the clouds. The peaks, like people, appear separate and individual, but one has only to watch the clouds disperse to realize the mountains are joined at the base. As individuals we are the same. We may walk, talk, and act as a totality, but we are a part of the collective race. In the seventeenth century John Donne explained it well in *Devotions:* "No man is an island, entire of it self; every man is a piece of the continent, a part of the main." Still, the full implications of becoming a channel and thereby gaining true individuality cannot be described. Understanding comes only through personal experience. Think about offering yourself as a channel. Meditate upon it. You need not take the step this soon, for there is much to be said about the psychological makeup of humanity that might help you to make your decision with more ease.

Transmitting Psychic Energy

Certain exercises for transmitting psychic energy support Donne's statement, however. We are joined in our humanity. You can prove this for yourself by seating yourself in a circle with others who have learned to build their energies, and joining hands. In unison, inhale the light and, as you exhale, send the energy coursing through your right arm into your hand and then into the hand of the person on your right. The person on your left will be transmitting his or her energy through your left hand. Close your eyes and concentrate on the sensation and you should feel it, but do not become discouraged if you don't notice any difference at first. Psychic energy is a high, fine vibration, which takes some getting used to. Relax and you will feel it, just as you felt it on your face and hands when you were working alone.

After a few minutes, halt the flow. Build your personal energy stores again, and then reverse the prana, directing it through your left hand to the person on your left and receiving it from the right.

Also, while you are seated in the circle, withdraw your hands and place them on your lap in the customary meditational position. Then build your light, this time working with the light rather than the direct psychic energy. When you are completely filled with the light, do the exercise that expands your light to seven feet from your body. Each person in the circle will do the same. Then, with your eyes closed and without touching anyone else, you should be able to feel the energy. Relax then, and seek the silence while you feel the heightened vibrations that come from the mountains joining at the earth.

Before you start the following chapter, which will explain how to use energy to help yourself and others, work with your personal store until you can feel it and build it to the point where your body seems to be bursting with prana.

13

Retraining the Subconscious

Psychic energy can heal you or help you to eliminate any bad habits you may have acquired. Among the worst types of habits, three are the result of cultural conditioning. Through overexposure to sensory stimuli, we have been prevented from using our minds to the fullest. Because others smoke, we have come to accept smoking as natural. Because we live in a land of plenty, we are apt to overeat.

But what we have learned we can unlearn, with considerable help from our psychic energy. We begin by writing new instructions to our subconscious on the order of the following. For better concentration, we can tell our subconscious:

1. I believe I can concentrate.
2. I make concentration a habit.
3. I reduce distractions to a minimum when I read or study.
4. I have a good mind. I listen well and am interested in everyone and everything. (Visualize yourself possessing these attributes.)
5. I concentrate and thereby am successful in my endeavors. (Visualize yourself as a success.)

After a few meditations, reduce the steps to one, the simple visualizing of concentrating and earning the rewards.

To eliminate smoking, use or adapt this program:

1. Smoking is detrimental to my health.
2. Smoking is expensive; it literally requires money to burn.
3. I do not need this detrimental, expensive habit.
4. I do not delude myself by cutting down on smoking.
5. I am free of the habit, the desire to smoke.
6. I smoked because I was tense. Tension increased my desire for another cigarette, and this cigarette did nothing to alleviate the tension.
7. Requiring cigarettes caused more tension, of which I am free.

8. I thank my subconscious for eliminating this detrimental, expensive habit.

Actually you do not require a long program. Simply visualizing yourself as free of the habit should suffice, although many of us feel more secure when we expend greater energy for those bad habits of long standing. Use whatever works best for you, and don't hesitate to change the wording of any program to suit your personal needs.

Losing Weight

Obesity is a chronic ailment in affluent countries. But because it is unhealthy as well as unattractive, most of us search for ways to reduce. Before you devise a program for your subconscious, however, consider these suggestions:

- Make a definite decision about your weight. Decide you CAN LOSE, what you want to look like, how much you wish to weigh, and begin. DO NOT plan to start tomorrow or next week—DO IT NOW, this second. The only time available to you is NOW.
- If you haven't had a physical examination recently, see your doctor and follow whatever diet he or she recommends. But don't postpone starting.
- List all your reasons for wanting to reduce.
- Analyze your eating habits. Do you suffer from the "binge-or-bust" syndrome? Discover *why* you overeat and *when,* and plan to be where food is unavailable during your vulnerable hours, or at least be too busy to think of food.
- List all the foods you can eat on your diet. Memorize the list.
- Decide each morning what you will eat that day. Weigh yourself each morning.
- Keep a record of every morsel you consume during the day.
- Write yourself simple but brief instructions for RENEWing. A sample renewal to be used during meditation could be as follows:

1. My subconscious controls my physical body.
2. My body is a product of my subconscious, a result of what I've foreseen in the past, and can be altered.
3. My body is slim, lithe, active.
4. My body requires only those foods that keep it healthy and lean.
5. My body enjoys only those foods that keep it healthy and lean.

6. My body is (visualize yourself at the weight you wish, and see the weight numbers in lights at the upper right of your mental screen.)
7. I bless my subconscious for this assistance and my slim and beautiful body for acting on this wise suggestion.

No matter how fat you are at present, visualize yourself as slim and rejoice in the visualization. Expend all the emotion possible in your rejoicing, and then withdraw the emotion and simply watch yourself move as a slender person. Your present size is the result of foreseeing yourself as fat in the past, even though you desired to be slim. Don't repeat this error. SEE ALWAYS AND EXCLUSIVELY THE END PRODUCT, then release the picture so your subconscious can begin to manifest your desire. In other words, watch and wait. Don't hold a shotgun to your subconscious. Give it time to work. You didn't become fat in a day, and you can't lose a great deal of flesh in a few hours and remain healthy.

You may bolster your morale when tempted by food by repeating a slogan such as one of these:

Eat it today and wear it tomorrow. And tomorrow. And tomorrow . . .

A moment on your lips, a lifetime on your hips.

I can absorb all the energy I need from the atmosphere. Or a stalk of celery.

I am vital, alive, and slim, and my body is the servant of my subconscious.

I am slim, I am, I am, I am.

Use your slogan sparingly, however. Frequent repetition indicates you are dwelling on your dietary problems, and this is the worst possible thing you can do, because food and eating could become an obsession. Better to omit a slogan altogether than fall into this trap. And don't talk about your diet to others, for this is apt to destroy the energy building in your subconscious. Simply program yourself during meditations and forget about your weight the rest of the time. If you are tempted by a particular "poison" (cake, chocolate, ice cream, beer), close your eyes and see your slim self as turning away in disgust from the fattening substance. Know that your body doesn't need empty calories, any more than your essence does. Do not permit your body to rule you.

Whatever habit you wish to break can be overcome by proper programming of the subconscious. Just be sure that your instructions are simple and clear, do not infringe on the freedom of others, and add your thanks for the assistance. Recognition of your subconscious will facilitate your contacting it in the future.

Daily contact with your subconscious mind is one of the best ways to approach the essence, which is located in the subconscious region of the psyche, so do not hesitate to work on such practical matters as breaking bad habits.

Mind Over Body

One of the most important uses of psychic energy, or of programming the subconscious, is also personal. We can keep ourselves well and, if we are already ill, we can heal ourselves. We may not be able to find much evidence for this claim in scientific circles, although scientists are currently beginning to study the possibility and are learning that what psychics have been maintaining through the centuries is true: we can control our body as well as our desires.

At the Menninger Foundation in Topeka, Kansas, Dr. Elmer Green and his associates have monitored a subject who pushes contaminated darning needles through his flesh. The wounds heal within minutes; no sepsis results from the voluntary and apparently painless injuries Jack Schwarz inflicts upon himself. Mr. Schwarz further taught his technique to Dr. Stuart Twemlow, a psychiatrist at the Veterans Administration Hospital in Topeka, and Dr. Twemlow repeated the experiment with equal success.

Dr. Green has also investigated the Swami Rama, who can increase his heart rate to three hundred beats per minute, decrease it to twelve per minute, and stop the flow of blood from his heart for seventeen seconds, among other controls.

At Rosary Hill College in Buffalo, New York, Sister Justa Smith, who holds a doctorate in enzymology, conducted repeated tests on faith-healer Colonel Oskar Estebany and found he could alter the contents of test tubes containing enzymes (which accelerate naturally during the healing process in the body) by simply holding the stoppered vials for a period.

But such physiological controls are not confined to a few adepts. In classrooms across the country, students are learning how to master their bodies by using biofeedback equipment or through the simpler, less mechanical technique of programming the subconscious.

But the mind is capable of more than interior control. At the Stanford Research Institute in Menlo Park, California, Lawrence Pinneo, a neurophysiologist and electronics engineer, has added another chapter to the cybernetics saga. His subjects have electroencephalographic equipment attached to their skulls and by thought alone can control a computer that carries out their signals to move a dot on a screen. If one is able to mentally direct mechanical equipment, how much more easily can he or she alter a mind-susceptible instrument like the body? Many medical doctors believe that over 90 percent of illnesses originate in the mind. What is caused by thought, then, can be healed more quickly when thought is used to *assist* medicine.

Proceed with care. It is a future possibility that when you progress in your development, you may be able to avoid all illnesses as well as cure those you have. But you have not learned enough about the body and its responses to risk your health by forgoing your doctor's prescriptions. If you are presently under medication for either a congenital or a "self-inflicted" ailment, YOU MUST CONTINUE WITH THAT MEDICATION. The point cannot be stressed enough. But you can definitely assist in your healing and also build your confidence in the process so that you can remain well in the future. Psychic healing is potent medicine, but like all remedies it must be handled with care. Clear up current sicknesses with medication and meditation and learn to live in health, rather than trying to cure mind and body of *old* diseases simultaneously.

With these facts in mind we are ready to work with healing programs. We shall begin with headaches and minor ailments and work up to more major ones.

1. Offer a silent prayer.
2. Determine the cause or possible cause of the ailment and explain it to yourself. If you didn't have it at birth and didn't get it through an accident (which also originated in the mind), it is mental in origin, since the mind customarily exerts tremendous influence over the body.
3. Seek help from your essence in breaking the negative thought pattern or habit that led to your ailment.
4. Close your eyes in meditation and let yourself drift to the alpha state.
5. Anesthesize your hands:
   a. Drop both hands to your side.
   b. Imagine that your stronger hand, the one you use for writing, has an electrical current running through it. Feel the pulsations of the mild current and the tingling that results from it. Direct all your attention to your stronger hand and feel it vibrate from the mild current.

c. Forget your stronger hand and direct attention to the other, the "weaker" hand. Imagine it has received a shot of novocaine. Feel it become numb as the anesthetic takes hold. Concentrate on this hand and note what is happening. It may become numb or cold, or it may begin to prickle as the circulation of blood slows. If the response is not immediate, tell yourself you will count to five and after five you will feel the cold, the numbness, or the prickling. When you feel it, raise your stronger hand and pinch the back of the weaker lightly. Notice how leathery the skin has become, how stiff. You have induced in your weaker hand what is known as glove anesthesia and are now ready to heal.

d. Place your weaker hand on the stronger and feel the stronger become numb, too. Now place this weaker, healing hand on your forehead and feel the numbness or coldness penetrate the skin of your forehead and begin to draw off your tension or a headache.

e. After a sufficient time has elapsed—and in a couple of sessions you will learn to judge the time fairly well—drop your weaker hand and shake it vigorously from the wrist to shake off the pain of the headache.

6. Offer a prayer of thanks for your healing.

Add the exercise for glove anesthesia to your meditation routine. Practice will familiarize you with healing yourself and others and enable you to build healing power in your weaker hand so it is *always* available, rather than just during meditation—a distinct advantage in emergencies. When you become proficient, you will be able to staunch a heavy flow of blood from a wound by the simple laying on of hands. No elaborate preparations to induce the glove anesthesia will be required.

The following method is perhaps better for more extensive and interior ailments. Repeat the first three steps of the preceding exercise and then:

4. Close your eyes in meditation and drift into alpha. Imagine you are seated in a white light. As usual, the light shines down on you from above, although this light is a pure white with no colors streaking through it and is a ball about three feet in diameter. Spend as much time as required to clear your circle of color. If you have difficulty visualizing it, sit under a flashlight or strong lamp with your eyes closed for a couple of sessions.

5. Inhale slowly, letting the light from above enter your body and lodge in the area of the ailment. Hold your breath for a count of five.

6. Exhale. Visualize the pain or illness draining from you like sawdust from a doll as you exhale, and see your body as completely healed.
7. Repeat the inhalation/breath-holding/exhalation pattern seven times. Desire healing with all your heart. Expend all the emotion possible.
8. Withdraw the emotion, resume normal breathing, and visualize yourself as completely healed.
9. Offer a prayer of thanks for the healing.

Do this at least once a day, although twice-daily healings, one in the morning and one at night, are best. Keep working and believing until you are well. Avoid thinking about the healing outside the meditative state, and do *not* discuss this healing with others. As always, the secret is to foresee yourself in perfect health and never suffering from illness—as healed rather than sick. Then give your subconscious the time to effect the cure. This means you must forget about your ailment except in meditation, so your subconscious can build the psychic energy it requires to make it work. Thinking and talking about a project dissipates the energy and, what is even worse, brings the subject into the open where it can be attacked by the reasoning mind, which is always trying to exert its dominance. Remember both mind and body will resist being put in their proper places. Give your subconscious a chance to tame them and prove its worth.

Directing the light to a specific spot will heal a localized ailment, but a slightly different exercise is required for general body deficiencies.

Prepare for your cure by reminding yourself of developments in faith healing. For centuries people believed it beyond human ability to cure teeth. Brother Willard Fuller, who conducts faith healing services in Florida, doubted it was possible, too, until a man demanded relief from a tooth-ache. Since that time, Brother Fuller's faith healing has ended toothaches of audience members, filled cavities in their mouths, and occasionally transmuted their silver fillings to gold. The healer's belief in the possibility made the difference.

Thousands of cancer patients have combined meditation with medication to cure themselves of cancers that had metastasized. Hundreds of others, who learned the meditational techniques when they were in the final stages of the disease, eased their remaining days. Yet with faith and determination, even last-ditch efforts have cured generalized cancers like those of the bones and blood.

If cancers that might destroy the entire body can be healed, so can AIDS. The ailments are similar in that they affect the total physique, so the meditations will be substantially the same.

We will begin by taking ourselves down to an altered state of consciousness (if necessary, see the breathing exercises in Chapter 1) and then using whatever elements of the exercise are most suited to our conditions.

1. When you have breathed yourself down to the meditative state, visualize yourself as standing (or sitting) in the light and hear yourself say "I am in the healthiest possible state of being. I am using this state to return my body to full health."

2. Offer a silent prayer.

3. Determine the cause or possible cause of the ailment and explain it to yourself.

    a. For cancer patients: If you didn't have it at birth, it originated in the mind. (Even accidents are the products of the mind, so injuries from accidents are results or misapplied thought). What has been caused by the mind can be cured by the mind.

    b. For AIDS patients: Do NOT waste energy lamenting over the disease's cause or the unfairness of your situation. No matter how you acquired AIDS, you can cure it. The body is the servant of the mind, and your mind is already in its healing mode.

4. Seek help from your essence in breaking any destructive thought patterns or habits that might prevent you from instructing your body to heal itself of your present "dis-ease."

5. Seek help from your essence in breaking any patterns or habits that could prevent your body from responding to your instructions to heal.

6. Visualize before you a TV screen, and see it light up with a view of your body's interior. This X-ray–like picture will show you your bones first.

    a. Examine your bones closely, and if either their outsides or their marrows appear abnormal in any way, know you will return to work on them.

    b. As the screen focuses on your muscles, examine them for trauma.

    c. On viewing your veins and arteries, look for signs of abnormality in the blood.

    d. When the organs of your body flash onto the screen, starting with the brain and moving downward, note any that require healing.

    e. Let your screen go blank for a moment, and see it light up with a picture of the major disease and the part or whole of the body affected. Put this view on hold, so you can heal the disease.

7. Visualize the light attacking the ailment. Choose one of the follow-

ing to correct the problem. After a preliminary trial or two, you may decide to try another of the examples or even tailor one to your own needs.

   a. If the ailment is in your bones or blood, see the light entering the top of your head on the screen, and moving down through your bones or bloodstream to flush out diseased cells and replace them with light and life-giving cells.

   b. OR visualize the light bringing into the top of your head a stream of white cells, which become "Pac-men" that voraciously consume the malformed cells. Watch the healthy "Pac-mental" cells chomp their way down through your body until all the diseased ones are gone.

   c. OR let your television screen become a computer screen and watch the healing energies of the light turn into a kind of software spell-check that seeks out every malformed atom in your body, flashes it on your screen, and corrects it at your command.

   d. OR visualize the healing energy that comes in the form of light as a magic potion, slowly but steadily transforming the infected cells into whole and sparkling pinpoints of health.

8. Know that your mental screen is only a projection. A special kind of video camera is taking a picture of your inner body and showing it on the screen.

9. See your inner body glowing with pure and healthy light—completely, to indicate your dis-ease is gone. The screen shows the light starting three inches above your head, extending three inches on all sides, and ending three inches below your feet. Rejoice in this easy, healthful condition.

10. See the picture on your screen shift to an exterior view of your body. See yourself, glowing with light from within, running, dancing, and cavorting with delight in its perfect health. Using all your senses—sight, sound, taste, touch, feel, and the extrasensory one— experience perfect health. Rejoice in your physical perfection and know that what you foresee is what you get. But REMEMBER TO SEE YOUR HEALING AS HAVING COME TO PASS, rather as a future event.

11. Erase the picture on your screen, wrap up the mental apparatus, and put it away until your next meditation. Then feel the light pouring down on you from above, and with your eyes still closed, look down

into your body and see the effect these exercises are having. Know that the healing is not something you dreamed up on a screen, but has ALREADY happened inside you.

12. Say a prayer of thanks for being healed.
13. Know that when you leave this meditative state, your body will be putting your healing commands into effect. Repeat the meditations regularly, until your body understands that you are serious and the cure is manifested in the flesh.

Breathe yourself up to consciousness and come wide awake and feeling great.

Plan to repeat this meditation at least once a day until boredom with the exercise indicates your body has put your instructions to work.

Confining Thoughts

Whatever occurs, remember to confine thoughts of your disease to meditations alone. If and when you think about the condition during the day, tell yourself at once that you will consider it later, along with any pain, in meditation. Immerse yourself in some activity. Don't fight the thought or feel guilty or unsuccessful because the thought recurs; just postpone it until meditation and soon you will not think about your ailment except at the appointed time.

A fourth healing method is for less serious ailments, such as migraine headaches or localized pains. Begin this one by breathing yourself down to an altered state.

1. Picture yourself in the light and say, "I am in the healthiest possible state of being."
2. Offer a silent prayer for healing.
3. Ask yourself what caused this ailment.
4. Instruct your body to heal itself of this discomfort.
5. Inhale slowly, drawing in the light and directing it only to your hands. Focus all attention on your hands. Be aware of every nail, each finger, your thumb, and the palm through to the back of each hand. Feel how each part is related to the others.
6. Resume normal breathing, knowing you are breathing in the light and directing it just to your hands, which will increase in warmth until they are fairly hot. Retain the heat. Think of nothing but your hands. If they become painful, shake them vigorously from the wrists

and resume the exercise until your headache, or other localized pain, has evaporated.

7. Offer a prayer of thanks for the healing.

What you are doing can be explained simply. During a migraine headache, the blood is "trapped" in the head. You relieve the headache and get rid of it by drawing the blood from your head into your hands. You draw it off by focusing on another part of your body, in this case the hands, and you find that you can control the flow by redirection.

To keep from suspecting that you are only imagining the effects rather than experiencing them, you should test yourself. Doubt, the enemy of the psychic processes, can destroy every attempt you make at healing. By testing and receiving verifiable responses, you can eliminate doubt.

In *Experimental Hypnosis,* editor Leslie LeCron includes an article called "Dynamics in Hypnotic Induction." Its author, psychologist James A. Christenson, Jr., used a hypnotist to induce the phenomenon, but you can accomplish this yourself by using what is called autosuggestion. Say your prayer and then try this interpretation of Christenson's method:

1. Seat yourself with hands palm down on your thighs and begin your meditation.

2. Direct your attention to your right hand and observe all the sensations it experiences.

3. Let your mind explore your fingers, the nails, the palm. Feel the changes that occur. Is your hand becoming hotter or colder? Drier or more moist? Heavier or lighter? More sensitive or more numb? One or more of these sensations may be experienced.

4. The sensations will cause your hand to become progressively lighter in weight. When it does it will begin to rise from your thigh—slowly and jerkily at first, perhaps, but it will rise. Do not help or hinder it. Just relax, continue to focus on your hand, and let it do what it will.

5. As though it had a mind of its own, your hand will rise, your elbow will bend, and the movement will continue until the back of your hand comes into contact with your nose.

6. When you touch your nose, the test is over, and you can resume a normal meditation.

If your hand doesn't move the first time you try this exercise, do not become discouraged. Try again.

Another standard test establishes an immediate link between your mind and your subconscious. The techniques described by Leslie LeCron in *Self-*

Hypnotism and Sidney Petrie and Robert B. Stone in *What Modern Hypnotism Can Do for You* are easily adapted, as was Christenson's, for our purposes.

1. Attach a lightweight pendulum or button to a twelve-inch string.
2. On a sheet of paper, inscribe a circle with one horizontal and one vertical diameter that bisect each other at the center of the circle.
3. Position your elbow on a table. Grasp the loose end of the string between your thumb and forefinger, and drop your hand until it is parallel to the table and the pendulum or button is directly over the center of the circle and able to swing without touching the paper.
4. Ask your subconscious which of the four possible movements will signify *yes:* top or bottom on the vertical line or right or left on the horizontal plane.
5. Hold the string and wait. Do not move. The pendulum will start in motion of its own accord to indicate the yes position. When it does, write *yes* on the paper, since this will always be your movement for *yes* and you will want to remember it for the next time. Write *no* directly opposite your *yes,* on the horizontal line if your *yes* is to the right or left, on the vertical line if *yes* is above or below the center of the circle.
6. Ask which of the remaining two positions will indicate an "I don't know" response. Permit the pendulum to move when and how it will, and record the direction for *I don't know.* Directly opposite that, write *I don't wish to answer.* The subconscious is always able to give the correct answer, even for questions about which you know nothing. However, your conscious mind may not be able to handle all the answers until you have learned to live through your essence, and your subconscious may refuse to stir up psychic contents that it knows could harm you. If that's the case, you will receive an *I don't know* or an *I don't wish to answer.* Try wording your request more simply, but if you receive the same response, don't persist with the question.
7. Phrase your question carefully. As we've cautioned before, the subconscious is literal, so you must be clear and concise. It has no sense of humor, so don't use the pendulum for foolish questions or parlor games. Treat it seriously and with respect so it will be available for assistance on serious business.

Your subconscious neither rests nor sleeps. It never forgets. Everything you need to know about the past it can and will recall for you, for it's a gigantic computer that stores whatever information you desire to have even if it's unknown to your consciousness. For example, if you've lost an object, you can locate it via your subconscious. One method is to tell yourself before you fall asleep that you will recover the lost property. Help yourself by writing what you wish to locate on a slip of paper and repeat what you've written ten times. Place the paper under your pillow and consciously forget about it. This is similar to what happens when people pray to St. Anthony to find a lost object for them; the subconscious is instructed to find the object, the person has faith in finding it because of faith in the saint, and he or she leaves the project in better hands. In either case—whether you do it yourself or ask for help using prayer—the subconscious is freed to do its work.

Recovering Lost Objects

Our personal method of recovering what is lost is to draw a triangle on a slip of paper just before you go to bed. As you draw it, tell yourself you will remember where you left your property or otherwise find what is lost. On waking, draw a square, using the triangle base for the bottom and having the tip of the triangle touch the top line of the square. Repeat your instructions to yourself as you draw. At noon, draw a circle around your triangle-square, letting all points of the square touch the circle. Repeat your instructions, then forget about them so your subconscious can get to work on locating the property for you. Don't specify any time when your results will be forthcoming, for your subconscious is beyond time and immediately accepts as fact anything you decide is important enough. If you set time limits and your subconscious cannot produce on schedule because of outside influences or lack of "earth-time" to accomplish its task, you may become discouraged and lose faith. This will confuse your subconscious and cause you needless anguish.

Various other ideomotor tests can be used, but those mentioned should suffice. When properly employed, they will convince you that your essence, in your subconscious region, has infinitely more information than you are aware of. Do not, however, resort to automatic writing or Ouija board experiments. These can be dangerous, since they play games with your psyche, which is comparable to an onion that may be peeled, skin by skin, until one reaches the core. The layers of thought, emotion, and habit are the skins that protect our cores from the outer world. If we peel them away before we have completely eliminated the negativities that can wreak havoc with our lives, we leave ourselves exposed and defenseless and thereby open to disaster. Toying with automatic writing and the Ouija board may seem innocent enough at first, but those who have persisted in such games without cleansing their personalities of harmful effects beforehand often find the messages received from the writing or the board turning into a horror show. Many people have been driven to the verge of suicide as a result. Carol Liaros, a nationally known psychic from western New York, has rescued at least two individuals who were contemplating killing themselves as a result of the terrible messages they were receiving from automatic writing or the Ouija board. These people had stripped away their protection and were unable to handle the results of reaching their naked psyches.

Reaching the Subconscious

Don't uncover your core, your essence, until you are spiritually ready—which you certainly should be at this point in your development. Use your subconscious for good, retrain it gradually, and it will overcome all the problems you may encounter in life. It can help you find objects you've mislaid, locate missing information, and decide vital issues of the present and the future. If you refrain from using your subconscious for fortune-telling per se, it will amaze you and perhaps startle you at times. Yet there is nothing strange about its powers. It is simply a part of the self that is seldom relied upon.

In general, we could say that reaching the subconscious is a way of extending the mind—a natural, healthy way. People refer to it and its actions whenever they mention hunches or intuition, though *intuition* implies a haphazard use. What we are discussing is a permanent, reliable method of communication employed by thousands of our ancestors—some using it for the wrong purposes and coming to grief, and others employing it in a positive fashion in order to reap the rewards.

Fortunately for humankind, the twentieth century is becoming aware of the potential of the psyche and people are more willing to accept help in such areas as healing than they have in the past. This does not mean you should announce your ability along these lines. On the contrary, the less said, the better. All the psychic processes lose their psychic energy when they are discussed. Let results speak for themselves. Start by improving your personal health. Work on minor ailments, such as headaches, and when you've achieved some success and have faith in your growing expertise, you can tackle greater obstacles.

14

Healing Energy

The ability to heal oneself and others is not new. People have practiced it throughout the centuries, and some, like the early Christians, became highly proficient in the art of healing. The work was carried on, in a pseudo-scientific manner, by an Austrian physician, Franz Anton Mesmer, who lived from 1734 to 1815.

He is remembered chiefly for his interest in hypnotism, and his name comes down to us in the eponym *mesmerism*. His work was continued by the French physician and neurologist Jean Martin Charcot (1825–1893) from whom Sigmund Freud, the Austrian neurologist and father of psychoanalysis (1856–1939), conceived the idea of using hypnotism as a means of helping the mentally ill. However, Mesmer was considered a greater healer of medical ailments than either of his successors. Believing that one person could transfer energy to another and effect cures through what he called animal magnetism, Mesmer constructed a huge bucket that he filled with bottles containing magnetized water, glass powder, and iron filings. He covered the bucket with a circular top and rods, and the collected corporeal rays of the body were transmitted through the apparatus to heal the sick.

He also believed that healing energy could be transmitted directly. In *Magic, Supernaturalism and Religion*, Kurt Seligmann relates Mesmer's belief that individuals endowed with a powerful vital spirit can transmit their health to others if they know how to direct the rays that carry this force. They may lay their hands upon the sick or direct the emanation with an iron stick, the conductor. In short, energy can be transferred directly from one being to another.

Healing Others

The art has not been lost. Olga Worrall, like other such modern healers, carries on the tradition of the laying on of hands by directing "subatomic particles invisible to the naked eye" from herself to her patients. In scientific tests she has demonstrated her ability to heal, but her investigators required more proof and devised a cloud chamber, or glass-enclosed area, for her to work on. She placed her hands on the outer walls of the chamber and caused the clouds in the interior to form different wave patterns and later achieved the same feat through long-distance thought projection. To those who believe in Christ's healing, her feat is not surprising; it is merely another example of his promise that his followers would do greater miracles than he (John 14:12).

What others have done, you can do also. But caution must be exercised, for it is possible by will and desire to transmit one's energy and leave oneself depleted. This happens when the healer doesn't understand the process. Energy can be gathered from all forms of life, not just other humans. In *This World and That: An Analytical Study of Psychic Communication*, Phoebe D. Payne and her husband, Dr. Laurence J. Bendit, stress the point that the healer "neither gives his own vitality to the patient, nor does he draw on others around him. He relies on his ability to draw vitality from the atmosphere about him and acts as an impersonal channel for it." The simplest way to do this is to offer oneself as a channel for the Almighty, in which case nothing can go wrong. The famous healer Agnes Sanford did not go far enough in this respect at one time as she completed the work of God, for in her book *The Healing Gifts of the Spirit,* she told how her healings left her "utterly exhausted." She requested the gifts of the Holy Spirit to continue her work, and her prayers were answered for herself and two friends. Her experience was marked by a "deep burning within the head, as though a spiritual power were awakening even the physical channel of brain cells, nerves, glands, whatever they might be." Her own physical disabilities seemed to be healed, leaving her more peaceful and joyful, and thereafter the healing of others did not deplete her. She observed, "The entering in of the Spirit was a rounding out of the full personality, a quickening of life in every area of thinking and feeling." Obviously a spiritually healthy person, as Agnes Sanford was before her change, is a better channel once he or she is opened up by the Holy Spirit.

Entering of the Holy Spirit

Payne and Bendit also believe that the spiritually integrated person is the more effective healer and cite the Swiss psychotherapist C. G. Jung's remark that "in psychotherapy it matters more what one *is* than what one *does*." Being is more important than doing. The Holy Spirit helps one to be aligned with the maker. The entering of the Holy Spirit also presages a psychic change—the opening of the third eye—which brings with it psychic gifts such as healing, prophecy, clairvoyance, and psychokinesis, to mention a few. Christ may have been referring to this when in the Sermon on the Mount he told the multitude, "The light of the body is the eye: if therefore thine eye be single, thy whole body shall be full of light" (Matt. 6:22).

When the Holy Spirit descended upon the disciples at Pentecost, the third eye of each was activated. This enabled them, like Mesmer and Sanford, to heal others easily without tiring. Moreover, it made each more focused and directed in what he did. The interior presence of the Spirit shone out from the mystical body, and the individual aura became filled with more intense light.

If you feel you are ready for this step, you too can achieve a full third eye opening. Be certain, however, you intend to use it for God's good, to spread the light. It can be misused, of course, since every individual has the free will to choose between the opposites of the *daimon,* but those who abuse the privilege always pay dearly. They can leave themselves open to obsessions or possessions, as they are generally called, though we know that they are merely delving into the dark side of the psyche and coming up with contents that will harm themselves and others.

Those who opt for the light, on the other hand, need never fear the loss of their personalities. Becoming a channel is not necessarily permanent, for the individual retains freedom of choice. In short, one cannot become possessed by the spirit of light as one does by the forces of darkness.

A Christian who desires to become a channel can begin with the Jesus Prayer: "Lord Jesus Christ, Son of God, have mercy on me, a sinner" and can then proceed to ask to serve. A non-Christian can substitute any meaningful prayer that requests the aid of the Creator. The prayers may have to be renewed on occasion, however, since the higher power will not force itself on any person. This means you can experiment with being a channel without making a permanent commitment. We suggest you do so in the following exercises, but always with the understanding that your subject is receiving proper medical attention from bona fide doctors. As a beginner, you do not know and have not tested your healing powers, and you should encourage your fellow experimenters to seek medical assistance before it is too late for them to be helped. What you can do, in addition, is to reinforce the healing provided by doctors by using techniques similar to those you've used on yourself.

Beginning the Healing

Start by seating your subject in a straight-backed chair and ask your subject to relax as much as possible. Stand behind the chair. If you know the subject well enough, place your hands on the area of affliction. If the subject is only an acquaintance or if you feel in the least bit uncomfortable touching him or her, bracket the ailment with your hands, placing your healing hand in front of the area but not touching the body, and your stronger hand (the one you use for writing) behind and away from the body.

Close your eyes and drop gently to the alpha level. Offer a prayer for the healing, mentioning your subject by name. Visualize the white light entering at your crown chakra and inhale that light as you breathe. Forget yourself. You are not the healer. Our entire conditioning tells us that we cannot assist another person in this fashion and that we lack the ability to transmit healing. Do not fight this concept, for it is essentially true. We do nothing by ourselves. Know instead that you are a channel for the healing that comes from the light above you and is directed through you to the ailment.

You may feel the energy flow through you, as many healers do. But, like others, you may feel nothing and, in this case, you will know the healing is taking place because the light is present.

To help yourself detach so the light can do its work, see yourself sitting in the chair, being the patient rather than the healer. If this is difficult, imagine that you and your subject are mountains, with both your bodies being the observable peaks and the floor under you the earth at which the peaks join. Such a procedure helps you to establish contact with your subject, so the healing can work faster.

You should direct the light toward the ailment, but the cure won't necessarily take place at that site. Perhaps at the start of your work on this patient, the light will cure the cause of the trouble, the overall body rather than the specific complaint, so you will have to continue your ministrations until the whole body is receptive. You may be required to perform more than one treatment, though this is generally not the case; most of the time the cure will benefit the ailment itself, but you must not think you have failed if the subject doesn't feel immediate relief. Let the light work as it will. It knows better than you.

If at any moment your hands become painful because you have drawn the ache into your own body, shake them from the wrist and resume the treatment.

Keeping a Pure Mind

Work always with the best of intentions and a pure mind. This does not mean that you must become a saint before you can heal; if this were so, no one could assist anyone else in this world. To establish a state of pure mind, one must first eliminate all negativities. You should be doing this full time, anyway, but it's particularly vital when you are trying to aid others, since it enables you to throw off any aches or pains you may collect from them.

The second step in achieving the desired state of mind is to feel love for your subject, a fully compassionate love that will not tolerate any thought of his or her possible faults or any judgments about them that would explain their contracting such an ailment. The third pure mind ingredient is humility. You are in no way superior to your subject because he or she is ill and you are healthy, and you should take no pride in the work. After all, you are only the instrument through which the healing is accomplished, not the healer itself.

Remembering to Pray

A prayer at the start and conclusion of the healing session—even a silent one—will help you clear your mind of any negative thoughts and put yourself in the "pure state." After the healing—and you will learn through practice when to terminate a session—it is advisable to "preen your aura" and so cleanse your body of any negative thoughts or aches or pains transmitted to you by your subject. Your prayer of thanks will strengthen the cleansing of your body, so you will feel wonderful after a healing. But if you've picked up any discomfort, place your hands above your head with your fingertips meeting in prayer fashion. Separate your hands and bring them down over your shoulders as though you were tracing your outline and say, "I am created by Divine Light." Shake your hands from the wrist three times. Repeat the process, hands above the head with fingertips touching, then move the hands apart and down five times in all, for a full aura-cleansing.

The entire sequence is as follows:

> I am created by Divine Light.
> I am sustained by Divine Light.
> I am protected by Divine Light.
> I am surrounded by Divine Light.
> I am ever growing into Divine Light.

When you have advance warning of a healing, you should prepare for it by cleansing your physical body, by fasting for a time, and by prayer. When circumstances make this impossible, try to wash your hands before and after the healing. The body is the temple of the soul, and you should endeavor to bring to the task the purest temple possible. If water is unavailable, rub your hands together in a "dry wash," which will—at least symbolically—cleanse you and prevent you from transmitting any personal problems to your subject.

Absent Healing

You can use the aforementioned aura-cleansing for others as well as yourself, particularly when the other person is absent. Ask for the guidance and protection of the absent one by simply going into meditation, visualizing the person as seated in front of you, and then preening his or her aura.

Another effective method is to visualize the patient on your mental film screen as being well and happy, and by gesture or words surround him or her with the light.

An excellent prayer to use prior to a healing is that of St. Francis of Assisi:

Lord, make me an instrument of thy peace.
Where there is hatred, let me sow love;
Where there is injury, pardon;
Where there is doubt, faith;
Where there is despair, hope;
Where there is darkness, light;
Where there is sadness, joy.
O Divine Master, grant that I do not so much seek to be consoled
    as to console,
To be understood as to understand,
To be loved as to love;
For it is in giving that we receive,
In pardoning that we are pardoned,
And in dying that we are born to everlasting life.

This devotion need not be restricted to your healing sessions. In fact, it embodies all the attitudes and desires you should have developed at this point for your spiritual growth. Naturally you will be stronger in some of the areas mentioned than in others, but you can work on your weaknesses, knowing they can be overcome. The prayer, if recited daily during meditation, can help you enlist the aid of the highest powers. Moreover, it is sufficiently comprehensive to be used by Christian and non-Christian alike.

Building Up Energy

Once you have acquired the feel for it, you can replace the light with psychic energy for absent healing. During your private meditation, build your energy in one of the ways suggested in the previous chapter. Bringing the light into the upper three chakras and thus working on the lower four is one of the best methods for this purpose. When the third eye lights and the energies begin to flow unimpeded through your body, permit the prana to flow freely and form an energy circle. Build further energy with one of Weed's exercises (see page 122). This will saturate you with the energy, for it is the true healer. Of yourself you are powerless; the healing is actually from a universal source, and if you are not a channel at any other time in your life, you must be, temporarily, if you desire to heal. Offer a prayer or a positive thought before you start to send the prana. Then visualize the person. Do not see him or her as ill. Picture him in the best of health. Next, direct your energy toward the person, letting it come easily as you exhale and stream from the area that is about three fingers above the heart. Know that as it leaves you, more energy will be drawn in via your breath and through every pore of your body. You can never overdraw your supply. But if you attempt to hoard it and set up resistances to prevent others from using this prana, you will exhaust it quickly and thoroughly and come away feeling emotionally and physically drained. When you expend it freely and without reservation, on the other hand, you will build the sort of stamina that will enable you to emerge refreshed from the most grueling schedule. Use your psychic energy for absent healing. Use it also during your waking hours to help others in your presence. You are a part of every living thing in the universe and therefore should assist the rest of life by transmitting what life forces are required by them or it.

Through healing others you refine your own body and keep it in perfect health. When you conclude your absent healing treatments, visualize someone who may be having problems other than health, which require energy. Note the approximate time you are sending, and check with these people the following day. If they, too, have been working with the psychic process, or are the least bit sensitive, they will not only know they have received a feeling of well-being, or an inrush of energy, but after a few trials may be able to identify you as the sender. Each of us has a unique quality that causes our energy vibrations to feel different to the recipient. And those who are still doubtful about the identity of the sender can discover their benefactors by simply asking their subconscious minds.

At the conclusion of each energy transmission or subconscious questioning, be certain to offer your thanks. This can be done with a prayer or a short statement acknowledging your appreciation, but every psychic exercise should be concluded with a thank-you. Gratitude paves the way for further development.

In Chapter 12 we spoke of prana and how to build it. In Chapter 13 and this section we have been dealing with present and absent healing. Now we are ready to combine your prana exercises and absent healing for inclusion in your meditations. A simplified program follows, but before you start, take yourself into meditation and by extending your index finger, strike your chest three times. Wait a moment and repeat the tapping, then wait another moment and do it again.

You will discover you have touched the same part of your upper chest each time. This is the place from which you will send your energy. Never permit the prana to escape from your hands or arms during an absent treatment of a subject, but send it always from this spot.

As we have said, the light and prana are synonymous, but you should be able now to feel the effects rather than see them, so relax in your meditation and let your body absorb energy from the atmosphere.

1. Feel the effects of the energy inrush on your body, particularly those parts which are uncovered—like the head and hands.
2. Forget your breath and concentrate on your skin. In previous exercises you deliberately built the energy through breathing, but you no longer need to do this. Simply think of your skin, and feel it become warmer, or cooler, or prickly, or numb—however your body reacts to the absorption. Failure to feel it may result from being too tense, so relax. In a few moments you will be able to perceive the difference.
3. Let the energy build until your entire body feels alive with it. Know that as you absorb it, any negativities in the form of aches, pains, worries, tensions, or fears will be expelled from your body at the point on your chest. Do not hurry the process. Take as much time as you need to ensure your body is filled with the life-giving prana.
4. Speak a prayer of your choice and ask to be permitted to use your energy to help another human being.
5. Visualize that person who needs physical, emotional, or spiritual help as being seated in front of you. Try not to use your mental film screen, but imagine the person as being there with you.

6. Place your hands, thumbs and forefingers touching, over the head of your imagined subject.
7. Think about the inrush of energy to your body. Feel it. Vibrate with it. Know that as it enters you, it will flow through you unimpeded and be projected from the spot in your solar plexus that you have tapped, to the subject. You may not feel it emerge from you, but it will nevertheless stream out like a laser beam, flowing steadily, just as you absorb it steadily.
8. Concentrate in a relaxed and confident manner as long as you are able to focus on your subject.
9. When your attention begins to flag, you will know that the treatment is concluded for that session. Give thanks for being a channel.
10. Release your subject and let your energy continue to flow to every human being and every other living thing within a mile of you and in all directions. Think loving, positive thoughts about everything within this mile radius.
11. Give thanks for being a channel of energy, and proceed to your other meditation exercises, particularly the one in which you seek the silence.

Working with your prana during meditation will enable you to build a supply for daily living. It should suffice to get you through the roughest day. However, if you should feel your energies flagging, simply stop what you're doing for a moment, close your eyes, and feel a fresh supply build within you.

Whether in meditation or during your waking moments, spend your energy freely. Nature will not tolerate a vacuum, and the more you use, the more you will get. Furthermore, continual use will refine your body, thus helping you as much as it helps others.

Those who need more specific directions for releasing the prana can use something like the following:

All-powerful Holy Spirit within me, I freely offer myself. Use my mind and body as a channel for thy will. Fill me with your purity. Let it stream through me clear and unimpeded to _____ (or to all the universe). I give thee praise and thanks for this blessing.

Don't expect trumpets to blare or bells to peal if you choose this offering. The Creator—whether conceived of as an anthropomorphic being or as a force—comes quietly and without fanfare—most appropriately, being a guest in every sense of the word and never staying when not welcome, and so gentle and undemanding that often we are not sure of its presence. But wait. Meditate. Repeat your desire to be a channel for several meditations, so the Creator will be convinced of your sincerity and, what's more, your subconscious will know the decision is not a passing whim. Then wait again, and soon the results of your partnership will begin to manifest. Then, be careful. So often we fall back into our old habits and congratulate ourselves on our efforts before we achieve any results. This can destroy any partnership, for we have petitioned to serve as channels, and whatever transpires is neither for personal glory nor for self-recrimination. We are not the cause—only the instrument. We are no longer egocentric—only God-centered, even though the effect can last only as long as a healing if we are not prepared to make a permanent commitment.

15

Personal Moral Codes

How is it possible, we might ask, for one individual to transmit energy to another separate being? We find the answer in the writings of Ralph Waldo Emerson, a Unitarian minister who lived from 1803 to 1882 and achieved his greatest fame as a transcendental writer. The word *transcendental* means "beyond or contrary to common sense or experience," and Emerson and his fellow authors, as C. Hugh Holman explains it in *A Handbook to Literature,* believed "that man can intuitively transcend the limits of the senses and of logic and receive directly higher truths and greater knowledge denied to these mundane methods of knowing."

Transcendentalism leaned heavily on the ideas that intuition was superior to reason, that the microcosm of the individual mind (i.e., the small part that has all the characteristics of the whole, the macrocosm) was attuned to the macrocosmic soul of the universe so a person carried in himself or herself the entire world, and that human beings had *a priori* knowledge, knowledge that existed before and independently of humanity's earthly existence. Each of these beliefs is a critical psychic theory, so it would seem that Emerson dealt with materials that psychiatrists and psychics later recognized as essential to the psychic process that comes with spiritual growth.

We find evidence of this in Emerson's "The Over-Soul," published in 1841. He says:

> The simplest person, who in his integrity worships God, becomes God; yet for ever and ever the influx of this better and universal self is new and unsearchable. . . . You are preparing with eagerness to go and render a service to which your talent and your taste invite you, the love of men and the hope of fame. Has it not occurred to you, that you have no right to go, unless you are equally willing to be prevented from going? O, believe, as thou livest, that every sound that is spoken over the round world, which thou oughtest to hear, will vibrate

on thine ear! Every proverb, every book, every byword that belongs to thee for aid or comfort, shall surely come home through open or winding passages. Every friend whom not thy fantastic will, but the great and tender heart in thee craveth, shall lock thee in his embrace. And this, because the heart in thee is the heart of all; not a valve, not a wall, not an intersection is there anywhere in nature, but one blood rolls uninterruptedly in endless circulation through all men, as the water of the globe is all one sea, and, truly seen, its tide is one.

Let man, then, learn the revelation of all nature and all thought to heart; this, namely: that the Highest dwells with him; that the sources of nature are in his own mind, if the sentiment of duty is there. But if he would know what the great God speaketh, he must " go into his closet and shut the door," as Jesus said. God will not make himself manifest to cowards.

About 1844, in "The Poet," Emerson referred to

. . . a secret which every intellectual man quickly learns, that beyond the energy of his possessed and conscious intellect he is capable of a new energy (as of an intellect doubled on itself), by abandonment to the nature of things; that beside his privacy of power as an individual man, there is a great public power on which he can draw, by unlocking, at all risks, his human doors, and suffering the ethereal tides to roll and circulate through him; then he is caught up into the life of the Universe, his speech is thunder, his thought is law, and his words are universally intelligible as the plants and animals.

In brief, what Emerson was describing is the fellowship of all humanity, or what C. G. Jung later called the collective unconscious. We are all one, not separate or distinct as we have been led to believe. And when we open ourselves as channels, we open our minds to others, whether they are in our immediate presence or distantly located, and so are able to learn easily and quickly what we must know. Since we are one with all humankind, we can assist others by sharing the energy of the universe and thus help those who have not yet learned to help themselves.

Nonverbal, nonkinesthetic communication is within the natural law because we are inextricably linked with one another, psyche to psyche. This is what makes it possible for us to see the auras of others, to communicate on a telepathic level, to transmit healing power. Each person in the universe and all who have ever lived or are alive are a part of us and we of them. Each is a child of God, even as we. Therefore we must be prepared to expand our horizons, to perceive the world about us as an essential part of ourselves, and to work for the good of the whole as assiduously as we would work for our personal benefit. We must regain the wholeness we experienced as children, but this time no longer on a limited, egocentric basis; now we must take the whole world into our "perfect circle."

Prejudice and Discrimination

This means we must seek the God in every living being and cease criticizing, envying, even hating those who represent the opposite sex, another race, a different color, an alien creed. We cannot afford a moment's anger or dislike, even when the God within another person is hidden beneath layers of negativities.

If we despise either our own or the opposite sex, we condemn *ourselves.* Each of us carries within ourself both male and female elements, as we have seen in our discussions of the chakras and shall see further when we deal briefly with the theories of C. G. Jung. We cannot afford to vent our anger on the half of the human race that represents the other sex because we are directing that anger toward ourselves. Also we know better than to criticize those who differ from us. Naturally, it is easy to spot the faults of those below us on the spiritual ladder, and as we progress we shall find we've passed many who were once our equals. Yet we have no right to condemn people for being what they are; they are at their levels, working toward enlightenment the same as we, and simple compassion for the human plight demands we withhold judgment of the person even when we abhor their deeds.

As students of the higher consciousness, we must do more, and this means to overcome racial, color, and religious bias. We cannot afford to dislike or distrust any group of people. Adherents of reincarnation believe that each of us consciously chooses the conditions of birth and that each of us has been a member of other races, other colors, other religious faiths in past lives. These people believe that race, color, and creed are all superficialities, mere conditions of birth that in the case of race and color were probably chosen in order to learn a lesson, and cannot be altered in this life as we know it. Even those who do not subscribe to the doctrine of reincarnation must realize that beneath the superficial and external we are one universal blood and sinew and bond, because we belong to one universal mind. What seems to be our separateness is what appears when we view the mountain range whose base is shrouded by mist. The peaks stand out individually, but when the sun burns away the fog—as mentioned before—the mountains can be viewed as one continuous flow joined to Mother Earth, just as we are joined. Spiritually and psychically, humankind is a continuum.

Unity of the World

Those who cannot fully comprehend the mountain range analogy will do well to study a grove of trees. Each tree is a separate entity—or so it appears to the casual observer. A pine may stand next to an oak, a cedar adjacent to a palm, a hickory nut beside a willow, each specimen having its unique characteristics and purpose so it looks not only detached and lonely but as different from the others as the races that inhabit our earth. Yet appearances are deceiving. Dig beneath the surface and you will discover that the roots of the various species mingle and intertwine to form a mass far greater than that of the visible bowers. Every individual is like a tree, for it is at the root level, in what we call the subconscious, that he or she is linked to the rest of humanity.

In previous lessons we have worked to eliminate negativities toward individuals who aroused our base emotions. Now we must complete the infinitely more difficult task of accepting classes of people toward whom we may be prejudiced in some way. This *must* be done. We are part of one another, although each at our own level of development and with our own perception of light. We must look for the light and ignore the rest. Whatever a fellow human being does or says or feels should make no difference to us. The other will live according to his or her level and develop as well as possible. We can help by seeing the other in increased light, but nothing we can say or do will withhold good from him or her, any more than the other's words or deeds can stop our good as long as we work in the light.

Withholding Judgment

Yet a word of caution is in order. As R. D. Laing explains it in *The Politics of Experience,* "Let there be no illusions about the brotherhood of man. My brother as dear to me as I am to myself, my twin, my double, my flesh and blood, may be a fellow lyncher as well as a fellow martyr, and in either case is liable to meet his death at my hand if he chooses to take a different view of the situation." A harsh statement, perhaps, though nonetheless true. Being a channel does not give you a license to ignore your other senses and expose yourself to situations where you might become the victim of those at the bottom of the evolutionary ladder. Being a brother or sister means to care as much for the rest of humanity as you do for your nearest and dearest. One must not expect to be loved in return, for that may be beyond the ability of those involved. This rule applies to every manifestation of love, but is most applicable when we deal with someone who behaves differently from us. If the behavior is of a criminal nature, we should abhor the deed but never the perpetrator. In all cases we must surround our fellow beings with light and leave them to work out their own salvation. We must expend our energies on correcting ourselves, rather than finding fault with others.

A similar rule applies to the 10 percent of the population that is impelled by nature, nurture, a dominating animus or anima, or whatever causes homosexuality. The search for a centered life does not entitle us to judge. If we are among the 90 percent of the population that is heterosexual, the actions of the 10 percent are none of our business. Place everyone else on earth in the light. We get back what we send out, the Bible tells us. Let it be an understanding of the human spirit.

The general feeling that people with AIDS "behaved like animals and got what was coming to them" is contrary to every principle of centering. The association of AIDS with animals is that it developed from an experiment with primates, which got out of control. Since people with AIDS are paying for experimental error, they should be treated with the respect accorded all fellow humans.

Admittedly, it is difficult to overlook the sexual implications of the disease—*but if we are on the path to personal wholeness, how anyone contracted AIDS is not our business.* We need to expend the energy of our psyche (the triad of body, mind, and spirit) on improving ourselves, not casting stones. The psyche's message is clear: If you don't have AIDS, have compassion.

Whatever our sexual preference, each of us must come to terms with the third part of the psyche which we call the body. We defeat ourselves by remaining slaves of sex. It has its part in life, certainly, but is nowhere as important as contemporary media make it appear. On the path to wholeness, we must develop a personal moral and ethical code that may be more stringent than any imposed by the social order. As *The Gospel of Emerson* says, "The evolution of a highly destined society must be moral; it must run in the grooves of the celestial wheels. It must be catholic in aims. What is *moral?* It is the respecting in action catholic or universal ends. Hear the definition which Kant gives of moral conduct: 'Act always so that the immediate motive of thy will may become a universal rule for all intelligent beings.'"

Fidelity

Morality indeed consists of what is best for everyone, and the highest possible good comes from fully, completely, and spiritually loving every other human being—and reserving sexual affections for a chosen one. It is a psychic imperative that has shaped the mores, customs, morals, and religions of humankind. Though modern society has watered down its concepts of right and wrong, as well as its ethical and religious beliefs, the psyche holds its ground. It knows that if it harms another, it harms itself, for in the collective unconscious we are part and parcel of every other man, woman, and child.

Relaxed codes of conduct are dangerous to our health. Since the unconscious self contains both male and female elements, we harm ourselves by seeking gratification of the body alone. Even between consenting adults, unless there is a deep and abiding concern for self and partner, an "act of love" leaves lasting wounds on the minds and spirits of all involved.

The sex drive is necessary. It insures the continuation of the race. It is also the wellspring of creativity. Nonetheless, centered people are often "straight-laced" about sex. Some are celibate, preferring to use their energies for spiritual rather than bodily gratification and thus following the path chosen by people like St. Teresa of Avila and St. John of the Cross.

Yet sainthood is not the only way to achieve wholeness. A person need only abstain from sexual practice if single or respect the marriage vows if married. Again, the argument is not rooted in moral or ethical principles; the psyche has its own standards, which are more moral, ethical, and religious than the strictest social order. Centered people know that sex is just a part of living—a part best served when compassion, concern, affection, love, desire to protect, and the other emotions of the higher chakras are brought into play. In its proper place, sexual intercourse can develop in us one of the delights of the centered state: a deep and abiding love for every living thing—from the most exalted of persons to the lowliest form of the vegetable kingdom.

Deep Love

As we have stated previously, these views are not meant as criticism of any human being. Rather they are meant to protect oneself. No matter how disinterested a seeker of light may be in sexual matters, when the psyche begins to develop, an individual is confronted with possible danger. The lower chakras can heighten sexual awareness. But even the person who raises the energies to the higher chakras is vulnerable, for he or she experiences such a love for others, such a sense of belonging that he or she must beware of misinterpreting these urges, as well as of having others misunderstand them. One may think this psychic receptivity is sexual in addition to being spiritual; others may perceive it as a sexual advance. For this very reason one type of yoga that deals with love of humankind is prohibited to all but those who have been happily married for years. This tremendous love is what the Christians called *agape*. Be careful with it at first encounter. It is beautiful. It is powerful. It is a sign of great spiritual advancement. Don't mistake it for a lower urge and misuse it. After a time you will become accustomed to it, and these warnings will not be needed. Then you will be so deeply involved in the human condition and so attuned to the collective mind and heart that the most mundane encounter can become high adventure. You will absorb energy as you formerly absorbed the negative vibrations of the world that caused you to be tense, anxious, and fearful. In "The Poet" Emerson describes the results:

> How cheap even the liberty then seems; how mean to study, when an emotion communicates to the intellect the power to sap and upheave nature: how great the perspective! nations, times, systems, enter and disappear like threads in tapestry of large figure and many colors; dream delivers us to dream, and while the drunkenness lasts we will sell our bed, our philosophy, our religion, in our opulence.

Carlos Castaneda describes the experience as "stopping the world." Perhaps a better expression would be "owning the world," for this is the feeling. Every person, every circumstance, every wonder down to the last blade of grass exists for the joy of the enlightened.

Jung's Theories

But we needn't take Emerson's words for it. Fortunately his theories were continued by such modern scientists as Carl Jung, who was born in 1875 near Basel, Switzerland, and died in 1961. Originally a follower and close friend of Sigmund Freud, Jung disagreed with his teacher over the existence of paranormal forms of energy. Freud rejected Jung's ideas because they did not completely fit his theory of sexual energy, but Jung persisted, convinced that other forms of energy exist that are different from and beyond the sexual; from his own experience he knew they could result in such psychic phenomena as telepathy and precognition. In *Memories, Dreams, Reflections,* Jung recalls a telepathic experience in which he wakened with a "dull pain as though something had struck my forehead and then the back of my skull." He later learned that at the exact moment of his sensation, one of his patients had shot himself. This and other experiences led to his breakup with Freud, after which he struck out on his own, using myths in literature in an entirely different way from his friend to underline their differing ideas about energy and to sketch out his idea of the collective unconscious. But considering Freud's discovery that memories locked in the unconscious could make people ill, Jung began to investigate the possibility of elements in the unconscious that could heal them. In his own dream analysis and that of his patients, he discovered that the subconscious or unconscious process did try to heal as often as it tried to harm. He saw in dreams "an anticipatory or prognostic aspect" that fascinated him, and he eventually came to the conclusion that there was something in the unconscious that had not been supplied by the individual but was beyond him and transpersonal. He became aware of a vast pool of information and insights available to everyone if the individual could tune into it. Emerson had called this the over-soul. Jung named it the collective unconscious, and the separable elements in this collective unconscious he termed archetypes (primordial images that were the most ancient and most universal human thought forms.)

Employing the Unconscious

It is this universal unconsciousness that we tap when we assist others in healing, and the personal unconscious (the subconscious) that we employ when healing ourselves. But healing is not the only benefit to be derived. We can use it for other worthy purposes, such as locating an article of clothing or a book, or finding the answer to a personal problem. When you encounter a difficulty, ask for help from the collective unconscious. You will be surprised how easy it is to find the right solution, either in deep meditation or in dreams.

Specific techniques for contacting the greater awareness in dreams will be given in a later chapter, but the following exercise will serve for meditation. When you are ready, take a deep breath and tell yourself that as you exhale you will descend to the proper level for contacting your essence and thereby the collective unconscious. Then say something like this:

Lord, my need is _____.
I know the answer will be supplied.
It may come in a flash of insight or a thought of a person, in a particular writing to which I am led, or in another way I can understand.
I know you will supply the answer in your own time.
Thank you, Lord.

As always, dismiss the problem from your mind, and if you do not receive an answer, repeat your question in subsequent meditations. Don't set a timetable. Have confidence that you will know whatever is needed at the appropriate time, even if your knowledge concerns a future event. The collective unconscious, like your subconscious, is above time and contains all the knowledge of the past and the future, yet it has no sense of earthly time and placing a deadline on it will block it. Have faith. It will be rewarded.

Additional information on the collective unconscious will be outlined in the next chapter, but you can prepare yourself for understanding how it works by using it now.

16

Structure of
the Human Psyche

◆◆◆

"Man's task," as Rollo May explains in *Love and Will*, "by virtue of the deepening and widening of his consciousness, is to integrate the daimonic into himself." The *daimon*, you will recall, is the potential of any material thing (such as food or money) or abstraction (such as an urge or emotion) to be used for either good or bad by the individual. We integrate the *daimon* by learning to live for ultimate good rather than ephemeral whims. We turn our backs on whatever is negative and evil, for that is the dark side of the *daimon*. But there is also a light, indeed a light-hearted side, which we follow as children of the light.

Strangely enough, the two extremes are found in positions that are the reverse of what we'd expect. The dark is often manifested by the exterior facets of the personality: the persona (masks) and the false ego, while the light streams from our innermost depths, the essence. Nonetheless, there are dark aspects of our being that must be plumbed before we can uncover the light, and these have been described by Freud and Jung.

According to Sigmund Freud, the human psyche resembles an egg in which consciousness occupies the upper half, subconsciousness the lower half, and the ego separates the two, as shown in the diagram on page 164.

Of itself the egg shape is reminiscent of the "world egg" and could be termed a microcosm of the universal, or macrocosmic, unit. To state it more simply, one could say "as above, so below," for whatever exists on the greater scale is found on the smaller in human beings themselves. The same rule applies to consciousness, with the universal or collective unconscious applying to all living matter and the personal unconscious to the individual.

Before we deal with the unconscious, however, we must understand how the personality is formed and how it interacts with other personalities

FREUD'S MAP OF THE PSYCHE

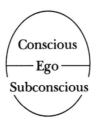

in our world. Jung developed a theory that individuals are basically intro-verted or extroverted, the former preferring solitude and the latter enjoying being with people.

Introversion and Extroversion

The introvert exhibits his or her greatest strengths and energies when alone. One might say that the person's psychic energy flows inward, while in the extrovert it flows outward. The extrovert is attached to people, things, events. Environment plays a controlling role in his or her decisions. Today we often call this type of person "outer-directed," being more re-sponsive to the desires of others and willing to submit to peer pressure. He or she is apt to be too sure of the self, whereas the introvert is inclined to be doubtful of relationships with others. Both types undervalue the oppo-site, and too often what works for one is wrong for the other. If Jung was correct that Easterners are mostly introverted and Westerners extroverted, as he claimed in *Psychological Types,* the basic meditations of the Orient, being designed for introverts, would not be suited to Western extroverts— an assumption that appears to be valid.

Introversion and extroversion result from the interplay of the ego and the conscious mind more than the subconscious, but the terms do not ex-plain the whole of the psyche. Jung also proposed the theory of the four basic functions that are responsible for our dealing with the world. These give the index to our conscious behavior. We use them to orient ourselves in the extra-mental world, though they further determine inner orientation.

He described them, according to Frieda Fordham in *An Introduction to Jung's Psychology,* as "*sensation,* which is perception through our senses; *thinking,* which gives meaning and understanding; *feeling,* which weighs and values; and *intuition,* which tells us of future possibilities and gives us information of the atmosphere which surrounds all experience."

Sensations

Each of us has one of these as a dominant function, but none is superior to another. They are simply ways in which we orient ourselves to the world and learn to react to it. Nevertheless, we all begin with sensation, for this is the door through which outside experiences, people, and things are percei-ved. A thinking, feeling, or intuitive type of person cannot be completely divorced from sensation, for he or she still experiences life through the senses. Indeed, each of us participates in all four functions. First, our senses are stimulated by a person or event. Then we reflect upon it or interpret it; this reflective function is thinking. Next we evaluate or orient the experience in our psyche; this is the function of feeling and answers the question, how do I feel about it? These three—sensation, thinking, and feeling—are conscious activities. They are followed by the fourth: intuition. This is what Jung called the "immediate awareness of relationships," and it takes place in the unconscious.

He further separated the functions into two categories: rational and nonrational. Those that pertain to reason and are rational are thinking and feeling, since they involve action and intention toward an object. The nonreasoning (nonrational) are sensation and intuition because the relationship with persons or object is passive. Neither sensation nor intuition takes any action. Instead, they most often receive the effects of one's meeting with a person or situation.

In *Jung's Psychology and Its Social Meaning,* Dr. Ira Progoff explains:

> Each individual, according to his nature, tends to specialize in one of the four functions. It may be any one of the four; but whichever one it is, whether rational or non-rational, the individual raises it to a conscious level in keeping with other aspects of his psychological development. Most important is the fact that the individual uses his leading or dominant function not merely as a means of experiencing the world, but as the basis around which he organizes his personality. The individual uses the dominant function as a focus for orienting and building his psychic life.

Whatever our orientation—and we discovered it in the attitudinal profile in Chapter 2—the dominant function is well developed in our consciousness. Its opposite lies deeply in the unconscious. Therefore it is possible to draw a diagram of any one of the functions. For example,

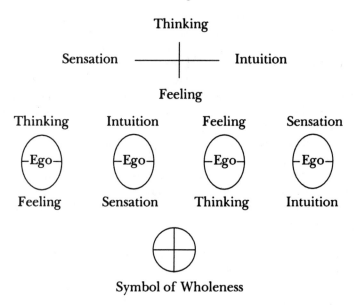

INTERPRETATION OF JUNG'S FUNCTIONS

Symbol of Wholeness

if thinking is the dominant function, its opposite, feeling, will be at the bottom. If intuition is dominant, its opposite, sensation, will be submerged. No single orientation is correct for everyone. However, the goal is to operate at each of the functions when circumstances require it.

Wholeness

These thought functions revolve about the ego as the center. The ego is the personal "I" that lives in the hope of becoming a self through the process of individuation. The latter term is synonymous with wholeness, and the goal is to absorb the inferior function into the dominant in a way that can best be described as scrambling the contents of the egg while it is still in its shell. When this occurs, the egg will lose its elliptical shape and become a circle, the symbol of wholeness.

Most of us can identify individuals who have specific dominant functions. We have all encountered intellectuals who are so thought-oriented that they appear cold and unfeeling, because the opposite of the dominant function, the feeling, is buried within them. Those individuals who operate mainly on intuition can seem to be at a loss to perceive through their five senses, because their sensation function is inferior. Feeling people, who rate high on weighing and valuing, do not appear to do much thinking. The sensation-oriented, who learn so much through their five senses, are deficient intuitively. But when any individual seeks to become whole through meditation and the other exercises used to "put the world to rights," he or she can begin to operate at any of these points—in short, to inscribe a circle about Jung's four functions and use whichever is needed.

It is essential to bring the psyche under such control, for in every human there is the possibility of mental illness if the dominant function becomes too powerful. In such cases there is the danger that the inferior function, which opposes the dominant, may break out of the unconscious and master the personality, whether the dominant likes it or not. What has been repressed can rise to the surface, and in ways that may be harmful to the individual. This is the inferior function's means of compensating for neglect. Disregard of the inferior, the dark side lodged in the unconscious, can cause complexes, serious mental difficulties, and sometimes psychoses.

The Shadow

Each of us has a dark side in the individual psyche. It is the negative aspect of the *daimon* (mentioned in Chapter 8); it is associated with the unconscious region and has been termed the shadow. Even the positive side of the *daimon* can cause trouble when taken to extremes—pride in telling the truth can evolve into brutal honesty for its own sake, for example—but the dark side causes even greater trouble when it exerts temporary control of the ego and invades the light, or the world of consciousness. Thus an understanding of the shadow is crucial to all of us. We hide it, often refusing to admit its existence because it is a denial of the ascent to God, the path of light. But the shadow is a necessary aspect of all humans. Even Christ recognized it in himself, for when he was alone in the desert meditating in preparation for his work in the world, the devil tempted him. He commanded, "Get thee behind me, Satan." When he faced the light, the shadow was indeed behind him, as it is with all of us.

Furthermore, the shadow contains positive aspects. As Joseph L. Henderson explains in "Ancient Myths and Modern Man," this personality aspect

... cast by the conscious mind of the individual contains the hidden, repressed, and unfavorable . . . aspects. . . . But this darkness is not just the simple converse of the conscious ego. Just as the ego contains unfavorable and destructive attitudes, so the shadow has good qualities—normal instincts and creative impulses. Ego and shadow, indeed, although separate, are inextricably linked together in much the same way that thought and feeling are related to each other. The ego, nevertheless, is in conflict with the shadow, in what Dr. Jung once called the battle for deliverance.

We must recognize that there is a dark side to our natures, that, as Jung says, "there is something in me which can say things that I do not know and do not intend, things which may even be directed against me." How often do we hear ourselves blurting out information which we do not wish others to know? When we use our own tongues to slit our throats, it is because the shadow has taken over, and even a brief takeover can be disastrous. If we wish to avoid such incidents, we must study our shadows and learn how to control them.

Recognizing the Shadow in Dreams

One of the best places to contact the shadow is in dreams. In fact, all the subconscious is readily available to us in dreams, and we can advance quickly if we learn to interpret the messages sent by the subconscious during sleep.

We can recognize the shadow because it appears as the same sex as the dreamer and it is usually lacking a face, since it is the shadowy counterpart of the ego. Most of us have difficulty visualizing our physical faces, so it is no wonder that the shadow leaves his or hers blank. If a figure in our dreams has a recognizable face, we can assume it to represent some aspect of ourselves that we identify with a particular person of our acquaintance. If it is the face of a stranger, we can still assume it to be a specific person. But if the face is blank or the features indistinguishable, we should pay attention to what has been repressed in our psychological makeup, bring the repression to the conscious level, and deal with it. If with such a warning we continue to ignore the shadow, it can become a terrifying adversary, although here we are talking about extreme cases, as not all shadow contents are threatening. Nonetheless, we cannot afford to ignore the appearance of the shadow in a dream, for it is telling us something we should know. When it becomes hostile because of severe repression, it can, as Progoff explains, become "identified with the negative, unpleasant side of the personality. The opposite of the conscious attitude reaches the surface . . . the complex operates with a power of its own, and acts to embarrass the ego by foolish and tactless errors."

The shadow is a part of the personality we would prefer to ignore. Still, we must bring it to the light, for it cannot stand the light any more than Satan could. Bringing it into consciousness where the light will not vanquish it, but merely permit its integration into the total personality, enables us to progress to wholeness.

The shadow is rooted in the personal unconscious. The dominant function is also personal, though conscious, and both the dominant and inferior functions combine to determine the mask or persona adopted by every individual. The ego is the buffer, that bit of consciousness floating on the surface of the personal unconscious that separates these parts of the psyche. As the personality is formed the persona takes on the characteristics of the dominant function, while the shadow that represents the inferior function remains in the unconscious. The contents must be blended to prevent "invasion" from, or by, the dark side.

Revelations from the Psyche

Such invasions can occur when people attempt to force their psyches to reveal information they are not equipped to handle. This often happens when the unenlightened work with Ouija boards or automatic writing. They dig deep into their personal unconscious and, because they have not eliminated the negativities in their thought and feeling processes, they permit the dark aspects of their natures to surface. Fortunately, you will not have this trouble. You have learned how to react to life positively, and your delving into your shadow domain is merely an extension of your work in eliminating negativities. For you it is a safe process. You are ready for it.

This is not to say you will be freed of discomfort while you deal with your shadow. The dark can be upsetting and disruptive, for a time, though without it you would have no free will, no ambition, no creativity. But your safety lies in seeking the light of the essence, which will illumine even the darkest of the deep-seated urges and release them so that you can advance both spiritually and psychically.

Once you have raised the affects of the personal unconscious, you are ready to attune yourself to the universal unconscious and its vast store of knowledge. We all participate in the collective history of our peers, our parents, and indeed all humankind. Even in asserting our individuality we identify with the human race. We are not, as the seventeenth-century philosopher John Locke claimed, born with *tabula rasa,* that is, minds that are blank slates on which experience writes. Instead, we enter the world with a few common concepts that are as instinctual as our urge to survive. Some of these are our affinities with the circle, square, and triangle, which have been found in the most primitive societies. Another is the catabasis, the need to go into the depths in order to emerge with the solutions to our problems, as we do in meditation. One more common and vital concept is that of the hero. Every civilization in all eras and parts of the world has its hero myth, for the idea of an admirable and all-conquering individual is ingrained in our psyches. In fact, we ourselves are seeking the hero within us as we search for our essences.

Universal Consciousness

Such universals as the circle, square, triangle, catabasis, and hero motif are the perceivable links between us and the general human race. As John Donne stated in the seventeenth century in *Devotions,* "No man is an island entire of itself; every man is a piece of the continent, a part of the main." It is as if we were elliptical corks on the sea of the universal unconscious. Above the waters, separate and individual, is the personal consciousness. The waves lap around the center, the ego, but the personal unconscious rests in the sea, as illustrated in the following diagram.

CONSCIOUSNESS

COLLECTIVE UNCONSCIOUS

The universal consciousness has its impact on the personal conscious, thus permitting us to be affected by our particular culture and so be culturally conditioned for survival, but it is at the deeper level that the collective unconscious is strongest. And when we have come to grips with the personal unconscious, we are ready to dip into this collective, universal sea, which teems with the knowledge of all times and every place. From this sea we gain the information of the past or the future that we term precognition or retrocognition, or have the ability to know what is happening at the same time in a distant place, which we call telepathy.

Male and Female Attributes

Our first contacts with the universal unconscious in dreams, however, are marked by the presence of a person of the opposite sex. The shadow of the personal unconscious represents the problems usually associated with our own type and sex, but our troubles often arise from our dealings with the opposite gender. Thus it is that in dreams a woman's unconscious appears as a man. Jung termed this the animus. In a man's unconscious, it emerges as a woman, or anima. As even the ancient Greeks knew, every man has a woman within him, every woman has a man within her. Though a man may glory in his maleness and identify with the dominant male attitudes of his culture, he cannot rid himself of his female characteristics. Similarly, women identify with the culture's dominant idea of femaleness, though they contain male as well as female attributes. Experiencing both sexes of our nature enables us to live in a world where roughly 50 percent of the population is composed of the opposite sex, though the other-sidedness, or opposite of the sexually dominant, undergoes a repression. Specifically, we repress this "inferior" and identify it with the opposite sex. The process takes place in the collective unconscious.

The theory is Jung's, but in *Man and His Symbols* he admitted it was not original. As far back as

> . . . the Middle Ages, long before physiologists demonstrated that by the reason of our glandular structure there are both male and female elements in all of us, it was said that "every man carries a woman within himself." It is this female element in every male that I have called the "anima." This "feminine" aspect is essentially a certain inferior kind of relatedness to the surroundings, and particularly to women, which is kept carefully concealed from others as well as from oneself. In other words, though an individual's visible personality may seem quite normal, he may well be concealing from others—or even from himself—the deplorable condition of the "woman within."

Like the shadow self, the animus or anima can cause trouble. It represents the undeveloped side of the personality attempting to assert itself. Like the shadow, too, when it appears in our dreams, it is faceless or not recognizable as any individual we know. It is part of that greater tension of the opposites of the conscious and unconscious, and before we can achieve integration of our personalities and find our true selves at the center (the essence), we must come to grips with it. We may well complain that it is enough to be faced with the shadow self of the same sex without being plagued by a figure of the opposite sex, and wonder if we must face it in order to become whole. The answers are in the affirmative. Of course, if we have surrendered to the essence, we need not be concerned about the battle. The essence will handle the problems without any overt effort on our part. Then the struggle between conscious and unconscious will not be bypassed as much as taken over by the higher power. But for those not ready to commit themselves, wholeness is still possible. For both the uncommitted and the committed, however, knowledge of the process is beneficial. As we have said before, we are dealing with mind stuff, and we should endeavor to understand the workings of our minds.

In *Jung's Psychology and Its Social Meanings,* Ira Progoff interprets the origin of the animus/anima as follows:

> . . . when the Shadow is brought into the lower levels of the unconscious and the collective psychic contents are added to it, it can no longer be expressed by a figure of the same sex as the Ego. Having gone more deeply into the unconscious, it must turn completely into the opposite of consciousness. The Shadow-side of a man, previously expressed by a masculine figure, is now represented by the image of a woman; and the Shadow of a woman now comes out of the unconscious in the form of one or more male figures. The Shadow, in short, changes into an Anima or Animus.

The anima/animus contains both good and bad and represents the daimonic in our lives. Jung believed the *daimon* could surface in either the shadow or the anima/animus, bringing with it great energies. Properly harnessed, the energies can be used to advance our creative work. Indeed, the psychologist Rollo May maintains that the *daimon* we observe in its shadow-anima-animus manifestations is absolutely essential to creativity. Though it may temporarily victimize us or embarrass us by bringing unwanted psychic contents into our conscious force fields, the ultimate result of successfully confronting it is a deeper and more satisfying integration of our personalities and the possibility of greater spiritual progress.

Anima

On the positive side, the anima helps a man find his true mate; helps him dig out facts hidden in the unconscious, both personal and collective; keeps him attuned to inner values; and thereby assists him in his growth by acting as a guide to the inner world of the self.

This personality aspect develops early in life. Dr. Marie-Louise von Franz, one of C. G. Jung's closest confidantes, explains it best in *Man and His Symbols.* The anima patterns itself after a man's mother. If the mother's influence is felt negatively,

> . . . his anima will often express itself in irritable, depressed moods, uncertainty, insecurity, and touchiness. (If, however, he is unable to overcome the negative assaults on himself, they can serve to reinforce his masculinity.) Within the soul of such a man the negative mother-anima figure will endlessly repeat this theme: "I am nothing. Nothing makes any sense . . ." These "anima moods" cause a sort of dullness, a fear of disease, of impotence, or of accidents. The whole of life takes on a sad and oppressive aspect. Such dark moods can even lure a man to suicide, in which case the anima becomes a death demon.

If the relationship of a man to his mother has been too strong, the anima may make a man too effeminate for his culture or so weak that he may be preyed upon by women. Frequently the anima can surface in men in the form of critical or "bitchy" remarks. Men who gossip like old women, as the term goes, can be far more vitriolic than the opposite sex. At a time like this, they are suffering from an invasion by the anima.

Nevertheless, as von Franz maintained,

> The most frequent manifestations of the anima take the form of erotic fantasy. Men may be driven to nurse their fantasies by looking at films and strip-tease shows, or by day-dreaming over pornographic materials. This is a crude, primitive aspect of the anima, which becomes compulsive only when a man does not sufficiently cultivate his feeling relationships—when his feeling attitude toward life has remained infantile.

Animus

Just as a man is most influenced in his anima-life by his mother, a woman is affected by her father. The animus in a woman causes feelings of power, coldness, obstinacy, force—even in the most feminine-appearing of the sex. The animus generally doesn't surface in erotic fantasies or moods, however, so centerfold pin-ups of males don't have the same attraction for women as such pictures do for men. Rather, as von Franz says, "One of the favorite themes that the animus repeats endlessly in the ruminations of this kind of woman goes like this: 'The only thing in the world that I want is love—and he doesn't love me'; or 'In this situation there are only two possibilities—and both are equally bad.'" It too can become "a demon of death." A wife in the grip of her animus can propel her husband and children toward illness, accident, or even death. The animus, like the anima in a man, can paralyze feeling and tell a woman, "You are hopeless. What's the use of trying? There's no point in doing anything. Life will never change for the better."

Yet, von Franz adds, "the animus does not merely consist of negative qualities such as brutality, recklessness, empty talk, and silent, obstinate, evil ideas. He too has a very positive and valuable side; he too can build a bridge to the self through creative activity."

Of the two, the negative side of the anima appears worse than that of the animus. Progoff notes, "Jung has pointed out that when usually masculine traits are expressed in women they come out in maladapted form. When the feminine side comes to the fore in a man, it does so in moods by which the unconscious overtakes the conscious attitudes and introduces unpleasant effects."

Coming to Terms with the Anima/Animus

Before wholeness can be achieved via this route, everyone must come to terms with his or her animus or anima. Dealing with the man or woman within also helps one to deal with the world without. The appearance in dreams of the blank-faced single anima to a man, or the numerous blank-faced men to a woman, is a good sign. It indicates that the old shadow self, which is the same sex as the dreamer, has been pushed aside and replaced by the anima or animus. The unpleasant effects of dealing with this personality component when it first emerges are only temporary. Progoff gives us even better news in that the

. . . emergence of the Anima or Animus as an autonomous factor means that the creative readjustment of the psyche can now be begun. The Anima figure tends in time to become identified with the unconscious as a whole . . . The first effects are unpleasant, but the larger aspects involve the process by which the unconscious is brought to terms with consciousness. The integrations of the personality can be accomplished only *via* the Anima or the Animus, since they are the autonomous personification of the unconscious in the male and female.

The reward for confronting the animus/anima is the finding of the self. Dr von Franz observes also that "if an individual has wrestled seriously enough and long enough with the anima (or animus) problem so that he, or she, is no longer partially identified with it, the unconscious again changes its dominant character and appears in a new symbolic form, representing the self, the innermost nucleus of the psyche."

One exception must be noted for both Progoff's and von Franz's theories. Personality integration does involve the animus/anima, but the struggle need not take place on a conscious level if the seeker has offered the self as a channel; in such cases he or she has already become separated from animus/anima identification, and the self—the essence—is free to emerge when it will.

Completing the Circle

However one goes about it, by becoming a channel or by grappling with the shadow and animus/anima, the result is a return to one's original completeness. The elliptical or egg-shaped psyche flattens out into a sphere, a circle, for the person has come full circle and is self-actualized, holistic, individuated, synthesized, having completed the process.

This is the point you have reached—you stand ready to complete your circle, if you have not already done so. Jung, in *Analytical Psychology*, identifies the rewards accruing to a person who is fully integrated. He says:

> When the unconscious brings together the male and female, things become utterly indistinguishable and we cannot say any more whether they are male or female. . . . Conflict has come to rest, and everything is still or once again in the original state of indistinguishable harmony. You find the same idea in Chinese philosophy. The ideal condition is named Tao, and it consists of complete harmony between heaven and earth . . . On one side it is white with a black spot, and on the other it is black with a white spot. The white side is the hot, dry, fiery principle, the south; the black side is the cold, humid, dark principle, the north.

This fusion of male and female, light and dark, south and north is known as the yin and yang. As Clae Waltham explained in *I Ching: The Chinese Book of Changes,* the yin is "dark, moon-like, the Great Obscurity, weak, female, earth, soft" and the yang is "bright, sun-like, the Great Brightness, strong, male, heaven, hard." The yin and yang combine to form the Tao, the symbol for completeness and wholeness. None of us can be whole until we fuse the maleness or femaleness within us to the femaleness or maleness that is dominant. The fusion is shown in the Tao circle, a smooth, tight junction of the dark and the light with the dark being pinned by a dot of light and the light skewered with a pin-point of dark.

The Tao symbol and its separate parts work on all levels. In the greater society of the world, the male and female complement each other, forming the world circle we know as the globe. In the smaller unit, the micro-cosmic human being, the male and female are likewise present. Yogis describe them as the Pingala, the masculine, and the Ida, the feminine, which rise up through the chakras to twine about the spine and intertwine with each other to form the kundalini. Thus the Orientals have known for centuries what Westerners are just learning: that it takes the interaction of the masculine and the feminine to achieve wholeness.

However much our culture stresses the separation of the sexes, we are one with the opposite gender, and for this reason neither male nor female chauvinism must color our attitudes. Neither must we criticize or judge the opposite sex, for it is the shortcomings of our inner selves that we find fault with, the deplorable man or woman within that we project onto others.

Psychic Negativities

Before we begin the meditation planned for this point of your development, one more aspect of the personal and collective unconscious must be considered. This is the result of delving into the unconscious on both levels, which can be good or bad, depending on what the individual is seeking. As one of the *illuminati,* you are a child of the light and seek only what is best for yourself and the world. When you explore your personal unconscious, it is in search of the light. Therefore you need never fear what is called obsession or possession. Your essence will never obsess or possess you, for the higher power that is the light within you works on absolute free will and allows you to choose at all times. But those who seek self-interestedly and with ill will toward others may certainly become what is known as obsessed or possessed, though these are only terms to explain the psychological results. Actually, there are no demons that can jump into a body and take it over, and "possession by the devil" is a misnomer. Those who exhibit such possession are actually people who have gone into their own personal unconscious and dug out all the negative contents, the psychic garbage contained therein.

Abnormal Phenomena

Continuing, they have progressed beyond the personal and into the universal unconscious and have attracted to them, because they were so inclined, all the negativities and dirt of the universal. The marks of possession" —the speaking in foreign tongues, the levitating of objects or people, and all the other phenomena that can occur when one is in this state come from the same universal unconscious also manifested in those who seek the light. The phenomena in themselves are not evil. They are natural and healthy attributes, which can be used correctly by those who wish to use them for good. But they can also be misused by the self-centered, the negatively inclined who wish to gain power or revenge or to otherwise deprive their fellow-beings of their rights.

For this reason you have worked to eliminate the negativities in your actions and thoughts during your conscious moments and have sought the light in your meditations. When you progress, as you shall when you are ready, you will be able to use all the knowledge of the universal unconscious for the good of yourself and your world. You will be able to tap into the universal mind, just as holy persons before you have done throughout the ages.

Stilling the Mind

To assist yourself in reaching the stage where you can avail yourself of universal knowledge, begin your meditation. This time do not work on any projects, such as foreseeing or sending energy to others. Begin with a prayer and then clear your mind of everything. In short, seek the silence. Let your mind be a blank, and if a thought attempts to cross it, do not fight or resist that thought, but let it pass, and gently but firmly bring your mind back to blankness. When you perceive a new scene or when an entirely new thought flashes across your mind, do not attempt to hold it or contemplate it, but let it come or go as it will, for you will be receiving the picture or thought from the collective unconscious.

The goal is to still the mind completely and to retain the stillness as long as you are able. This is true meditation, and all your duties, such as improving yourself and helping others, can be attended to at another time— particularly during your conscious moments. As you persevere, you will find your moments of silence lengthening into minutes and the minutes into an hour of deep, relaxing, and rewarding meditation. During this period you will contact your essence and it will guide you safely into the collective unconscious, from which you will emerge with new-found abilities and intelligence. Seek the light. Work with the light, and it will enlighten every moment of your life.

17

Working with Dreams

Wholeness is a round-the-clock activity. In the past chapters you have learned how to cope with your conscious activities by reforming your personality and to assist in this process with your meditations. Now we are ready to investigate the third of our lives that we customarily neglect—the hours when we are asleep and feel we are "dead to the world." Yet there is no such death, and sleep, too, comes under the psychic laws of cause and effect and can provide important clues to our advancement.

Our culture has largely ignored the sleeping state, believing that in sleep we lose all contact with the "real" world while we refresh our minds, bodies, and spirits, making ready for the next encounter with "reality." The facts indicate otherwise. The seven or eight hours each night when our egos are at rest are potentially the most fruitful of the twenty-four, for then the subconscious may reveal significant messages that escape us in the hurly-burly of the day. These messages come to us during our dreams and are often clothed in symbolic language, which we must interpret on a personal basis.

Fortunately, we do not have to accept on hearsay the fact that we all dream. Each of us dreams during every period of sleep longer than a momentary catnap. Science confirmed this long-suspected truth in 1953 when Eugene Aserinsky, a student of the famous sleep expert Professor Nathaniel Kleitman of the Physiology Department at the University of Chicago, "noted that an infant's eyes moved rapidly and jerkily under the closed lids for short periods during sleep. He reported this finding to Kleitman, and together they decided to extend their study to the sleep of adults to discover whether or not similar rapid eye movements would be observed, and if so, what might be their significance," as Dr. Ann Faraday recounts in her book *Dream Power*.

Rapid eye movements, later termed REMs, occur when one reaches the alpha state of brain activity, between eight and thirteen vibrations per second—the state achieved in successful meditation. Faraday recounts that Aserinsky and Kleitman continued their research and made

> ... the striking discovery that during the course of seven or eight hours of normal sleep, there were *four* or *five* periods of "emergence" from the deeper stages of sleep back to Stage 1. They found that as the subject falls asleep, he passes quickly through "descending" Stage 1, spending perhaps five minutes in this stage, before progressing rapidly through Stages 2, 3, and 4 to deepest sleep. He may spend half an hour or more in Stage 4, before ascending through Stages 3 and 2 to his first period of "ascending" or "emergent" Stage I sleep. Usually, he spends no more than a few minutes in this stage before once again descending to deeper sleep.
>
> During this second cycle, he may not even reach Stage 4, but if he does, he spends much less time here than he did during the first cycle. He then ascends once more to Stage 1, this time spending perhaps twenty minutes or so in this stage before once again descending into deeper sleep. This cycle of descent and ascent is repeated through the night in cycles lasting approximately ninety minutes. The periods of Stage I sleep become progressively longer, and Stages 3 and 4 become shorter as morning approaches. Indeed, toward the end of the sleep period, a person is spending most of his time in Stage I and 2.
>
> It must be emphasized that the above is an idealized picture of the sleep cycle. Actual sleep patterns vary somewhat from one individual to another, or for the same person from night to night. But the fact remains that the cyclic nature of sleep generally has never failed to appear in all the thousands of subjects who have taken part in sleep experiments throughout the world during the past two decades. It seems to be an in-built mechanism dependent on some biological rhythm within the body.

Stanley Krippner and Montague Ullman of the Maimonides Dream Laboratory at the Maimonides Medical Center in Brooklyn confirm the fact that each of us dreams regularly and, moreover, that severe psychological disturbances can result from dream deprivation. Since it is generally acknowledged by scientists that we do dream, the problem is what should be done if we cannot remember dreaming or are unable to recall the specific content of dreams that will aid us in our spiritual and psychic growth.

You are well prepared for dream interpretation. It is analogous to learning to read; meditation is the alphabet or phonics system that has taught you to identify letters or sounds. Knowledge of a few of the universal symbols (such as the circle, square, triangle) provides those "flash cards" through which you have learned to combine basic letters or sounds into words like "girl," "boy," and "run" and to associate those words with the pictures on the cards. Now you are prepared to open your first "Dick and Jane" reader and to identify such sentences as "Run, Dick, run. Dick, see Jane run." And, just as when you learned to read, you will begin slowly and with the simpler concepts to build your symbolic vocabulary until you can handle the most abstruse messages from your subconscious. This takes time, so do not expect to become a dream expert overnight.

Recalling Dreams

Learning to recall your dreams is simple. Tell yourself just before dozing off that you will remember them. Have writing materials at your bedside, along with a night-light that can be easily switched on and off to facilitate writing, unless you have the rare ability to write legibly in the dark. Say a prayer and reiterate your instruction to your subconscious to remember your dreams.

If you wake up during the night, immediately think about what you were dreaming and record it. If you sleep through to the morning, when you awake, lie back in bed and lazily think about dreaming. Do not make any sudden moves or put your feet on the floor until you have recalled your dreams as fully as possible. Write them down. If you wake up and recall nothing, go into a light meditation and ask your essence for the content of your dreams. Give it a firm order. If that doesn't work either, do not become discouraged. It may take you a couple of nights to break your old habit of not recalling dreams and to retrain your psyche, but within a few days you should be getting some messages. Record them on paper (you may use a tape recorder later, when the details become abundant), and retain your copies. A dream log in written form is advised at the start, because you will want to refer to it often to learn what your personal symbols mean. At first your symbols may strike you as being gibberish, but after a few sessions a pattern will emerge and you will understand them. Remember that you will have your own particular symbols. Universal symbols will, of course, emerge, but these, too, will be subject to your personal interpretation, so you do not require and should not use a dream book to interpret them. Your essence will provide all the data you need for dream interpretation. Just give it time to make itself clear. Ask to have the dream message repeated if you don't understand, and be prepared to receive the same message in a different form. You will find a knowledge of universal symbols of great assistance in establishing your personal symbology, and that knowledge, coupled with common sense, will suffice. Even if you are not conversant with universal symbols, it doesn't matter. You can discover what you need to know through repetition of symbols recorded in your dream log along with an explanation of some of the important ones, which we shall discuss shortly.

Dr. Ann Faraday suggests an exercise to assist you in remembering dreams:

> Lie flat on your back in bed, but keep your arm in a vertical position, balanced on the elbow, so that it stays up with minimum of effort. You can slip fairly easily and deeply into the hypnagogic state this way, but at a certain point, muscle tonus decreases, your arm falls down and wakes you up. Write down immediately whatever was going through your mind just prior to waking. The results can be amusing and may even provide some useful material for interpretation.

David Graham, in *Dream Your Way to Happiness and Awareness,* suggests the following:

> *Step one:* Decide to take a catnap. Now I could have told you to relax, but most people get up-tight wondering if they're relaxed enough. We're all used to taking catnaps. There's no great mystery. And you can't take a catnap without relaxing.
>
> *Step two:* Apply the brake. We're going to take this catnap for a specific purpose, and we don't want to snooze so enthusiastically that we slip right past the dream level. We have to have some means of holding ourselves at the desired level without interrupting the action. So lie on your back with one arm bent at the elbow, hand toward your ceiling up there. It's not difficult to keep the hand in this raised position, nor is it at all uncomfortable. When you get into the alpha level you won't even be aware of the arm—unless you start to slip past—at which point the upraised arm will begin to lower. It will probably only be the slightest of movements, but it will be enough to snap you back to level and not so much that you'll pop back awake.
>
> *Step three:* Find a trigger. Something that genuinely piques your curiosity and will get you to asking questions. A window. If you walk over to that window, what will you see outside? A garden? A grave-

yard? Are there people? Is the window open or closed? Try a road. Is it paved, or is it a dirt caravan trail? Are there other travelers, or are you alone? What is the countryside like around the road? What time of day or night? Where will it take you?

Step four: Observe all the detail you can possibly cram in your head. This is really part of Step Three, but so important that it deserves its own heading. In fact, I seriously doubt that the technique will work if you miss this step. It's careful observation of detail that pulls your outer mind inward, away from outside distractions and down to the alpha level or deeper. If you don't concentrate on detail in the pictures presented by your inner mind, your outer mind will still be hearing the tick of the clock, the passing car, the low-flying plane, and you simply won't be at the working level for which you're aiming. *Observe all details!*

Step five: Testing, testing, one-two-three. This is not what you would call scientifically established fact, but I use a little test periodically throughout the dream experience that, as far as I can tell, gives me a reasonably accurate check as to whether or not I'm at this alpha level. I try to change something the inner mind presents. For instance, upon seeing a bright-red door in the hallway of my mind, I decided I'd prefer to have it a soft blue. The door would quiver and the color would fluctuate—and hold on red. To me this indicates that while the outer mind is active and participating in the experience, the inner mind is the one in control of the action. Which is what we want. It's from the inner mind that we wish to obtain information, and the outer mind is all too eager to rationalize and distort. This little test tells me that, at that point at least, the outer mind can't play its tricks.

Step six: Go with the action. Once you're down to level and the testing shows the inner mind is in the driver's seat (however much the outer mind flashed the backseat driver's license) then you can just flow with what the inner mind is presenting for you. You won't need to try to structure the experience—in fact, if you can, you aren't there. Your outer mind sets up the opportunity by following the above steps. Your inner mind will respond by taking you on an adventure that instructs, informs, and intrigues. Don't worry about what form the adventure will take. Your inner mind is quite capable of giving you the message with wisdom, and accuracy, though some of the most uncanny symbolism, as well as with literal statements. And the inner mind has a knack of presenting information about you in a much more objective manner than the outer mind can muster.

Graham also stresses the importance of taking notes in both catnap and regular dream states, so that you can master the dream codes.

A prayer before starting your catnap and one at its conclusion are also advised. Prayer clears the mind of negativity and enables you to dream in a positive and constructive fashion. But the same applies to every sleeping state. You must continue to work daily in the light and to sleep in the light, for it is your comfort and protection.

The preceding exercises are meant as aids to developing dream recall, rather than substitutes for the deep-sleep dreams, which will prove most fruitful. It is in regular sleep-dreaming that your subconscious is most free to remind you of your waking condition, warn you when you are about to make mistakes, and guide you toward a higher level of development. Once you have mastered your personal symbols, do not be surprised if you begin to dream clairvoyantly or precognitively, for your essence, the God within you, knows what is happening throughout the world and time. It is, as Jung told us, capable of aligning itself with the universal unconscious and can as readily report on people at a distance and advise us about the future. We contact this essence in meditation, but we should not ignore it during the vulnerable third of our lives when it can spontaneously reach out to help us. Work with your dreams as assiduously as you have worked with meditation and with the same cautions: that *you seek what is best for you, do not interfere with the free will of others, and desire that all humankind should profit from your efforts.*

Dream Types

When you start to record your dreams in full detail, you must remember that not all of them are of equal importance. We can classify them as to four general types: digestive, physical, psychic, and spiritual, in order of their increasing importance.

Digestive Dreams

Digestive dreams are those which normally occur one to five hours after you've overloaded your stomach with food. They reflect the body's attempt to assimilate whatever you've eaten and are of little significance. Since they are most apt to occur during the earlier hours of the sleep period, you probably won't remember them unless you wake up prematurely. Dreaming of going to the lavatory also falls in this category, but in this case the dream indicates you should wake up and relieve your body of its burden.

Physical Dreams

Physical dreams arise from the worries, tensions, and fears that people accumulate during their conscious hours. Like the digestive dreams, they are a mish-mash of events and unreliable. If you recall one, do not become upset. They stem from illness or some negativity that you haven't succeeded in eliminating, and the only notice you should take of them is to work with the problem that caused them. For instance, if you dream of being fired from your position, the dream has been caused by worry and is not a forecast of what you should expect.

Nightmares

Nightmares fall into this category. They are the result of a feeling of oppression or of living in a hostile atmosphere. If you suffer from nightmares —which is extremely unlikely, since you have conquered your negativities—or know someone who does, reexamine your situations. Take the problems of your daily life, or those of the other person, into meditation and deliver them over to your essence. Ask for the strength to accept what is happening in your conscious life that you cannot change. Ask what it is that you are supposed to learn. Bless the situation. Say something like this: "I am a child of God. No evil can befall me, for he is with me waking and sleeping. I thank God for his love and protection and for correcting my situation." During your waking moments be sure to think positive thoughts only. Bless the unfortunate situation and those involved in it, and stop injecting negative content, which can only make it worse.

If you dream you are being chased by some creature, turn and confront your pursuer. Whether man or beast, the enemy will change into something tame that you can handle or even something that is friendly toward you. Or if you have not succeeded in establishing such control over your dreams, review the nightmare during the day or when you meditate, and write yourself a satisfactory conclusion. A dream is a manifestation of your unconscious, so if you don't like the results, you can use your subconscious to set matters to rights. Nightmares are not necessary for those who think and work in the light.

Psychic Dreams

Psychic and spiritual dreams are those that you will most easily remember at the closing periods of your sleep time or that are important enough to wake you from a sound sleep so that you can recall them in detail. They are rich in imagery, often appearing in three-dimension and full color, thus distinguishing them from digestive and physical dreams. This happens particularly if people are attuned to color in their lives; those who are not as observant may experience their psychic and spiritual dreams in black and white but still in more detail than they do the lesser and unimportant types.

Psychic dreams can warn us about events to come or otherwise assist us in our daily lives. If you dream about death, for instance, you must not take the message literally. What your psyche is telling you is that something in your present life is dying and will be replaced by something better. A dream of birth is not necessarily a signal that a child will be born but that something new will come into your life shortly. A dream of your automobile breaking down is probably a warning for you to attend to your health, though it may also be a warning that you are being careless with your property. If you dream of an accident, it won't hurt to pay more attention to your driving in the days to come, though your message is more likely to be aware of actions that will lead you to disaster in your emotional life or your everyday responses to situations.

In all cases, the figures of your dreams represent you. Every dream is about you, so if you dream of a teacher lecturing you for some misdeed, know that the teacher is the part of you that identifies with some *characteristic* of another person and that *you* are the teacher, not the pupil alone.

Spiritual Dreams

Spiritual dreams are those in which some wise individual imparts certain information to you or those in which you are involved in some learning situation with groups of others. If a relative or close friend comes to you in a dream with certain information, pay close attention. He or she may be telling you something about the future. If any figure clothed in light appears and gives you information, be certain to remember what is said, for this, too, is for your benefit. Many advanced souls dream of going to school during sleep and in their dream logs can record the details of the school as well as the instructions they received. This is the most beneficial of spiritual dreams, for it indicates that the dreamer is working during the night to gather the knowledge needed for waking moments.

The signs and symbols we encounter during our important dreams must be interpreted individually, but some are based on the universal language and might bear mentioning before we proceed to those which apply to you alone and require your specific interpretations.

For example, we can be reassured by a dream that has symbols of wholeness such as stones (jewels or otherwise), pairs, and mandalas.

Stones have a religious significance, and the Renaissance alchemists' pursuit of the philosopher's stone was really a religious quest as well as an attempt to change base metals into gold. The alchemist was often a seer seeking the key to the secrets of the universe, a religious mystic seeking Christ, the "pearl without price." For most dreamers, stones indicate God.

A dream of a king and queen or any other royal pair would signify that the disparate halves of the dreamer have been united, just as the masculine and feminine elements have been successfully combined in an individual, and indicate that the negative aspect of the animus/anima has been vanquished. Jung refers to the "royal pair" as a dream symbol of approaching personality integration.

Mandala in Dreams

Mandala is from the Sanskrit and means a circle, particularly a magic circle. In the Eastern world, ground plans of temples are usually in the form of mandalas. So are the pictures drawn in the temple on the days of religious festivals. In the center of the mandala there is always the god or the symbol of divine energy, the thunderbolt. Around this innermost circle is a cloister with four gates that represent the gates of the world. Then comes a garden, and around this there is another circle, the outer circumference. However, you may not see anything this elaborate. If you dream only of a circle you will know that health and wholeness are near and that the process of becoming whole is being completed. In the Western world we think of the Garden of Eden as being perfect, and Carl Jung, in Edward F. Edinger's *Ego and Archetype,* describes the legendary place as having "certain features of a mandala with four rivers flowing from it and the tree of life in its center. The mandala-garden is an image of the Self, in this case representing the ego's original oneness with nature and deity. It is the initial, unconscious, animal state of being at one with one's Self. It is paradisal because consciousness has not yet appeared and hence there is no conflict. The ego is contained in the womb of the Self." Thus if you dream of a circular garden, the message is even clearer than if you dream of a simple circle.

The story of the Garden of Eden is important to us because we learn of the origin of consciousness. Similarly we realize, on examining the myth, that Adam was an androgynous person before Eve was created out of his rib. The task of men and women is to recognize these universal concerns, to accept the double nature of our masculinity and femininity, the opposition and cooperation of our consciousness and unconsciousness, and to transcend the limits of body and mind by the vehicle of our spirits. By going into the depths, whether in meditation or in dreams, we are put in touch once more with our original wholeness and are directed to the goal of becoming one. To our meditative techniques we add those of dream analysis. Our minds are not separate from God's. We recognize that he can help us.

In *Dream Your Way to Happiness and Awareness,* David Graham cites Roy Eugene Davis, an expert on yoga, meditation, and creative imagination, who claims that "yoga masters teach that everything (all cosmic manifestation) this side of the Absolute non-dual aspect of Consciousness is taking place in the universal mind and is, therefore, God's dream."

Foreseeing the Future in Dreams

Even if we cannot agree with the yogis, dreams can be perceived as merely another way of realizing the presence of God. They may give us clues or answers to our problems. If you dream about a person and later have an argument with him or her, for example, the dream was warning you to be careful. The future can be read in dreams and altered during your waking hours. Tales abound of prophetic warnings given to parents about the danger of an accident to their children, thus enabling them to avert the catastrophe. Dreams, according to Jung in *Analytical Psychology,* "bring out everything that is necessary."

The hero frequently occurs in the dream pictures. Sometimes, as Jung explains in *Analytical Psychology,* the dream contains a universal element that indicates the subject has gone beyond the layer of the personal unconscious into the collective, and his or her problem is no longer a personal matter but one having to do with all humankind. The hero is one of these, and Jung explains him in *Man and His Symbols* as "a powerful man or god-man who vanquishes evil in the form of dragons, serpents, monsters, demons, and so on, and who liberates his people from destruction and death."

The Hero

Whether in myth or dream, the hero varies according to the time and culture. The Greek hero, for instance, had special qualities that set him apart from the common man and made him an object worthy of envy. He was highly successful in all his endeavors, but he had a tragic flaw of character that included the specific flaw of pride. He could make an error in judgment, his flaw would betray him, and he would suffer a reversal of fortune that would force him to atone for his sin or error and thereby achieve a cleansing known as a *catharsis*. Oedipus in Sophocles's play *Oedipus Rex* was such a hero, but the myth of the hero is not unique to the classical world. It occurs in all cultures: Egyptian, Indian, Eastern, Eskimo, American Indian, and other American cultures alike. Throughout the world among the world's people it occurs spontaneously because it expresses a basic psychic process. In *Analytical Psychology* Jung identified

> . . . the figures of the Hero, the Redeemer, the Dragon (always connected with the Hero, who has to overcome him), the Whale or the Monster who swallows the Hero. Another variation of the motif of the Hero and the Dragon is the Katabasis. . . . You remember in the Odyssey where Ulysses descended *ad inferos* to consult Tiresias, the seer. This motif . . . is found everywhere in antiquity and practically all over the world. It expresses the psychological mechanism of introversion of the conscious mind into the deeper layers of the unconscious psyche. From these layers derive the contents of an impersonal, mythological character, in other words, the archetypes, and I call them therefore the impersonal or *collective unconscious*.

The heroes in modern dreams may appear quite different from those of the myths, but they are always powerful people who can overcome every obstacle. Moreover, they are ourselves.

The hero is, of course, joined to the monster he fights. To Jung the hero and the dragon were inseparable figures from the same myth. Now we generally interpret dream snakes or dragons to mean a confrontation with evil, but this need not be the case. Evil serpents are most often symbolized by the serpent in the Garden of Eden, which is identified with the principle of evil, but even in the Christian context a serpent is not necessarily bad. Christ told his disciples to "be ye therefore wise as serpents, and harmless as doves" (Matt. 10:16). Thomas More, the sixteenth-century author of *Utopia,* conceived of Christ, savior of the world, as a "holy, wholesome serpent that devoureth all the poisoned serpents of hell."

The Caduceus

The ancient Egyptians used a coiled snake as a symbol of royalty. They also associated the snake with healing and used it as the emblem of the healing god, Thoth, who, in later tradition, changed into Hermes or Mercury, the messenger of the gods. Another serpent-healing connection is the snake wound about the staff, symbol of Aesculapius, the Greek god of healing. The staff used by both Thoth and Aesculapius is called the *caduceus* and is familiar to moderns as the official symbol for the U.S. Army Medical Corps, the Navy Pharmacy Division, and the Public Health Service of the United States. A single serpent wound about a staff is used as a symbol by the American Medical Association, the World Health Organization, the U.S. Air Force Medical Services, and the British and French armies.

The appearance of a snake in a dream, therefore, need not be considered frightening. Rather, like the mandala or the simple circle, it can be an indication of approaching wholeness and our ability to place ourselves satisfactorily in our relationships with the world.

Another symbol which may be found in dreams, since it is so important in our conscious lives, is Leonardo da Vinci's man in the center of a circle against a background of a square. The Florentine painter (1452–1519) drew a man with his feet together and arms uplifted so he touched the square within the circle that surrounded it. Yet a second set of arms and feet was drawn with the arms at the side and the feet spread, with the arms touching only the square and the feet only the circle, as though the subject were trying to maintain his balance on an uneven plane. The symbol has reappeared in modern times, for instance as the emblem of the Montreal Exposition in 1967 as a single upright line connected to two "legs." Since then the symbol has sprouted a head and arms to form the human figure, while Leonardo's original drawing is being used extensively as the logo for media publishers. With the dawning of the Age of Aquarius, the human figure has progressed from an emblem typifying the theme "Man and His World" in Montreal to one that indicates our need to return to wholeness in conscious life as well as the dream state.

The Sign of the Cross

Wholeness can also be recognized in dreams by the appearance of a cross, an ancient and universal symbol. The Egyptian cross, the ankh, has the arms positioned midway, above a straight line and below a loop that may have represented the yearning of that ancient civilization for wholeness. A chain of these crosses can be found together with a representation of the god Thoth in the Great Temple at Karnak.

The Greeks constructed their cross with arms of the same length intersecting at the center like an arithmetical plus sign. After Christianity firmly established itself, it replaced the Greek cross with the Latin, where the horizontal bar has been raised and the vertical made longer below the cross-piece.

Naturally, other religious faiths have their own symbols of wholeness, such as the Star of David for the Jews or the Tao for the Orientals, but whenever one of these appears in a dream, it is an encouraging sign.

Because dreams impart their messages in symbols and archetypes rather than in plain speech, and because each of us is immersed in the universal unconscious, those phenomena found in myth and legend through the ages will aid us in our interpretations. However, as Erich Fromm points out in *The Forgotten Language,* "Whether the dreamer himself is able to separate the rational part of the dream from its symbolic veil or whether he needs the help of a dream interpreter depends on the degree to which the insight is veiled in symbols and on the strength of his reasoning power." Your reasoning powers have been developed, and you will not require a dream interpreter to assist you. You possess all the information required to understand the more important universal symbols, and if you spend some time studying your own symbols, you can perform the service on your own.

Doors and Ladders

Your dream log will provide all the help you require. You may discover that doors are important to you, for instance. Closed doors mean precisely what they do in conscious life: a block of some sort. Open doors mean the way is clear for you to proceed. Or you may dream of rooms, with cramped rooms indicating a confining condition in your life and high-ceilinged, spacious rooms ample opportunity for you to grow and expand.

Ladders will be important, depending on whether you are going up, to show you are rising in the world, or down, meaning that you fear a loss of status. Clothes are also used as dream symbols, and you can decide for yourself what it means to be wearing new clothes or shabby ones. Dreams of bathing or otherwise cleansing oneself might signal you it is time "to clean up your act" or indicate you have already done so.

You will, of course, experience the unimportant digestive and physical dreams and learn to ignore most of their contents. These are apt to be the unformed, lack-luster types. Your psychic and spiritual dreams, on the other hand, will be clear, startlingly real, and often in vibrant colors in order to impress you with their importance. Sounds and bodily sensations frequently accompany important dreams when you are oriented toward sound and feeling in your waking life.

Little more need be said. Your essence will take over the operation of guiding you on your path. It will be your guru. You will not need to seek another teacher, for it will help you to understand both universal and personal symbology; it will correct you if you start to falter; it will ensure your continued wholeness.

If you remain uncertain whether you have achieved this wholeness, this unification of body, mind, and spirit that Jung called individuation, you have simply to ask for the gift of the Holy Spirit which is the "spirit of wholeness." This was the comforter that Christ sent to his disciples after he ascended to God. This baptized the disciples with tongues of flame and conferred upon them various gifts as they sat in the upper room at Pentecost. But the gift is not just for Christians. God granted it to everyone for all time. It has never left us.

Making Requests

Like others before you, you may ask for the gifts identified in 1 Corinthians 12:8–10 as wisdom, knowledge, faith, healing, miracles, prophecy, discernment of spirits, tongues, and interpretations of tongues. All nine are yours for the asking. They were there for the earliest members of Western civilization. Indeed, every human being who has ever lived or is presently living can avail himself or herself of them, for nothing has been added, nothing taken away from us in our entire history. The old rules still apply: "Ask and ye shall receive." "This and greater shall you do." The promise is still in effect. We have only to ask for it.

To make your request, go into meditation. Be certain you have mentally cleansed yourself of all the negativities: hate, envy, anger, or whatever else you might harbor in the depths of self. Surrender yourself to the essence and then say,

> Heavenly Father, fill me with your light.
> Grant me the gifts of the Holy Spirit
> that I may spread your light on earth.
> All praise and glory be yours, now and forever.

You may not notice the difference immediately, but when the words of your prayer rise to God, he will come.

However you have achieved the victory of wholeness, it is now yours to enjoy. You have developed new methods of "seeing" along with new mental ability, having read through and worked on the assignments of this book. You have extended both mind and sight by learning what attitudes are required for self-fulfilment. You have exercised mind, body, and spirit in retraining for better habits and thereby exorcised whatever emotions or habits prevented your fusing the three parts into a workable whole.

You have extended mind and sight with meditation. By learning to relax you have discovered how to slow your brain waves to the point where creative thought and easy learning are possible. What was sporadic and accidental before has now become controlled and reliable alpha. And you have reinforced your meditations with your exploration of dreams.

If you have done your homework well, you have achieved synthesis, wholeness. And you can retain it forever, to be among the forerunners of the new and improved human race. Then you, like the early Christians, can benefit from the spirit: "your sons and your daughters shall prophesy, and your young men shall see visions, and your old men shall dream dreams" (Acts 2:17).

Moving Toward God

Conditions are changing rapidly to fulfill the prophecy. One evidence of this can be found in the Catholic Church, which is returning the service to the congregations, as it was in the first centuries after Christ. But the Catholic Church is not unique in this respect and is cited only as an example. Other organized religions are similarly finding their way back to "the living creed of God." And individuals professing no religion are searching on their own. The ranks of the enlightened are swelling, and you will not be lonely in your search and achievement. The world that you have begun to alter will change more rapidly as you find and work with others who are also motivated toward the light. These individuals will come into your life without any effort on your part. As you raise yourself to even higher levels, you will attract those working and living on those higher planes. When you require assistance in reaching the next levels, it will come to you naturally through individuals, books, other methods of information dissemination, or your own essence.

The worst of your struggles were over once you broke with your former self and learned how easy it is to function as a new being. For some, the process might be reversible. Years of cultural conditioning have taught us to play by the rules of society, and those who do not know what you have learned could slip back rapidly—even overnight. You need never fear this. So long as you are ready to work, to persevere, to surrender the worst of yourself so that a finer and purer person may emerge, you will release the power within and use it for your own and the world's good.

No longer are you a slave of negativities: hatred, greed, envy, laziness, heartbreak, or whatever else kept you in bonds; you have supplanted them with peace of mind, ease of soul, purposeful and inspiring communication with everyone you encounter. You live in contentment, with love and joy. You know what you must do: the duty of the moment. You do not expect bells to ring or trumpets to blare in recognition of your progress. Indeed, to the outer world your situation and circumstances may *appear* unchanged, although they are changed. The instant you changed, you attuned yourself to the infinite flow. Now nothing or no one can keep your good from you. Whatever you need, whatever you require for your advancement will be yours, whether it be health, fame, or fortune. Your struggles have ceased. What comes to you from this point on, as long as you continue to work in the light, will be for your ultimate good. Thus you have satisfied the conditions set forth by Jesus for all mankind: "I say unto you, Ask, and it shall be given you; seek, and ye shall find; knock, and it shall be opened unto you. For every one that asketh receiveth; and he that seeketh findeth; and to him that knocketh it shall be opened" (Luke 11:9–10).

Accept the blessings of God and live—in love, light, peace, and joy.

18

Attitudinal Profile 2

You can assess your spiritual growth in two ways. One is to compile a new list of fears and joys and compare them with those you wrote at the beginning of your study. You should find that your fears have diminished, while your joys have increased at an astounding rate.

The second method is to take the attitudinal profile that follows. As was the case with the first profile, there are no right or wrong answers. Each response merely reflects the way you react to situations. In this profile you are also asked to choose your first and most customary reaction to the circumstance, even though you might combine some possibilities given or find a much better solution. Write the letter for the answer you have selected in the space provided at the end of the questionnaire.

Attitudinal Profile 2

1. You are standing in line at a bank, with ample time to complete your business. However, an elderly person ahead of you asks the teller interminable questions about what sounds like a simple deposit. You

   a. Decide that in the future you will preview the customers *better* in order to determine which line is likely to move the fastest.

   b. Say nothing because there have been occasions when you, too, have needed explanations about monetary transactions.

   c. Observe what is happening without being annoyed, because a brief delay isn't worth getting excited about.

   d. Become highly impatient and request the bank manager to assign additional tellers to serve the customers.

2. You are in a store when a young mother begins to scream at her child. You

   a. Are terribly upset by the mother's behavior and feel like leaving the store.

      b. Are disturbed by the commotion and would like to ask the mother if there is something you can do to help.

      c. Quietly try to decide what problems are causing the mother to lose control.

      d. Are annoyed with the mother because she could have reprimanded the child without making a scene.

3. You are introduced to a candidate of your political party who wants your vote in the elections. Having no other commitments or knowledge of the other candidates, you decide whether you will support him or her on the basis of

      a. Whether the campaign promises sound interesting.

      b. Whether the campaign promises sound logical and sincere.

      c. The impression you got when you shook his or her hand.

      d. A feeling that he or she will do a good job in office.

4. You have invited some friends to be your guests at a show in which a member of your family is performing. The show is terrible

      a. At the intermission, you ask your guests if they'd like to leave.

      b. Somehow you knew this would happen, and you will pay more attention to such impressions in the future.

      c. You decide to take your guests to a good restaurant afterward, so the evening won't be a total loss for them.

      d. You watch the show, knowing that you are all present to learn something important.

5. You are out with your co-worker, who has too much to drink and insults you. You

      a. Know he or she is upset with something about himself or herself that you remind him or her of, so you ignore the insult.

      b. Forgive the insult, since your co-worker has always treated you well before.

      c. Know how he or she really feels about you, so the insult doesn't bother you.

      d. Attempt to get your co-worker home before he or she becomes even more disruptive.

6. You lend a favorite record to an acquaintance and when it is returned you discover it is ruined. You

      a. Suspect that something on the record, or your owning it, has upset the borrower, so you ignore the damage.

      b. Are not unduly disturbed, since you have played the record so often you know its contents by heart and no longer need it to be in good condition.

  c. Discuss the damage with your acquaintance and imply you expect a replacement.

  d. Are upset and can't help letting the world know it.

7. You are shopping with a friend who wants to buy the same article of clothing that you've selected to wear on a special occasion.

  a. If your friend wants it so badly, you will forgo the article because he or she has done many favors for you.

  b. You discuss the article and agree to toss a coin to determine who buys it.

  c. You decide the garment was not meant for you and that you will find something better.

  d. You decide not to buy it if your friend really wants it, since you can always find something you like as well as this one.

8. A relative has asked you to drive him or her somewhere, and on the way you are involved in an accident. Though it is plainly not your fault, the relative says that he or she will sue you. You

  a. Become very angry and argue with the relative.

  b. Know the relative is upset by the accident and would not really sue you, for you would not have offered to do this favor for someone in whom you sense a backbiting tendency.

  c. Are terribly hurt by the relative's attitude and refuse to discuss it further.

  d. Inform the relative that there are no logical grounds for suit and that you will not be threatened.

9. While sightseeing, you come across a particularly beautiful landscape. You notice

  a. The beauty of the scene and try to assimilate it as deeply as possible, at the same time feeling overcome by and grateful for such beauty.

  b. How the view affects your mood and lifts your spirits.

  c. Whether it is suitable for habitation and how it could be used to best advantage.

  d. The general atmosphere and general coloring of the scene.

10. At a party your spouse or beloved, who has always been faithful, completely ignores you and spends the entire time dancing with another person.

a. It's obvious the other person isn't your partner's type, so you aren't particularly upset.

b. Since you know nothing can deprive you of your rightful place, you enjoy yourself by talking and dancing with other people.

c. You understand that your beloved needs attention and he is trying to make you aware of it by his or her behavior.

d. You lose your temper and cause a scene.

11. A new neighbor accuses you of taking the lid of his or her garbage can, thus your relationship has started badly. Later, the neighbor goes out of the way to do you a great favor. You

a. Decide the neighbor was upset over unrelated matters when the lid incident occurred and is now trying to make amends.

b. Discuss the original incident with the neighbor and resolve the conflict.

c. Accept the neighbor for what he or she is in each instance.

d. Find it difficult to change your opinion of him or her, though you try hard.

12. You have lost your job, and you learn from newspapers and magazines that your skills are no longer in demand. You

a. Persist in looking for a job in your field, since you are very capable.

b. Assess your abilities and figure out how to use them in related work where jobs are more plentiful.

c. Investigate the possibilities of retraining so you can learn new skills.

d. Realize that nothing is denied you without something better replacing it, so you set to work to find a new and better job.

13. Alone in an unfamiliar place on a rainy day, you look for something to read. You find only four books available. Though none *really* interest you, you study the covers or read parts of books and then choose the one that appears to

a. Offer you the sort of insight you need at the moment.

b. Be able to give you some insight into the future trend of events.

c. Disclose alleged scandals in your government's affairs.

d. Analyze the problems of your country.

14. Your family is holding a gathering that you think may be disrupted by the presence of some relatives who are at loggerheads with each other. You do not have to go but would like to. You

a. Decide to attend, hoping you can help resolve the differences between them.
b. Know that although you can't solve their problems, your desire to see them reconciled will add good will to the situation.
c. Have more interesting things to do than listen to others argue, so you refuse the invitation.
d. Sense deep down that confrontation will not occur; attend the gathering and just enjoy seeing the rest of the family.

15. You have come up with a great idea that will save your company time and money. You discuss it with your superior before formally presenting it in writing and then find that he or she is claiming all the credit for it. You
    a. Complain about the injustice to your superior and if you do not get any satisfaction, pursue it with higher authorities.
    b. Become furious and engage your superior in an argument over the matter.
    c. Let matters run their course, since the success of the idea is more important than personal credit.
    d. Discuss the matter with your fellow employees and convince them that an injustice has been done to you, so you will have allies for your cause.

When you have completed the profile by filling in every blank, you're ready to score your results. You will find five boxes available for each question. Check the appropriate square and then count the number of check marks in each column.

Answers

1 _____   6 _____   11 _____

2 _____   7 _____   12 _____

3 _____   8 _____   13 _____

4 _____   9 _____   14 _____

5 _____   10 _____   15 _____

Question No.	Thought		Intuition		Feeling		Sensation		Centered	
1			a		b		d		c	
2	d		c		a		b			
3	b		d		c		a			
4	a		b				c		d	
5			c		b		d		a	
6	c		a		d				b	
7	d				a		b		c	
8	d		b		c		a			
9	c		d		b				a	
10	a		c				d		b	
11	a		d		b		c		c	
12	b				a		c		d	
13	d		b				c		a	
14	c		d		a				b	
15	a				b		d		c	
Total Number										

Using the following table, compare your scores from the original profile with this one.

	Thought Column 1	Intuition Column 2	Feeling Column 3	Sensation Column 4	Centering Column 5
Attitudinal Profile 1					
Attitudinal Profile 2					

The differences between your two scores will give you some idea of the progress you have made toward becoming centered. Do not expect great alterations this soon, however. In fact, *any* changes in your scoring pattern are cause for celebration, since it is so difficult to replace lifelong habits, emotions, and attitudes with superior ones. If you have any marks in the "centered" column, or have marks in *several* columns, you are progressing and are on your way to becoming whole, for the centered answers, or answers spread over several categories, indicate that you are capable of operating at any point in Jung's diagram and have succeeded, at least partially, in rounding out your personality so that it looks like this:

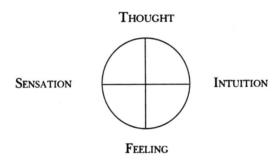

THOUGHT

SENSATION

INTUITION

FEELING

Do not retake the test if you are dissatisfied with the results. Instead, continue to work on your self-development and, six months or a year from now, complete the second attitudinal profile again. To use it often would destroy its effectiveness, for you would know what responses will give you the desired effect. If you forget about the test, on the other hand, you won't recall the answers, and your scores will provide a valid index of your psychological gains.

Whether your scores are satisfactory to you or not, continue your program of development. This course of study has been your introduction to the centered world. You have made a great beginning, but it is just that— a beginning. No one is ever finished with this work. All any of us can do is reach ever higher stages of growth, thus widening our personal circles until they encompass our towns or cities, our countries, our states, our nation, the entire globe, the complete universe. Only then will we be able to realize fully the glorious power within us and live eternally—in love, light, peace, and joy.

Bibliography

Benson, Herbert. *The Relaxation Response*. New York: Morrow, 1976.

Brothers of the Abbey of the Genesee. "New Day Prayer." Piffard, N.Y.: Prayer printed on the wrapper of Monk's Bread.

Christenson, James A., Jr. "Dynamics in hypnotic induction," in *Experimental Hypnosis*. Edited by Leslie LeCron. Secausus, N.J.: Citadel Press, 1972.

DeRopp, Robert S. *The Master Game*. New York: Delta, 1968.

Edinger, Edward F. *Ego and Archetype*. New York: C. G. Jung Foundation, 1972.

Emerson, Ralph Waldo. *The Gospel of Emerson*. Edited by Newton Dillaway. Lee's Summit, Mo.: Unity Books, 1949.

Evans, Bergen. *Dictionary of Mythology*. Lincoln, Nebr.: Centennial Press, 1970.

Fabun, Don. *Dimensions of Change*. New York: Macmillan, 1971.

Faraday, Ann. *Dream Power*. New York: Coward, McCann and Geoghegan, 1972.

Fordham, Frieda. *An Introduction to Jung's Psychology*. Harmondsworth, U.K.: Penguin, 1966.

Fromm, Erich. *The Forgotten Language*. New York: Grove Press, 1956.

Germain, Walter. *The Magic Power of Your Mind*. New York: Paperback Library, 1971.

Graham, David. *Dream Your Way to Happiness and Awareness*. New York: Warner Books, 1975.

Henderson, Joseph. L. "Ancient Myths and Modern Man." In *Man and His Symbols* by Carl G. Jung et al. New York: Pantheon, 1963.

Holman, C. Hugh. *A Handbook to Literature*, 4th ed. New York: Bobbs-Merrill, 1980.

Jung, Carl G. *Analytical Psychology: Its Theory and Practice*. New York: Random House, 1970.

———. *Memories, Dreams, Reflections,* rev. ed. Edited by Aniela Jaffe. Translated by Richard Winston and Clara Winston. New York: Pantheon, 1963.

———. *Psychological Types.* Princeton, N.J.:Princeton University Press, 1976.

———, and M.-L. von Franz, Joseph L. Henderson, Jolande Jacobi, and Aniela Jaffe. *Man and His Symbols.* London, Aldus Books, 1964.

Keating, Dr. Charles J. *Who We Are Is How We Pray.* Mystic, Conn.: Twenty-third Publications, 1987.

Koesler, Arthur. *The Roots of Coincidence.* New York: Random House, 1973.

Laing, R. D. *The Politics of Experience.* New York: Ballantine, 1967.

Leadbeater, Charles W. *The Chakras.* Wheaton, Ill.: Theosophical Publishing House, 1974.

LeCron, Leslie. *Self-Hypnotism: The Technique and Its Use in Daily Living.* New York: New American Library, 1970.

LeShan, Lawrence. *How to Meditate.* New York: Bantam, 1986.

MacNutt, Francis, O. P. *Healing.* Notre Dame, Ind.: Ave Maria Press, 1975.

Marshall, Catherine. *Adventures in Prayer.* Old Tappan, N.J.: Fleming H. Revell Co., 1975.

May, Rollo. *Love and Will.* New York: Norton, 1969.

Montgomery, Ruth. *A Search for the Truth.* New York: Morrow, 1969.

Moyers, Bill. *Healing and the Mind.* New York: Doubleday, 1993.

Orwell, George. *Nineteen Eighty-Four.* New York: Harcourt Brace Jovanovich, 1983.

Ostrander, Sheila, and Lynn Schroeder. *Psychic Discoveries Behind the Iron Curtain.* Englewood Cliffs, N.J.: Prentice-Hall, 1971.

Payne, Phoebe D., and Laurence J. Bendit. *This World and That: An Analytical Study of Psychic Communication.* Wheaton, Ill: Theosophical Publishing House, 1969.

Peterson, Severin. *A Catalog of the Ways People Grow.* New York: Ballantine, 1973.

Petrie, Sidney, and Robert B. Stone. *What Modern Hypnostism Can Do for You.* Greenwich, Conn.: Fawcett, 1972.

Pirandello, Luigi. *Six Characters in Search of an Author,* in *Naked Masks: Five Plays.* Edited by Eric Bentley. New York: E. P. Dutton, 1957.

Progoff, Ira. *Jung's Psychology and Its Social Meaning,* 3rd ed. New York: Dialogue House, 1985.

Puharich, Henry K. *Beyond Telepathy.* New York: Anchor, 1973.

St. John of the Cross. *Dark Night of the Soul.* Translated by E. Allison Peers. Garden City N.Y.: Image, 1959.

St. Teresa of Avila. *Interior Castle.* Translated by E. Allison Peers. Garden City, N.Y.: Image, 1972.

Sanford, Agnes. *The Healing Gifts of the Spirit.* New York: Jove Publications, 1983.

Sechrist, Elsie. *Meditation: Gateway to Light,* rev. ed. Virginia Beach, Va.: ARE Pr., 1972.

Seligmann, Kurt. *Magic, Supernaturalism and Religion.* New York: Random House, 1971.

Shealy, C. Norman. *Ninety Days to Self-Health.* New York: Dial, 1977.

Shinn, Florence Scovel. *The Game of Life and How to Play It.* Marina del Rey, Calif.: De Vorss, 1978.

Simonton, O. Carl., S. Matthews-Simonton, and J. Creighton. *Getting Well Again.* New York: Bantam, 1978.

Smith, Bradford. *Meditation: The Inward Art.* Philadelphia, Pa.: J. B. Lippincott, 1963.

Walter, W. Grey. "The Electrical Activity of the Brain," in *Altered States of Awareness,* readings from *The Scientific American.* San Francisco: W. H. Freeman, 1972.

Waltham, Clae. *I Ching: The Chinese Book of Changes.* New York: Ace Publishing, 1969.

Weed, Joseph. *Wisdom of the Mystic Masters.* New York: Prentice-Hall, 1962.

Worrall, Ambrose, and Olga Worrall. *Gift of Healing.* New York: Harper & Row, 1965.

Index

✦